#01 The Myth Contains the End

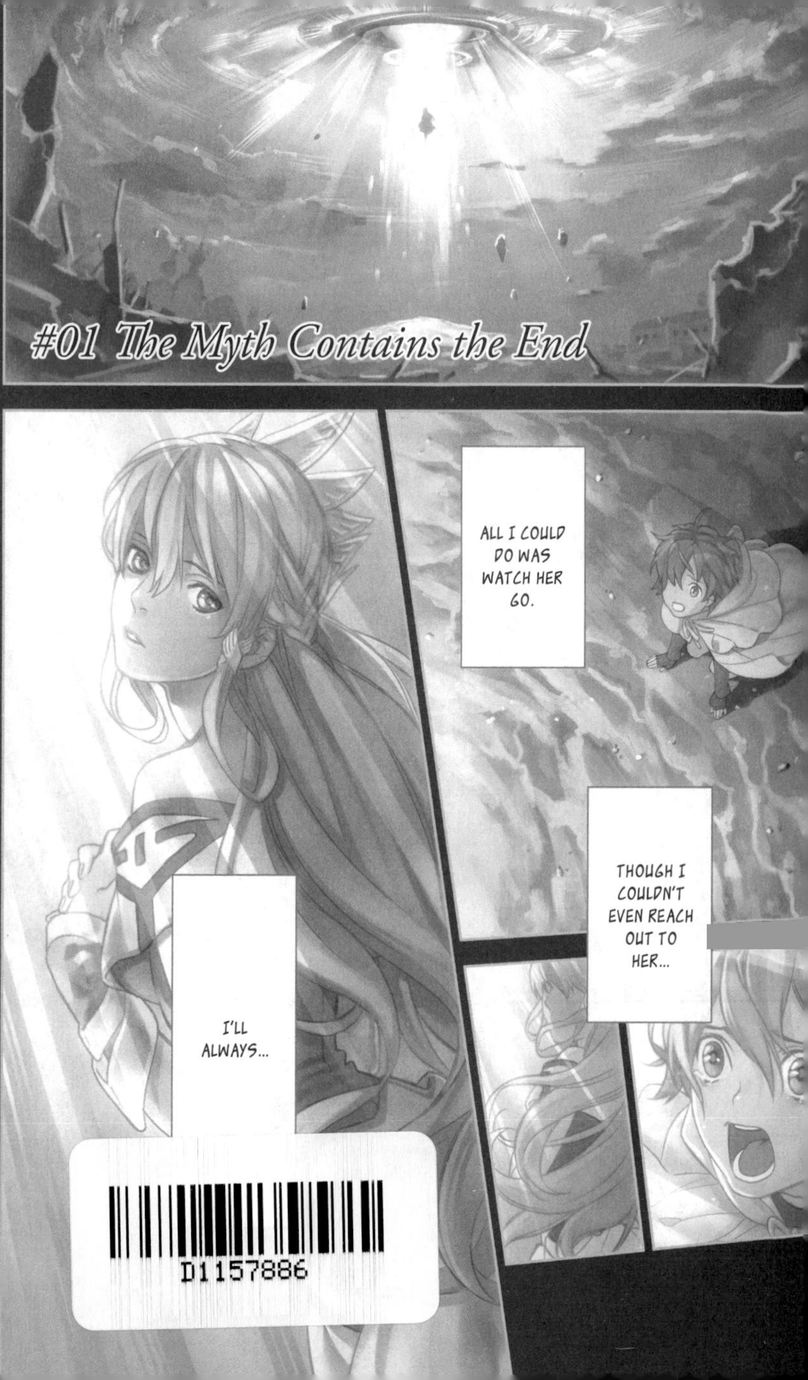
ALL I COULD DO WAS WATCH HER GO.
THOUGH I COULDN'T EVEN REACH OUT TO HER...
I'LL ALWAYS...

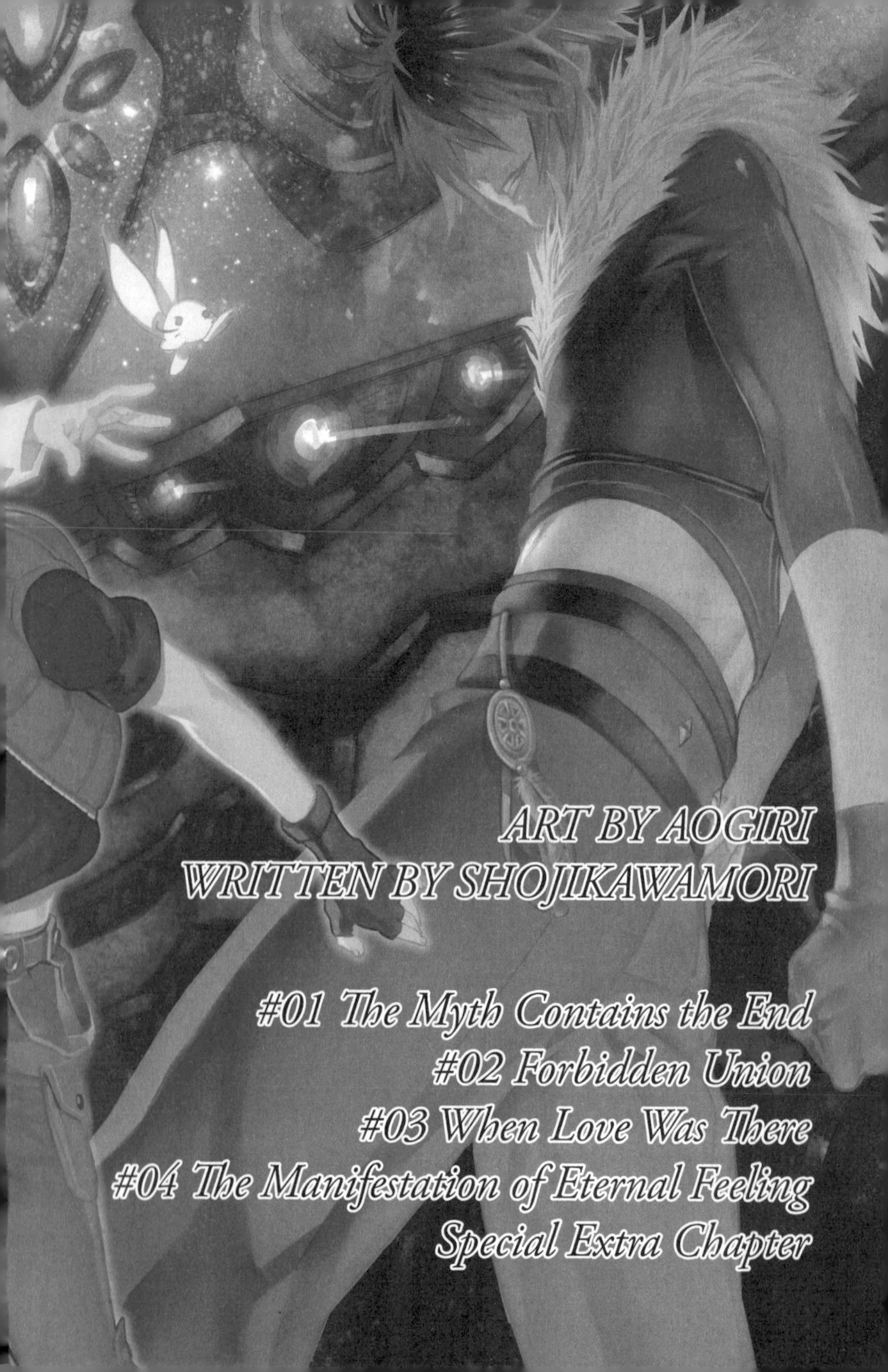
ART BY AOGIRI
WRITTEN BY SHOJI KAWAMORI
#01 The Myth Contains the End
#02 Forbidden Union
#03 When Love Was There
#04 The Manifestation of Eternal Feeling
Special Extra Chapter

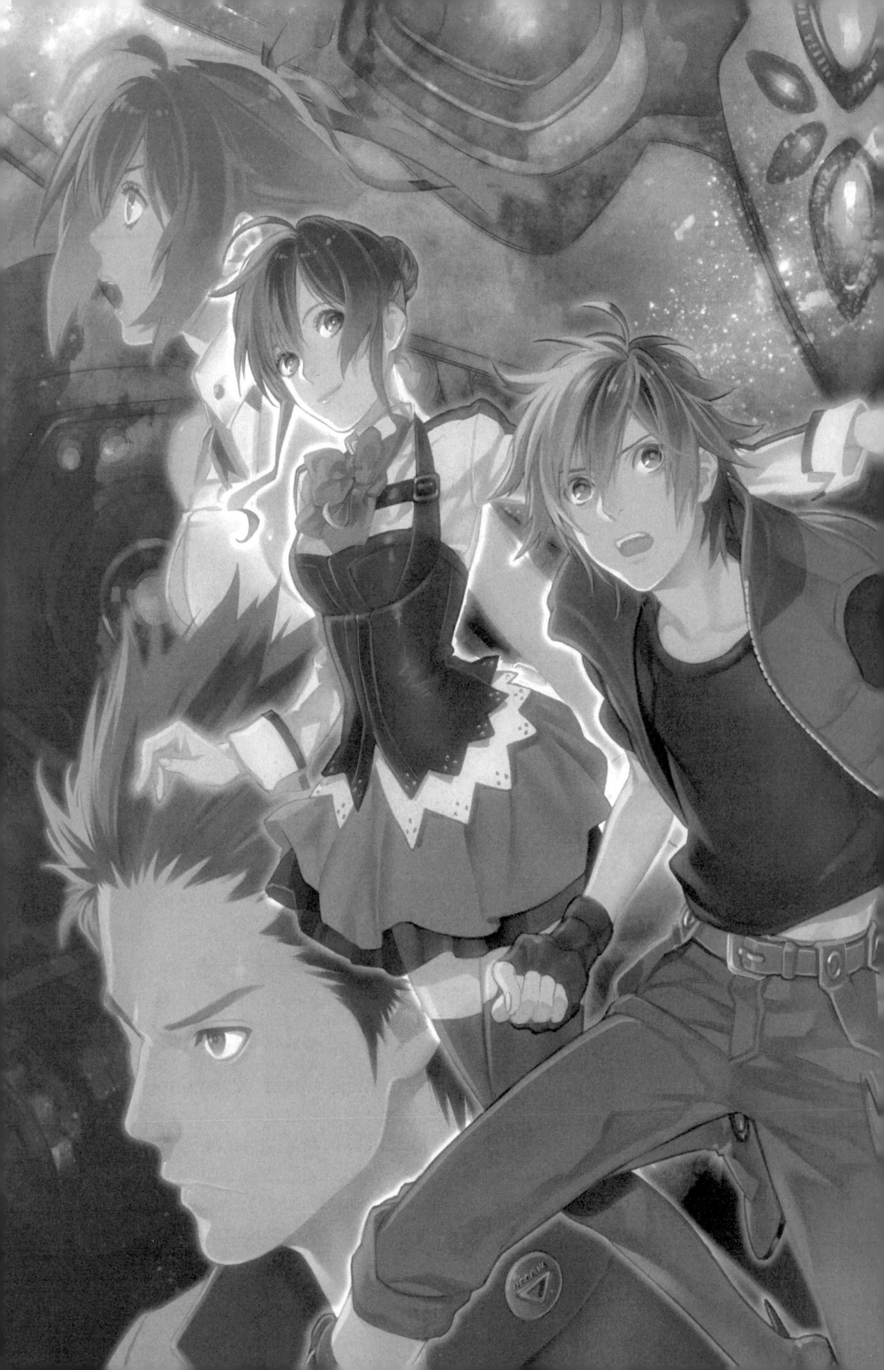

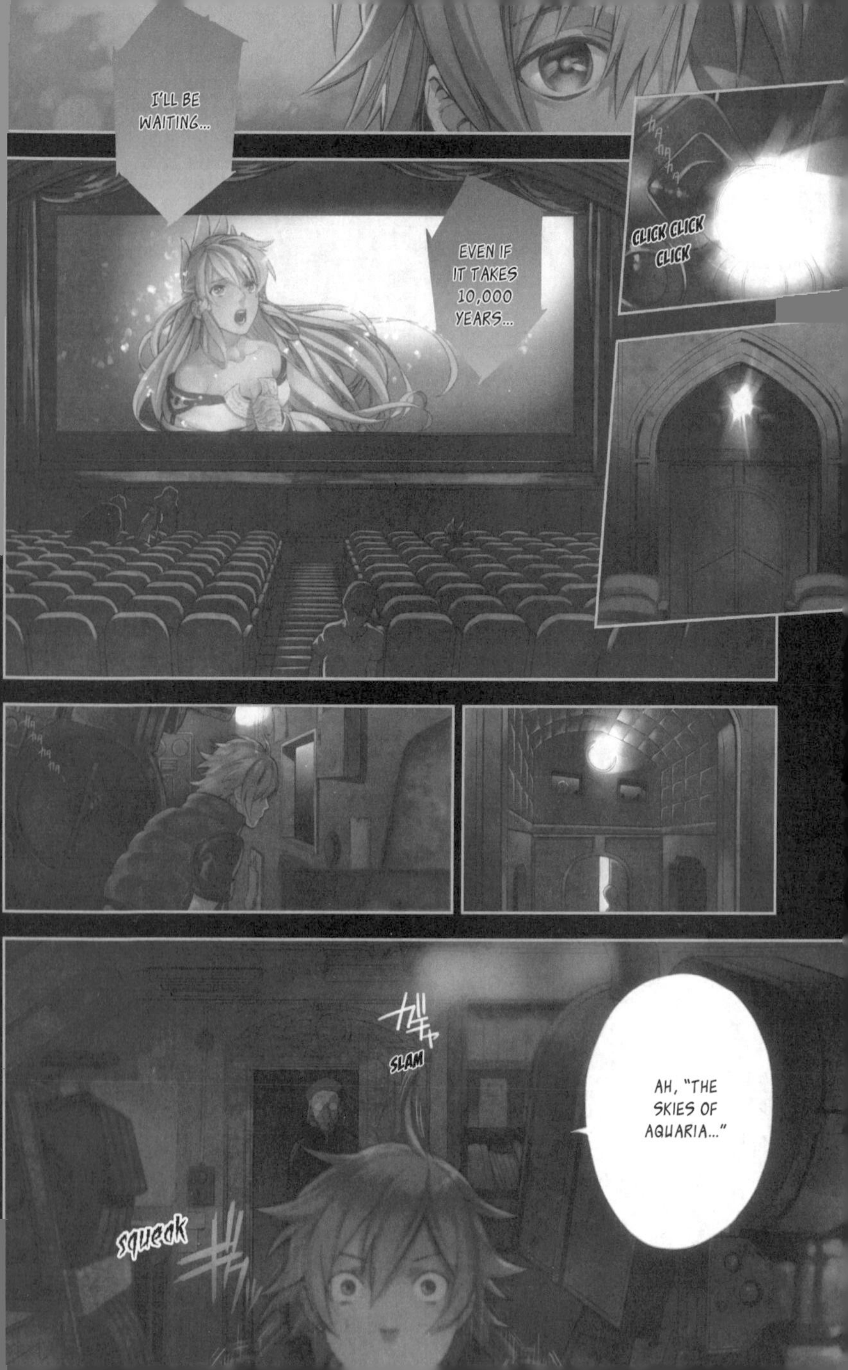
I'LL BE WAITING...
CLICK CLICK CLICK
EVEN IF IT TAKES 10,000 YEARS...
SLAM
AH, "THE SKIES OF AQUARIA..."
squeak

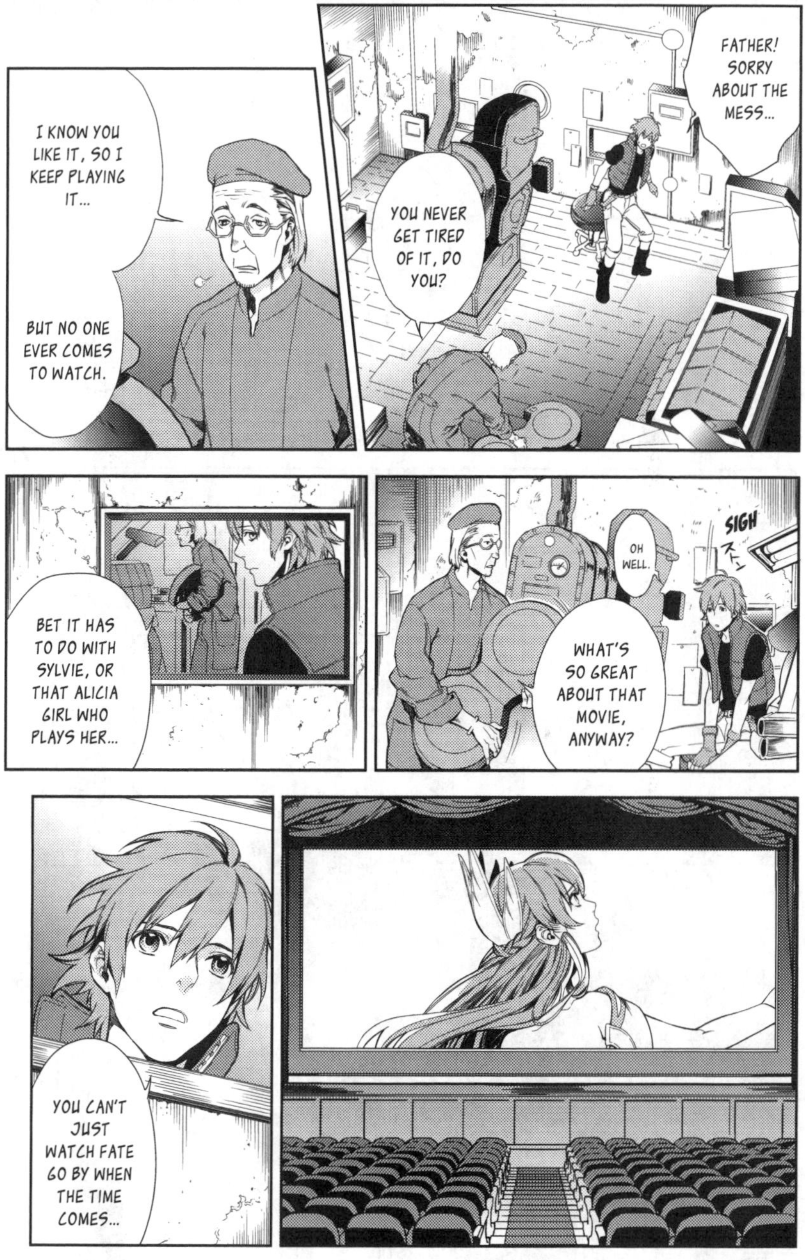
FATHER! SORRY ABOUT THE MESS...
YOU NEVER GET TIRED OF IT, DO YOU?
I KNOW YOU LIKE IT, SO I KEEP PLAYING IT...
BUT NO ONE EVER COMES TO WATCH.
SIGH
ストン
OH WELL.
WHAT'S SO GREAT ABOUT THAT MOVIE, ANYWAY?
BET IT HAS TO DO WITH SYLVIE, OR THAT ALICIA GIRL WHO PLAYS HER...
YOU CAN'T JUST WATCH FATE GO BY WHEN THE TIME COMES...

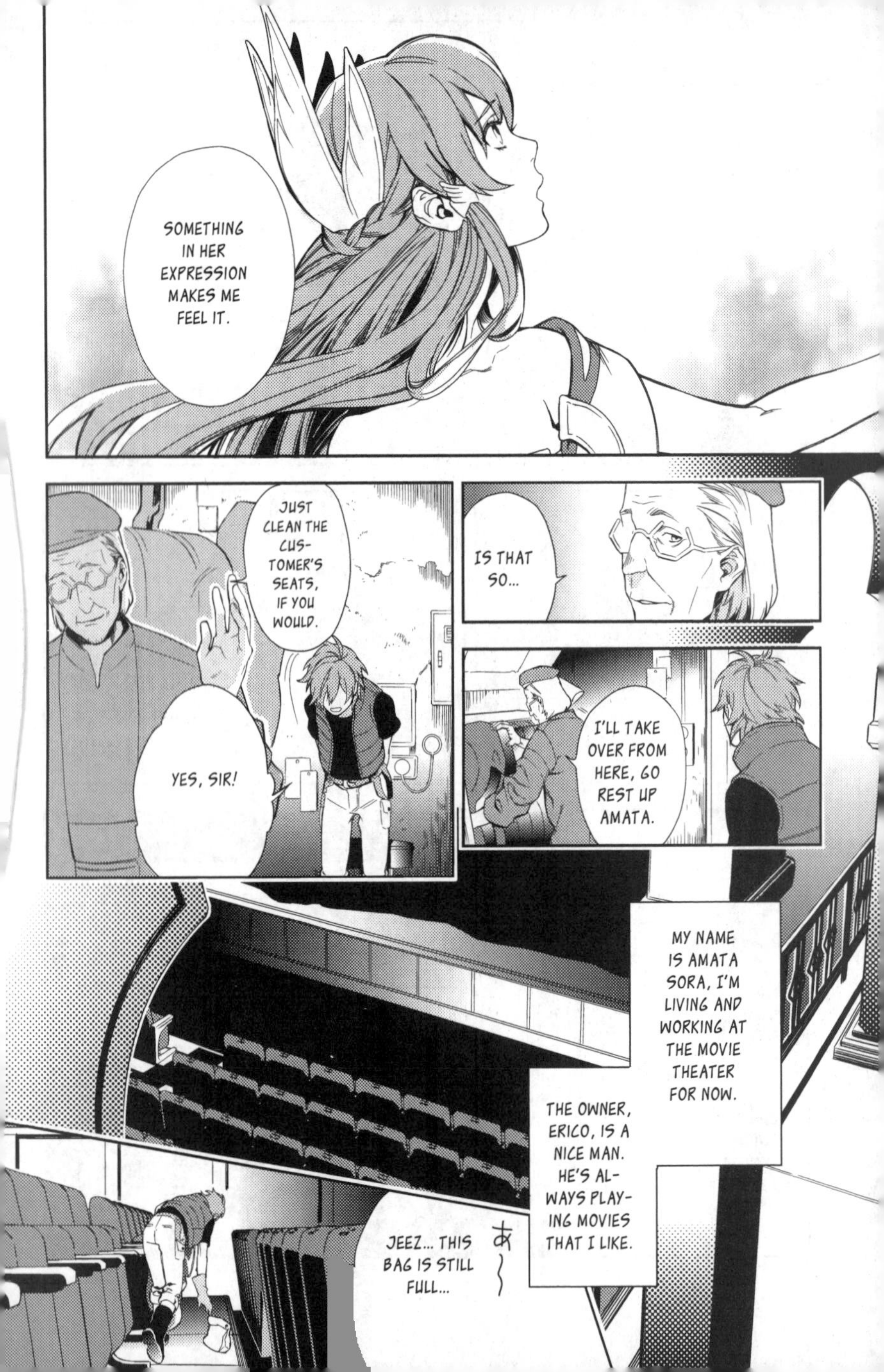
SOMETHING IN HER EXPRESSION MAKES ME FEEL IT.
IS THAT SO...
I'LL TAKE OVER FROM HERE, GO REST UP AMATA.
JUST CLEAN THE CUS-TOMER'S SEATS, IF YOU WOULD.
YES, SIR!
MY NAME IS AMATA SORA, I'M LIVING AND WORKING AT THE MOVIE THEATER FOR NOW.
THE OWNER, ERICO, IS A NICE MAN. HE'S AL-WAYS PLAY-ING MOVIES THAT I LIKE.
あ～
JEEZ... THIS BAG IS STILL FULL...

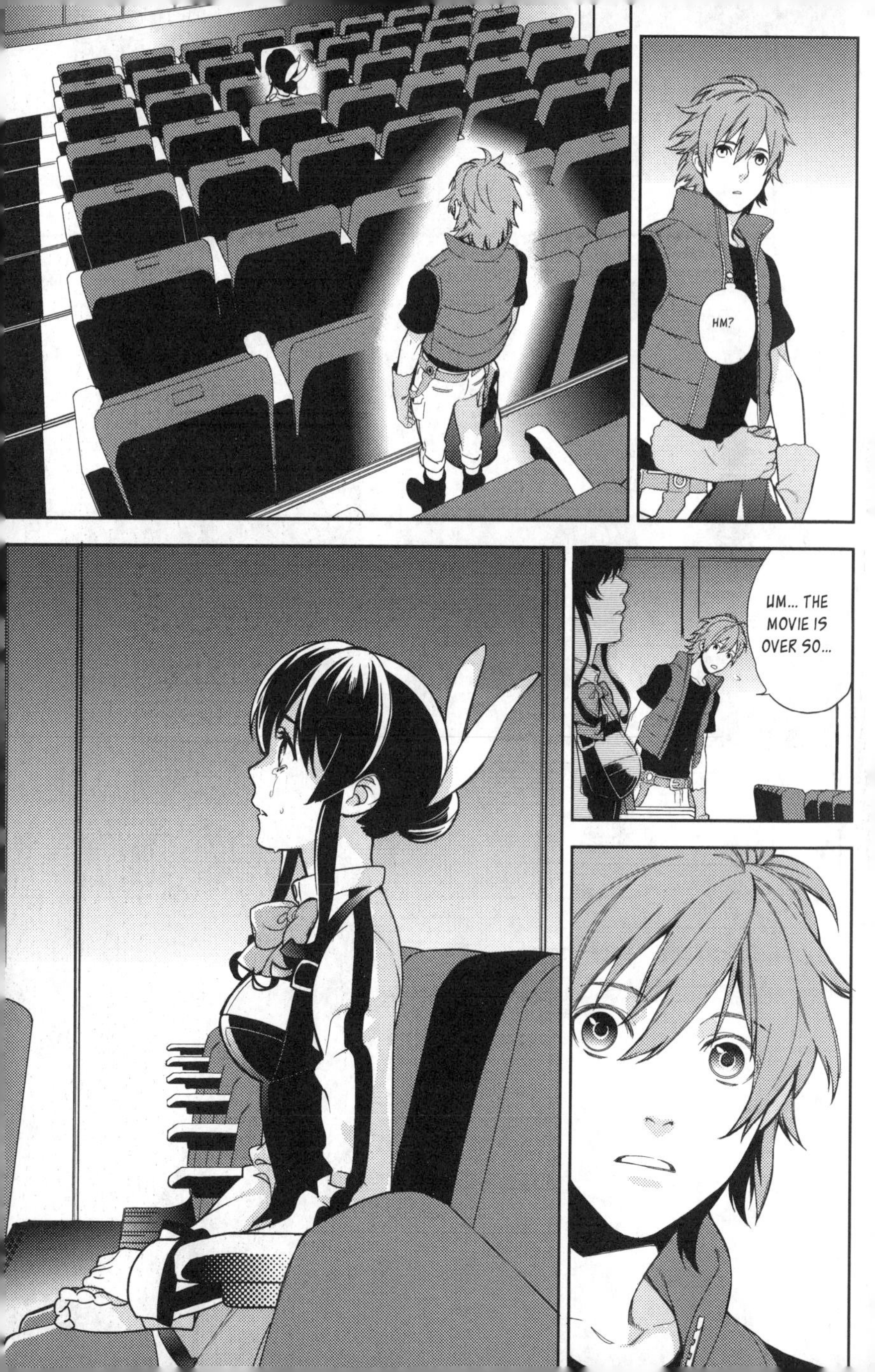
HM?
UM... THE MOVIE IS OVER SO...

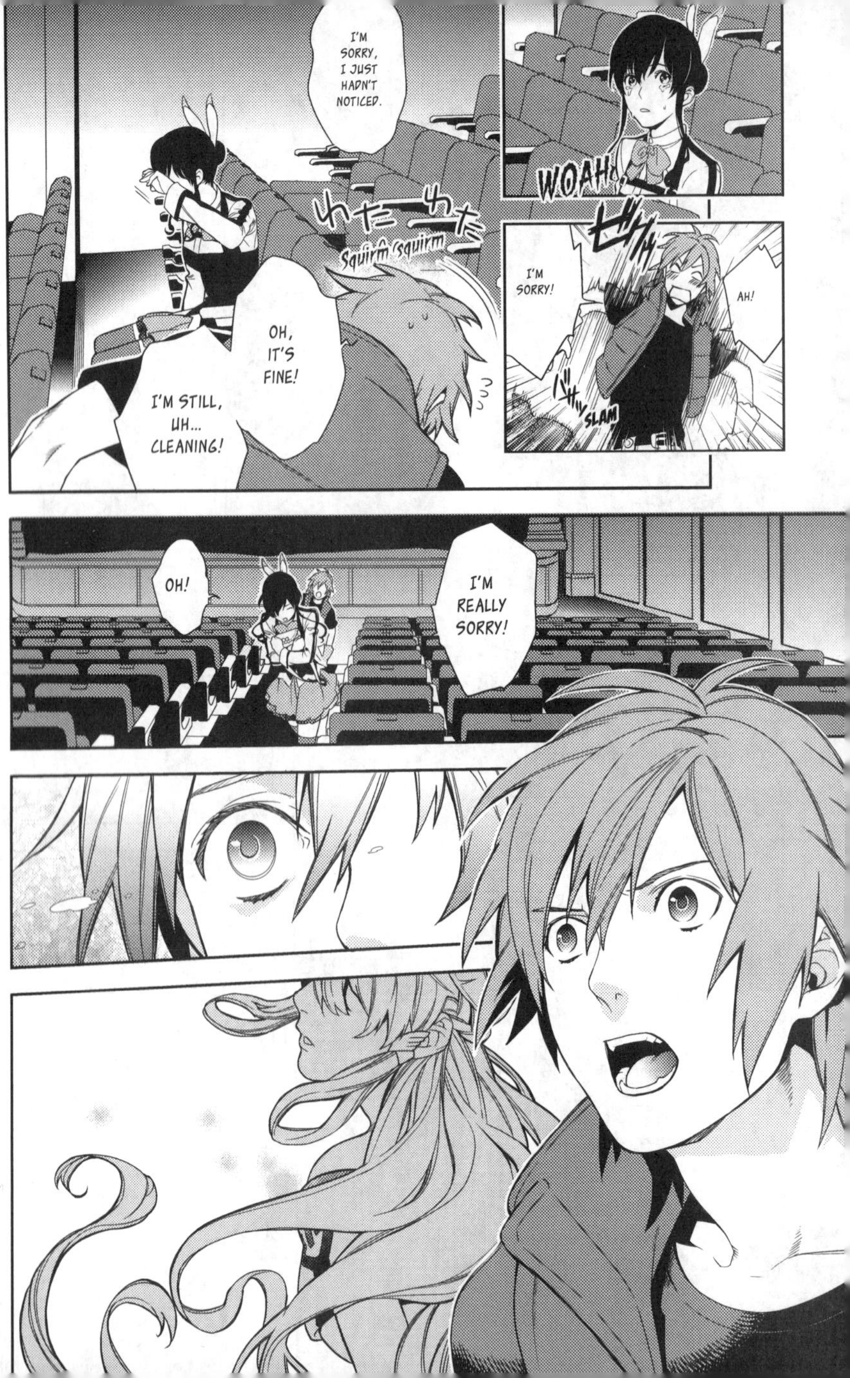
WOAH!
AH!
I'M SORRY!
SLAM
I'M SORRY, I JUST HADN'T NOTICED.
Squirm squirm
OH, IT'S FINE!
I'M STILL, UH... CLEANING!
I'M REALLY SORRY!
OH!

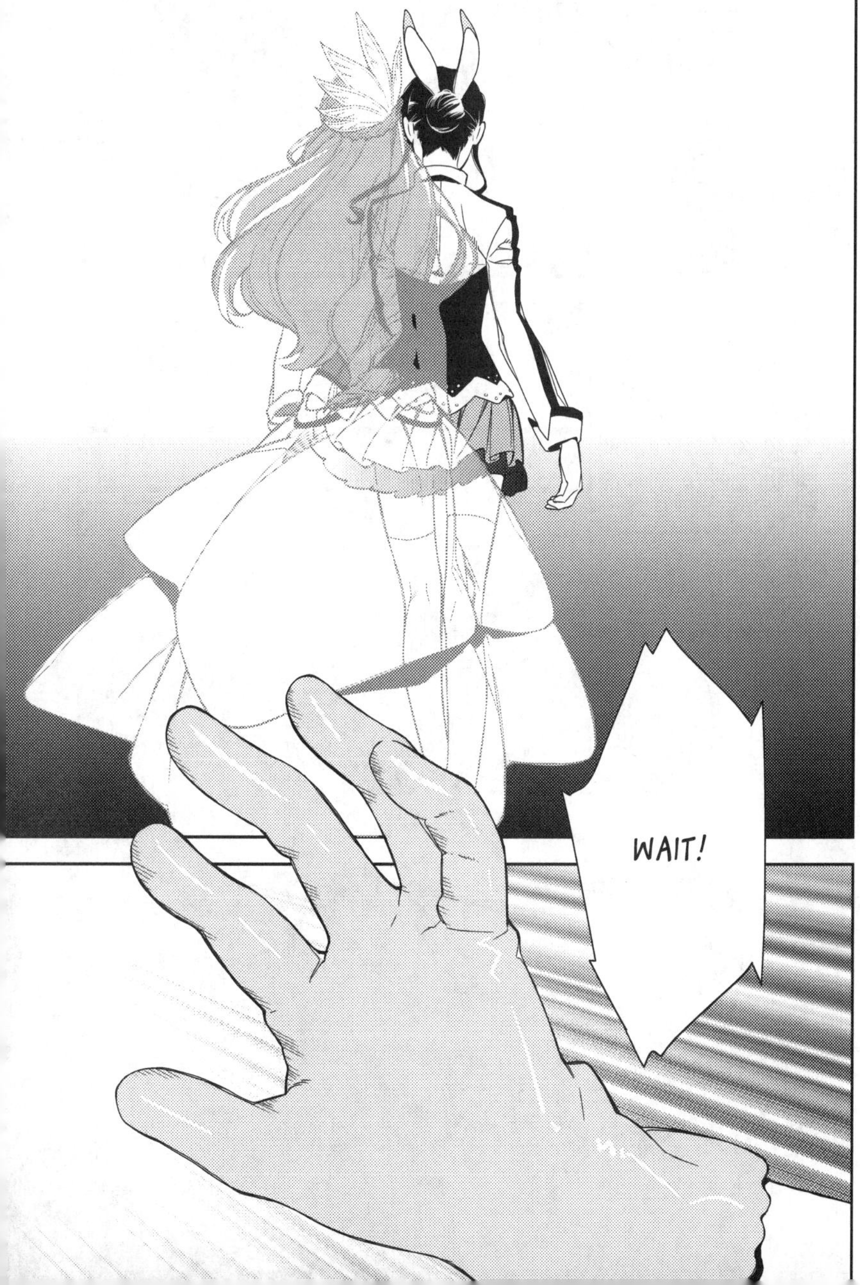
WAIT!

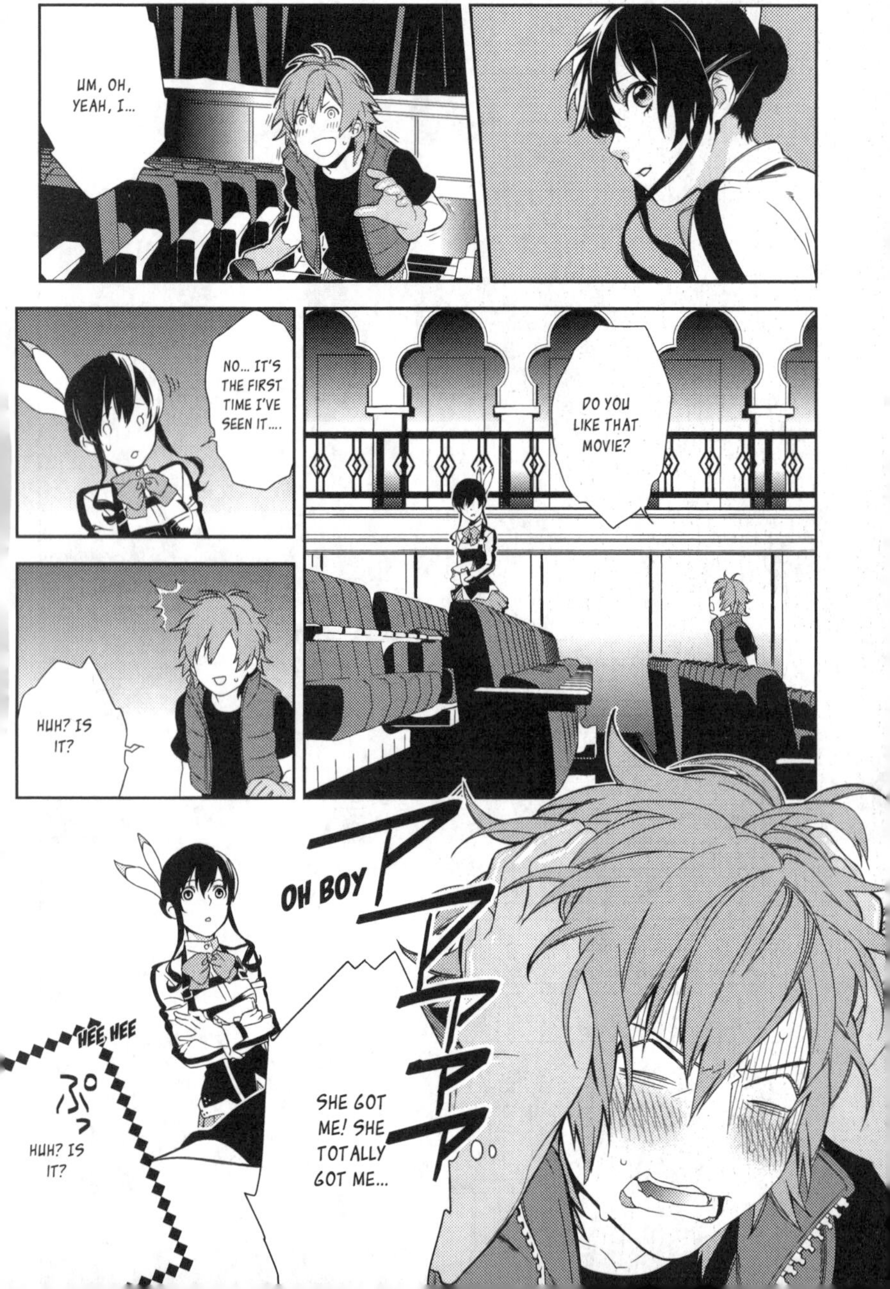
UM, OH, YEAH, I...
DO YOU LIKE THAT MOVIE?
NO... IT'S THE FIRST TIME I'VE SEEN IT....
HUH? IS IT?
OH BOY
SHE GOT ME! SHE TOTALLY GOT ME...
HEE HEE
ぷっ
HUH? IS IT?

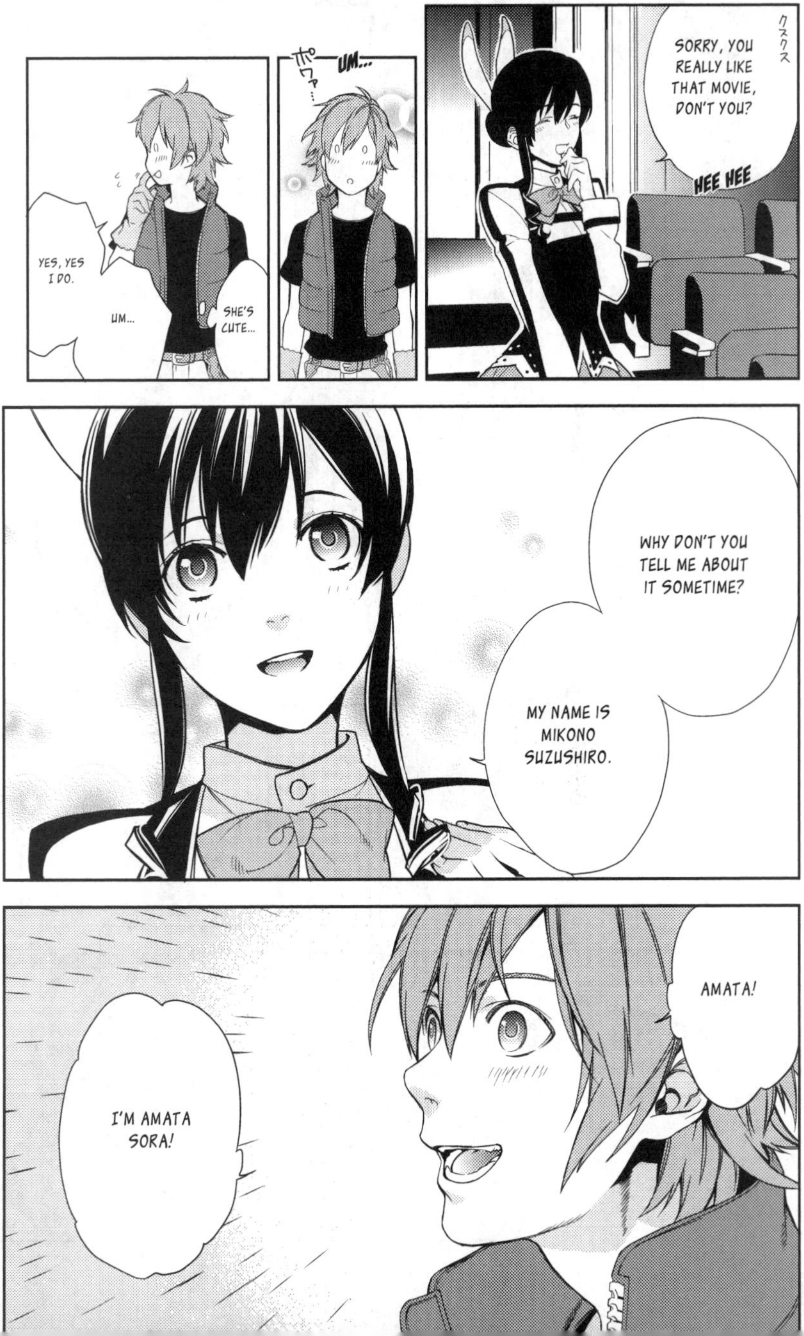
クスクス
SORRY, YOU REALLY LIKE THAT MOVIE, DON'T YOU?
HEE HEE
ポワァ…
UM...
SHE'S CUTE...
UM...
YES, YES I DO.
WHY DON'T YOU TELL ME ABOUT IT SOMETIME?
MY NAME IS MIKONO SUZUSHIRO.
AMATA!
I'M AMATA SORA!

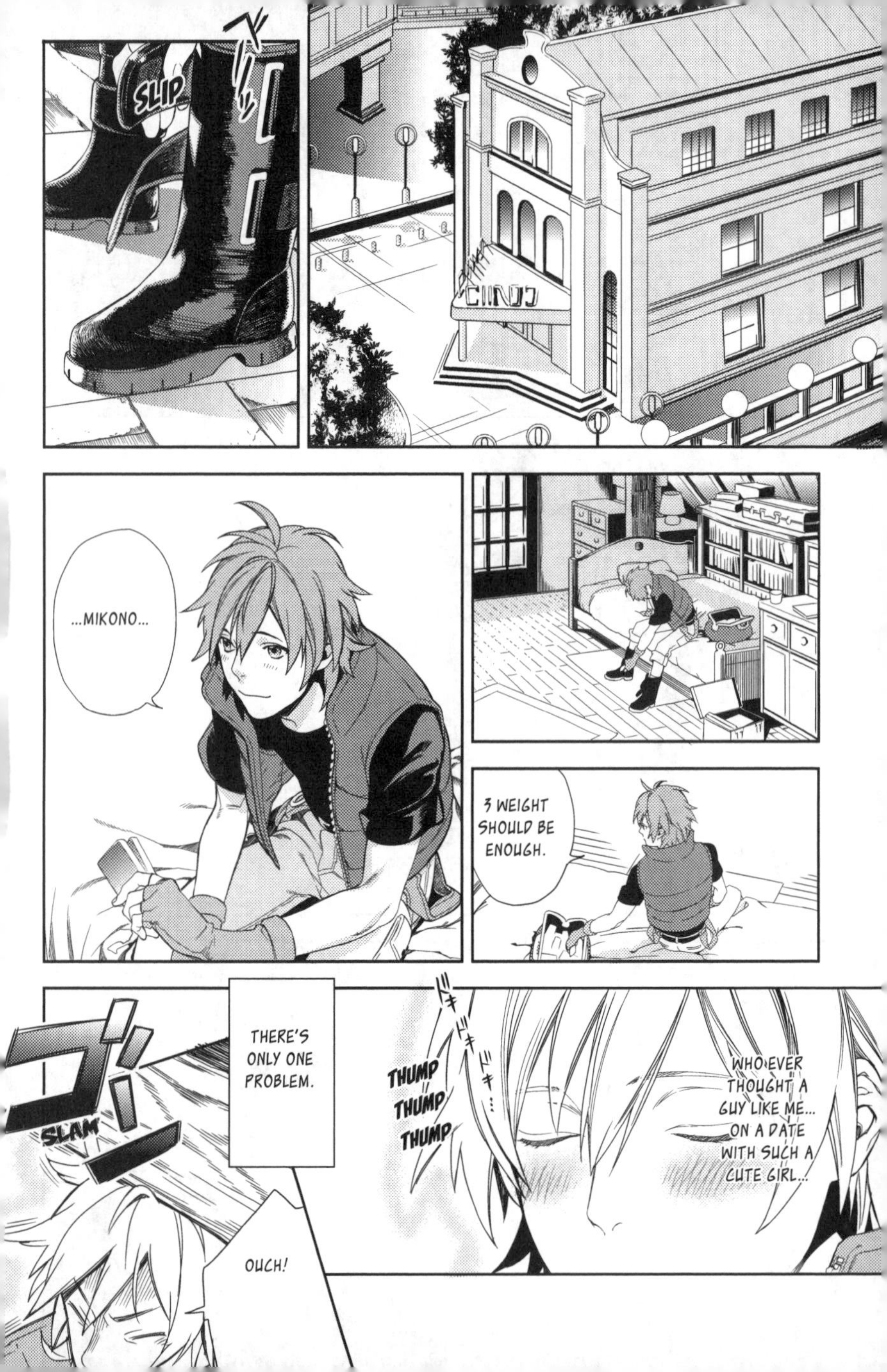
SLIP
3 WEIGHT SHOULD BE ENOUGH.
...MIKONO...
WHO EVER THOUGHT A GUY LIKE ME... ON A DATE WITH SUCH A CUTE GIRL...
ドキドキドキ…
THUMP THUMP THUMP
THERE'S ONLY ONE PROBLEM.
SLAM
OUCH!

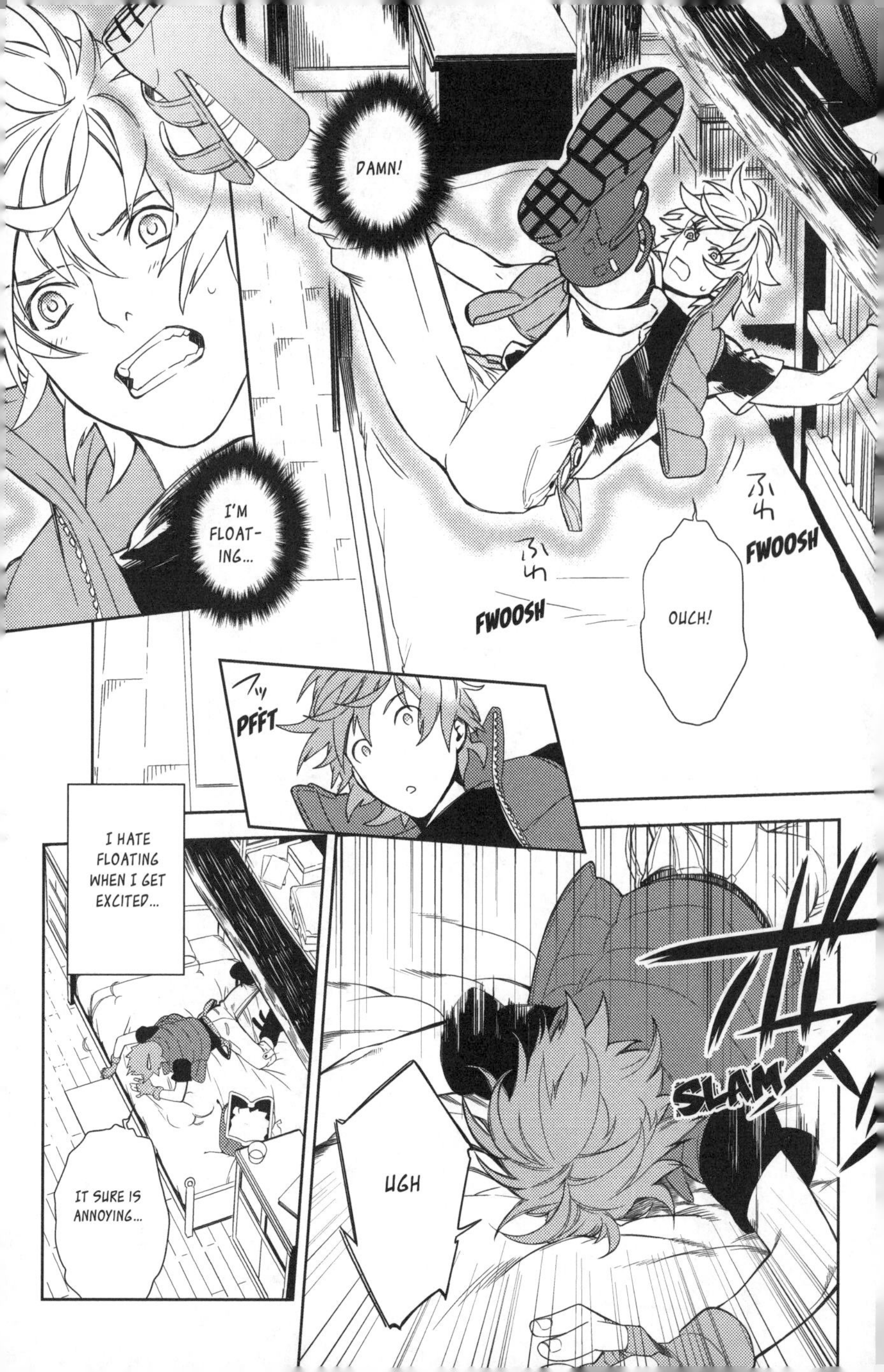

DAMN!
ふわ
FWOOSH
I'M FLOAT-ING...
ふわ
FWOOSH
OUCH!
ブッ
PFFT
SLAM
UGH
I HATE FLOATING WHEN I GET EXCITED...
IT SURE IS ANNOYING...

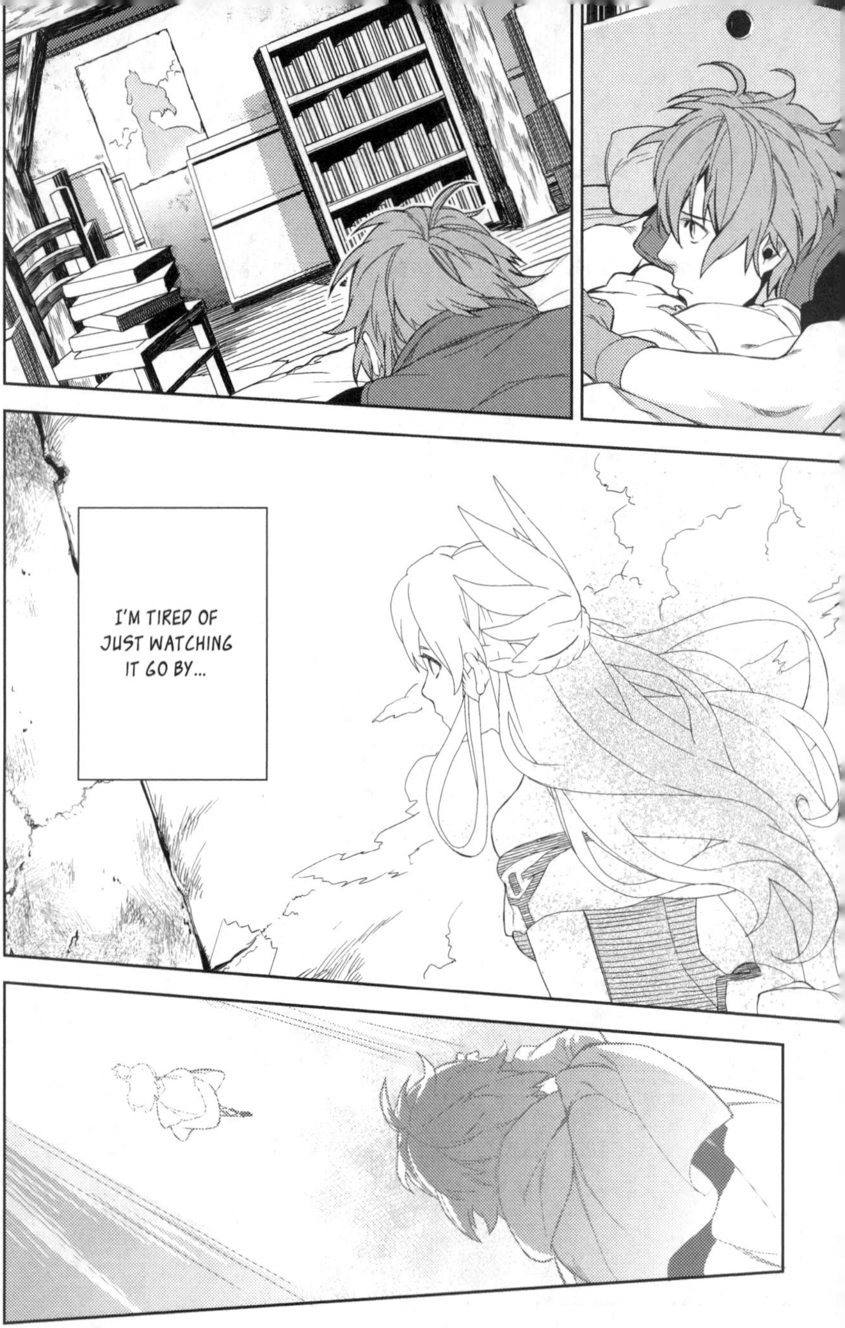
I'M TIRED OF JUST WATCHING IT GO BY...

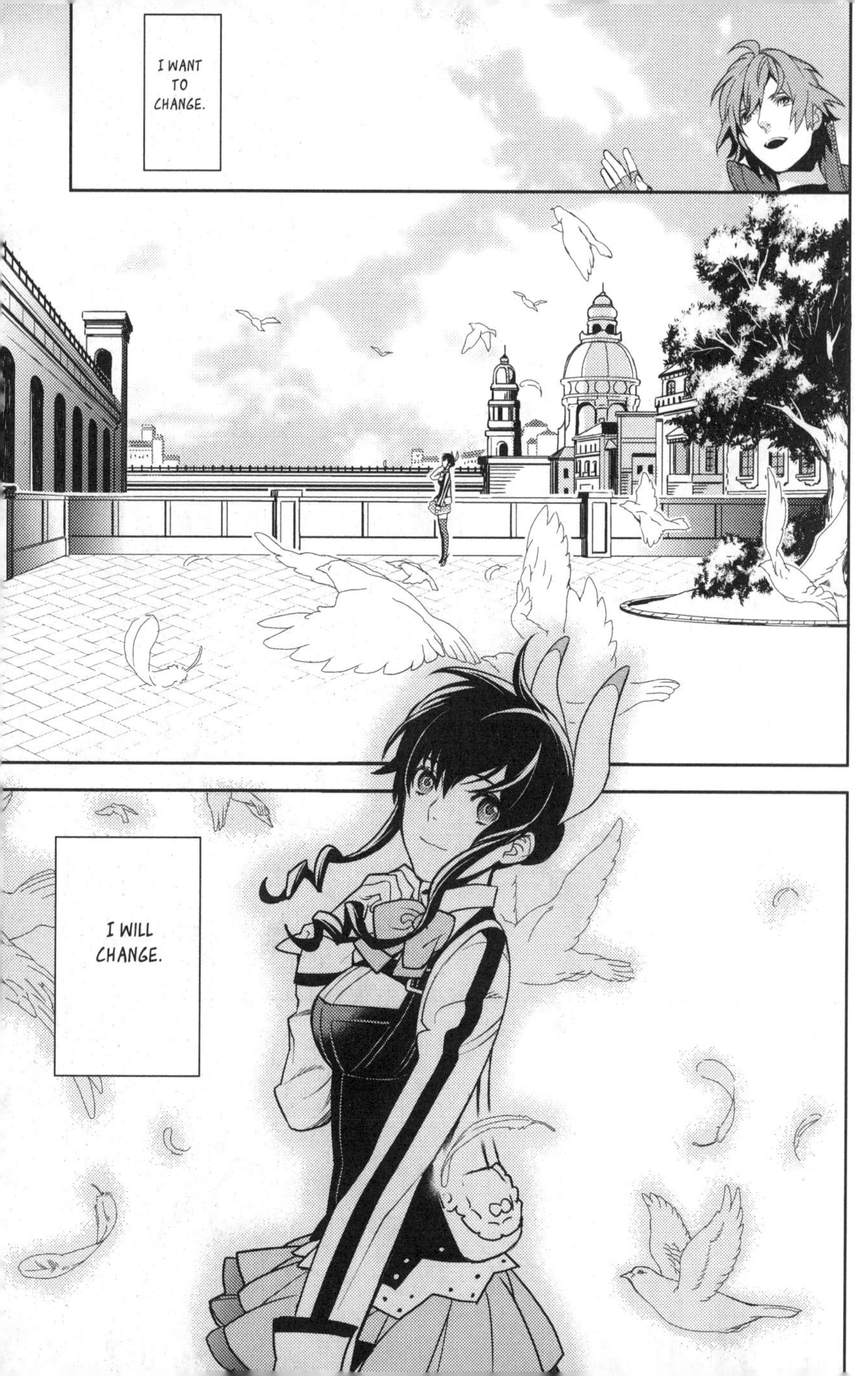
I WANT TO CHANGE.
I WILL CHANGE.

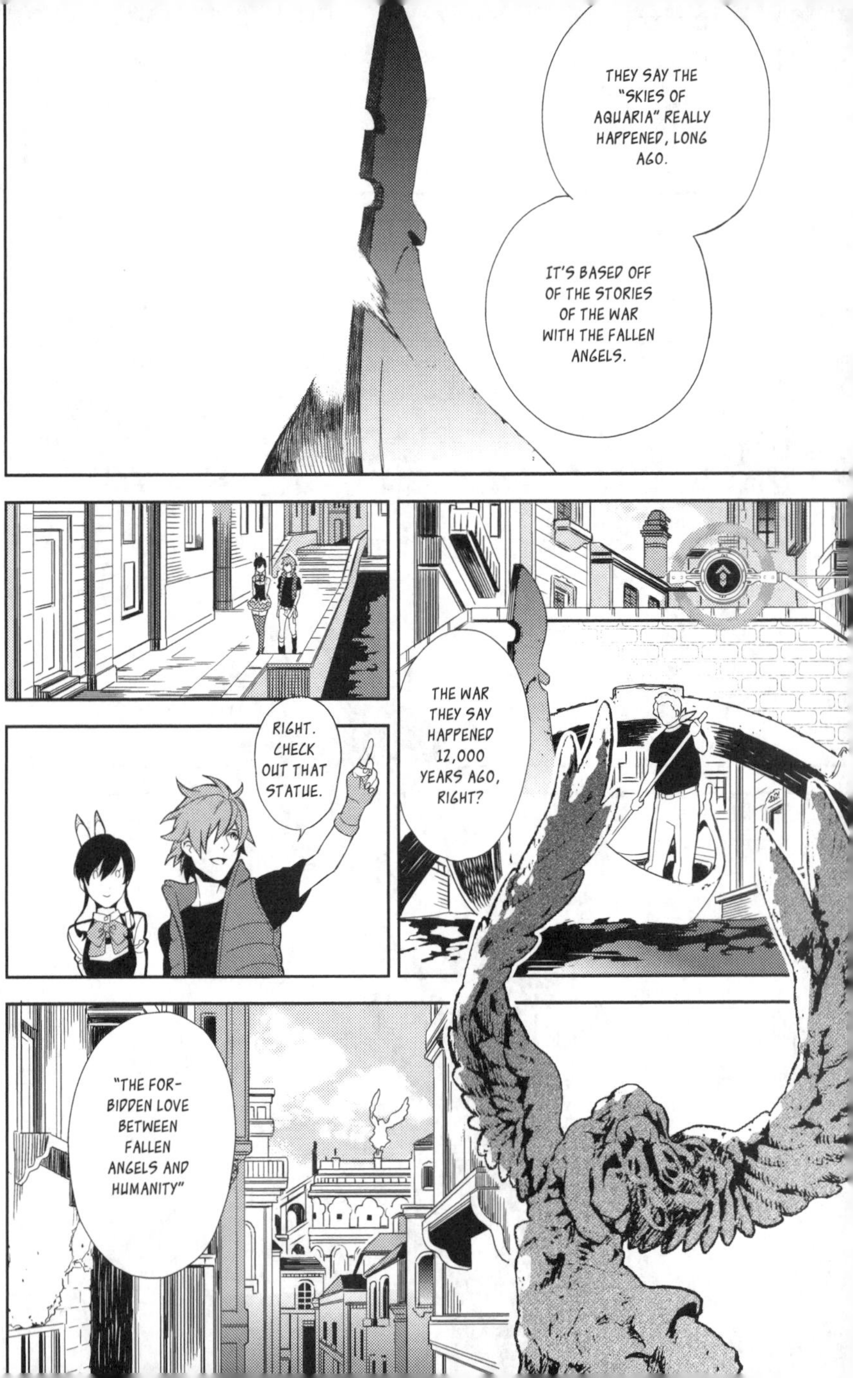
THEY SAY THE "SKIES OF AQUARIA" REALLY HAPPENED, LONG AGO.
IT'S BASED OFF OF THE STORIES OF THE WAR WITH THE FALLEN ANGELS.
THE WAR THEY SAY HAPPENED 12,000 YEARS AGO, RIGHT?
RIGHT. CHECK OUT THAT STATUE.
"THE FOR-BIDDEN LOVE BETWEEN FALLEN ANGELS AND HUMANITY"

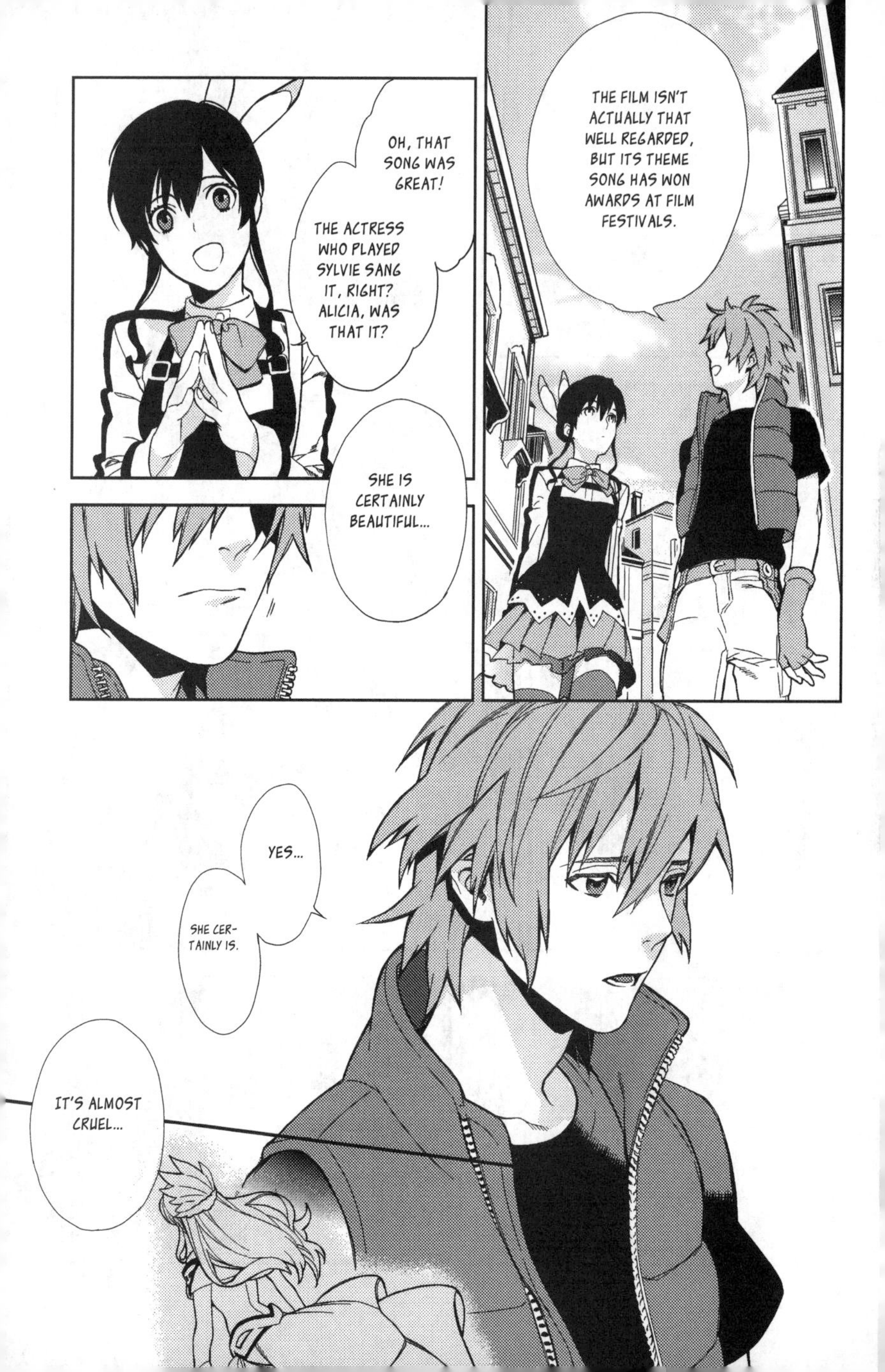
THE FILM ISN'T ACTUALLY THAT WELL REGARDED, BUT ITS THEME SONG HAS WON AWARDS AT FILM FESTIVALS.
OH, THAT SONG WAS GREAT!
THE ACTRESS WHO PLAYED SYLVIE SANG IT, RIGHT? ALICIA, WAS THAT IT?
SHE IS CERTAINLY BEAUTIFUL...
YES...
SHE CER-TAINLY IS.
IT'S ALMOST CRUEL...

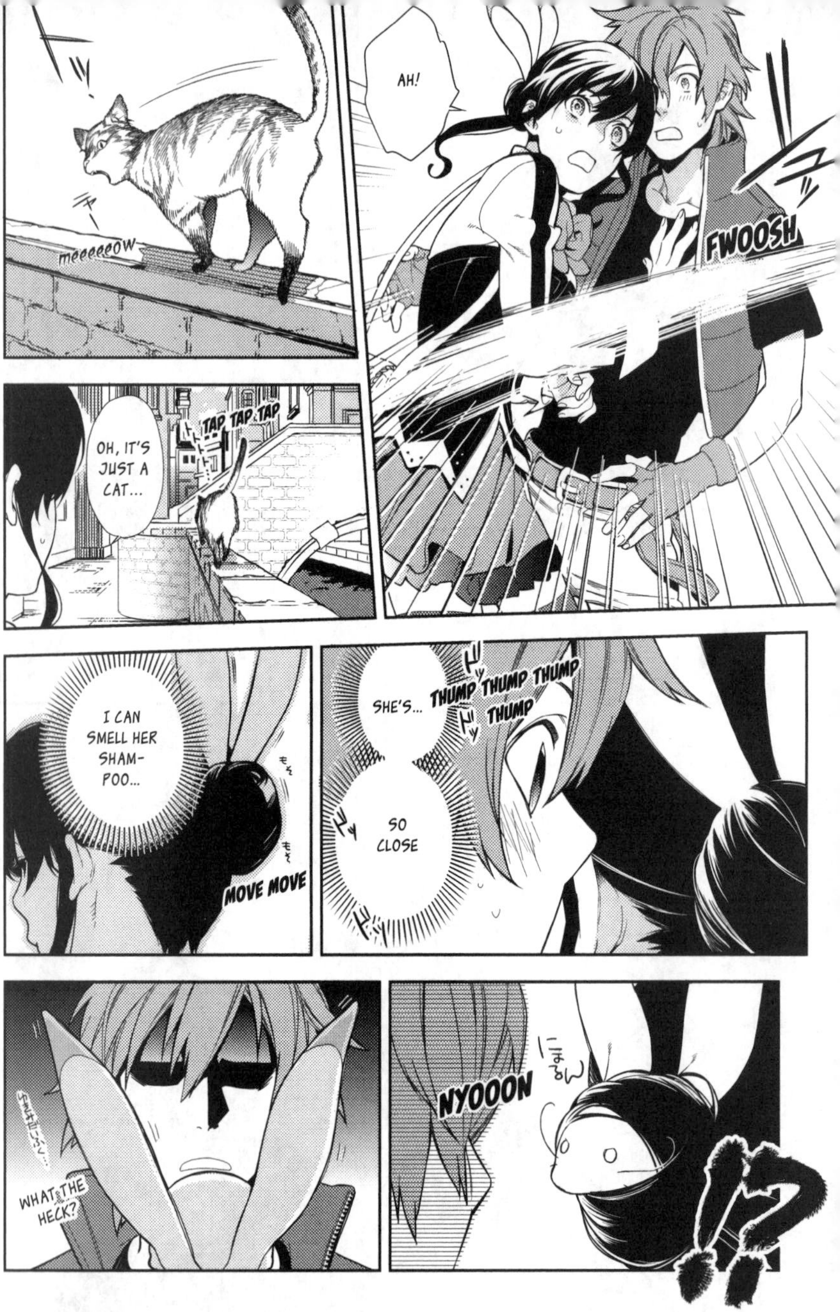
AH!
FWOOSH
meeeeeow
TAP TAP TAP
OH, IT'S JUST A CAT...
SHE'S...
THUMP THUMP THUMP
THUMP
SO CLOSE
I CAN SMELL HER SHAM- POO...
MOVE MOVE
NYOOON
!?
WHAT THE HECK?

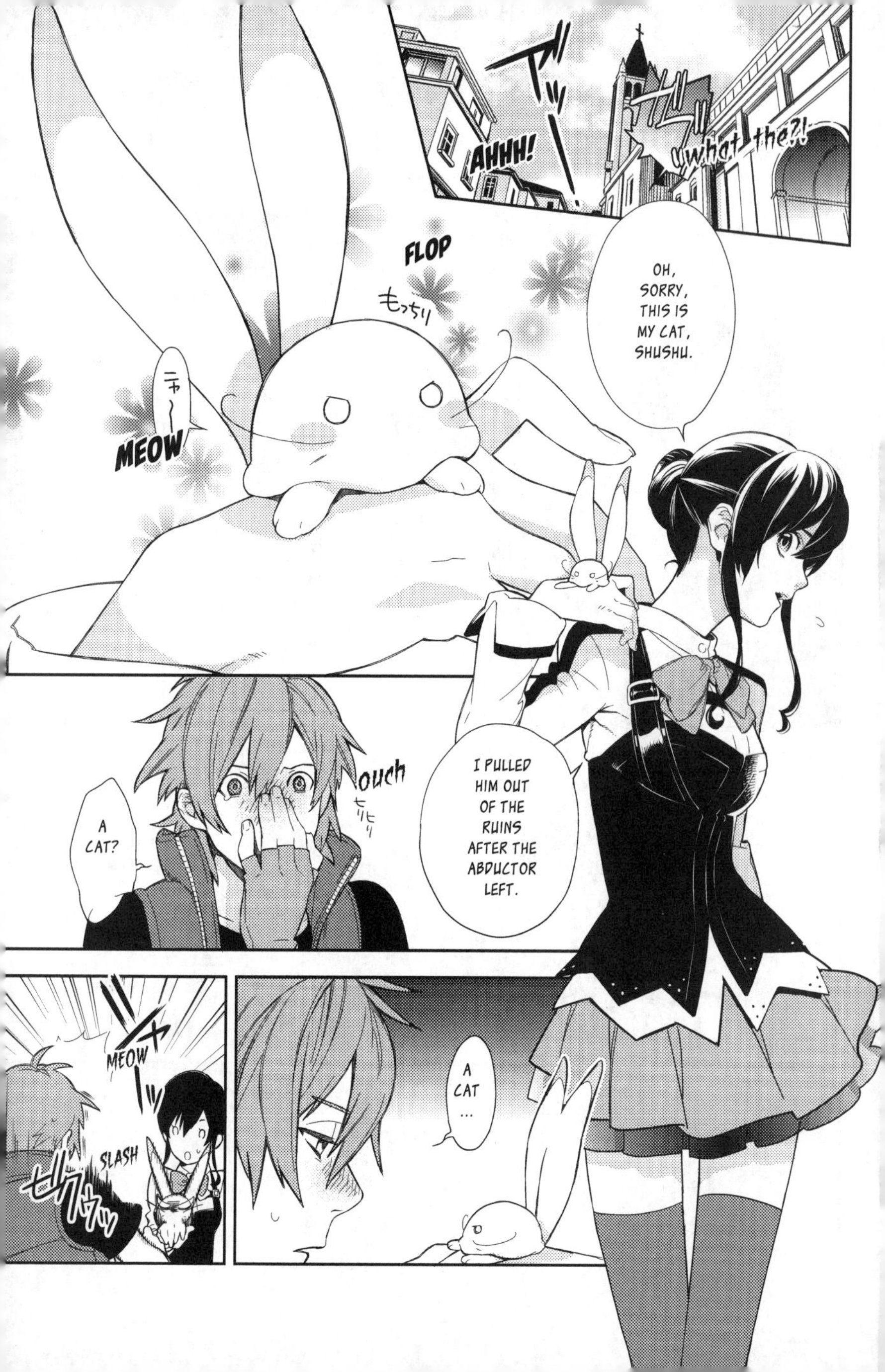
AHHH!
what the?!
OH, SORRY, THIS IS MY CAT, SHUSHU.
FLOP
もっちり
ニャ〜
MEOW
I PULLED HIM OUT OF THE RUINS AFTER THE ABDUCTOR LEFT.
ouch
ヒリヒリ
A CAT?
A CAT ...
MEOW
SLASH

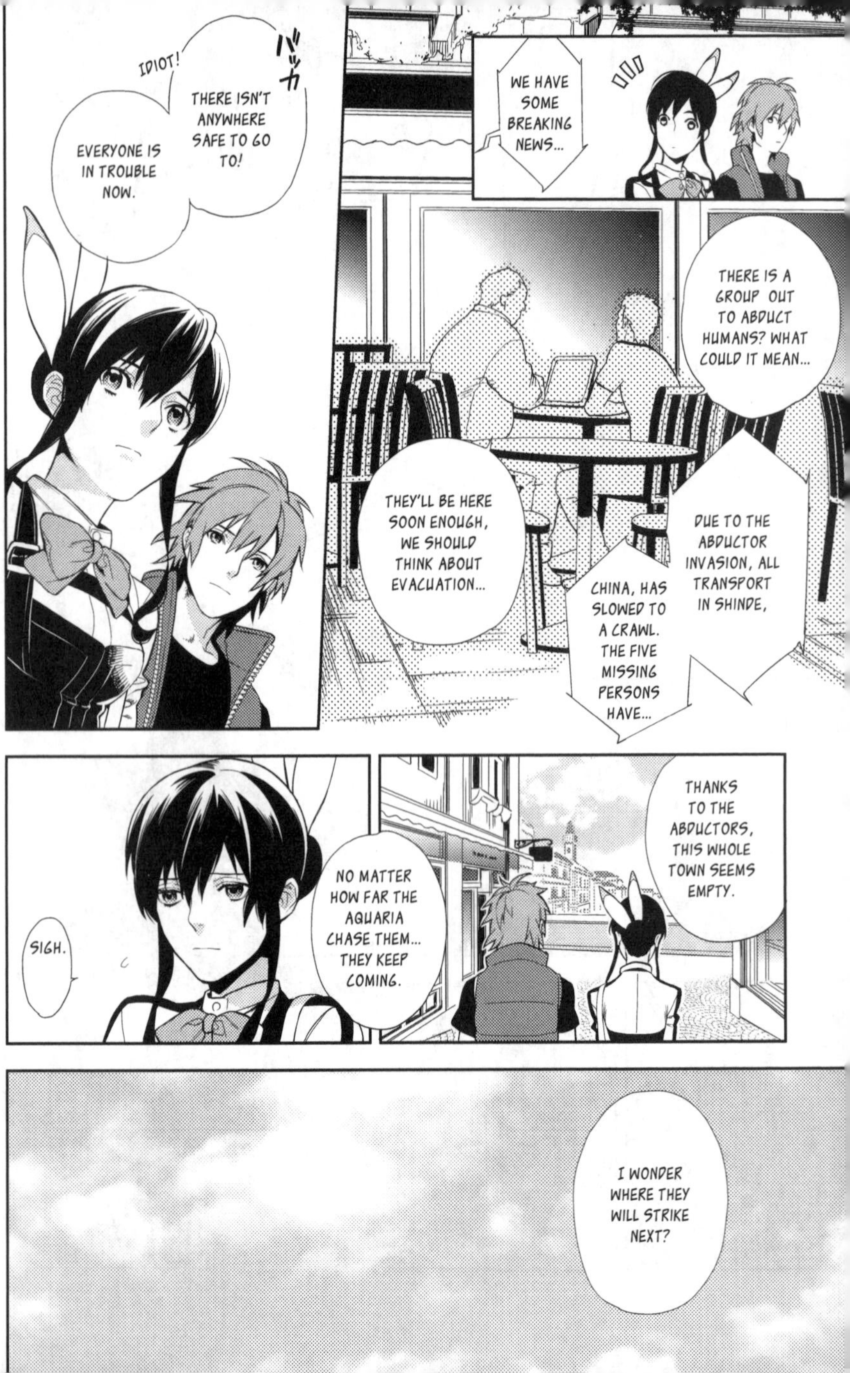
WE HAVE SOME BREAKING NEWS...
THERE IS A GROUP OUT TO ABDUCT HUMANS? WHAT COULD IT MEAN...
DUE TO THE ABDUCTOR INVASION, ALL TRANSPORT IN SHINDE,
CHINA, HAS SLOWED TO A CRAWL. THE FIVE MISSING PERSONS HAVE...
THEY'LL BE HERE SOON ENOUGH, WE SHOULD THINK ABOUT EVACUATION...
バッカ
THERE ISN'T ANYWHERE SAFE TO GO TO!
IDIOT!
EVERYONE IS IN TROUBLE NOW.
THANKS TO THE ABDUCTORS, THIS WHOLE TOWN SEEMS EMPTY.
NO MATTER HOW FAR THE AQUARIA CHASE THEM... THEY KEEP COMING.
SIGH.
I WONDER WHERE THEY WILL STRIKE NEXT?

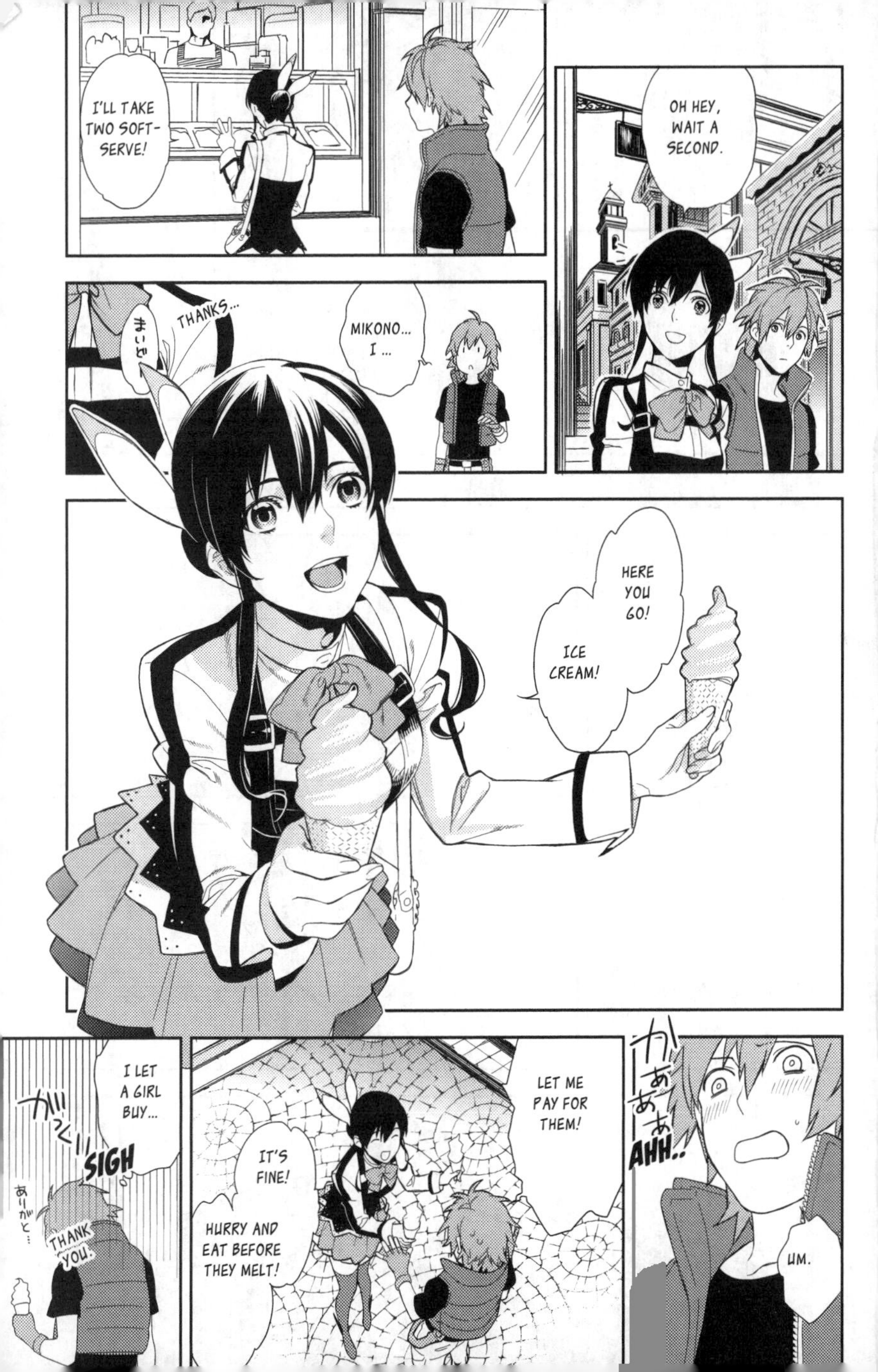
OH HEY, WAIT A SECOND.
I'LL TAKE TWO SOFT-SERVE!
MIKONO... I ...
THANKS...
まいど
HERE YOU GO!
ICE CREAM!
かぁぁぁ
AHH..
UM.
LET ME PAY FOR THEM!
IT'S FINE!
HURRY AND EAT BEFORE THEY MELT!
I LET A GIRL BUY...
がくっ
SIGH
ありがと…
THANK YOU.

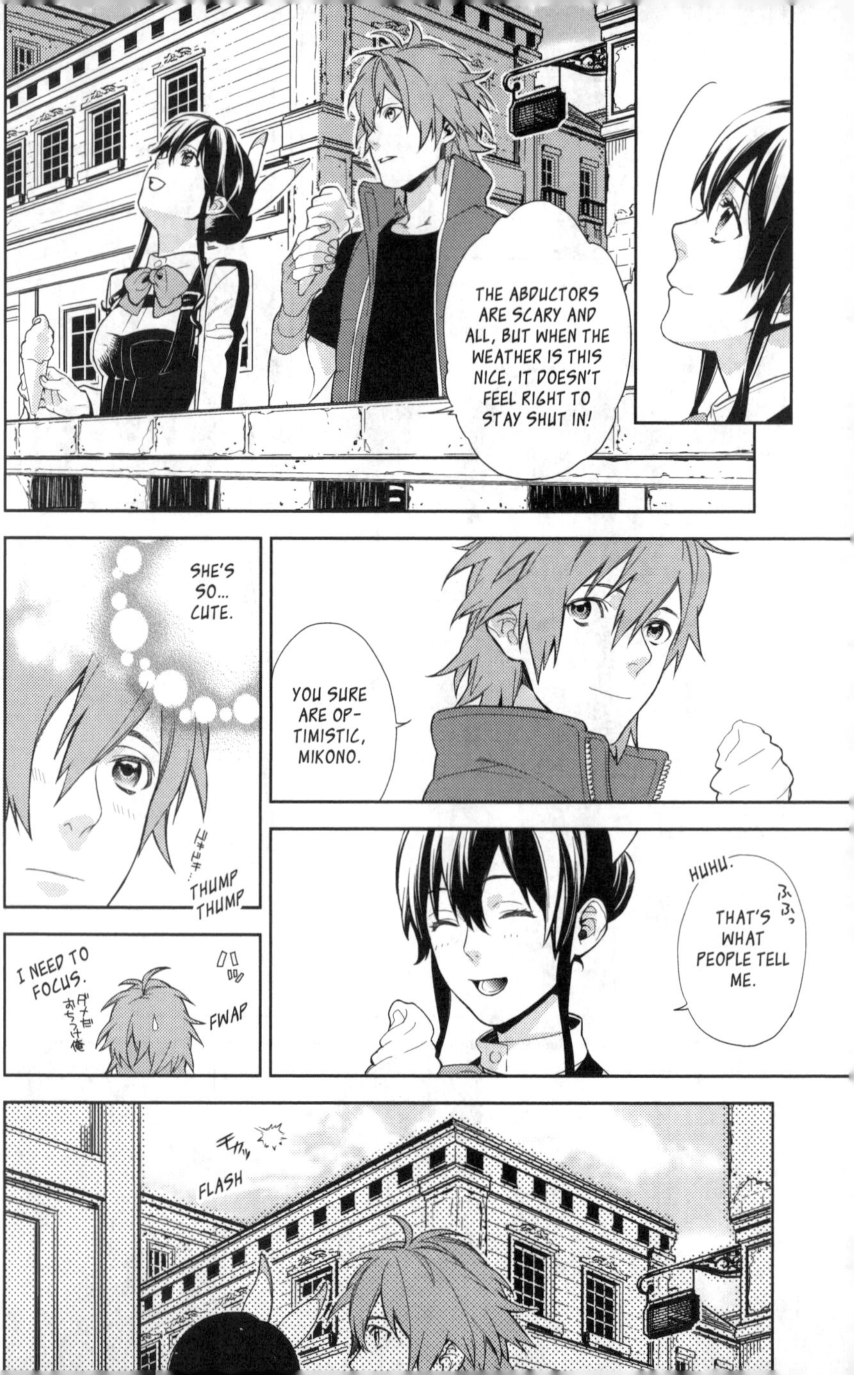
THE ABDUCTORS ARE SCARY AND ALL, BUT WHEN THE WEATHER IS THIS NICE, IT DOESN'T FEEL RIGHT TO STAY SHUT IN!
YOU SURE ARE OP-TIMISTIC, MIKONO.
HUHU.
ふふっ
THAT'S WHAT PEOPLE TELL ME.
SHE'S SO... CUTE.
ドキドキ…
THUMP THUMP
I NEED TO FOCUS.
ダメだおちつけ俺
FWAP
FLASH

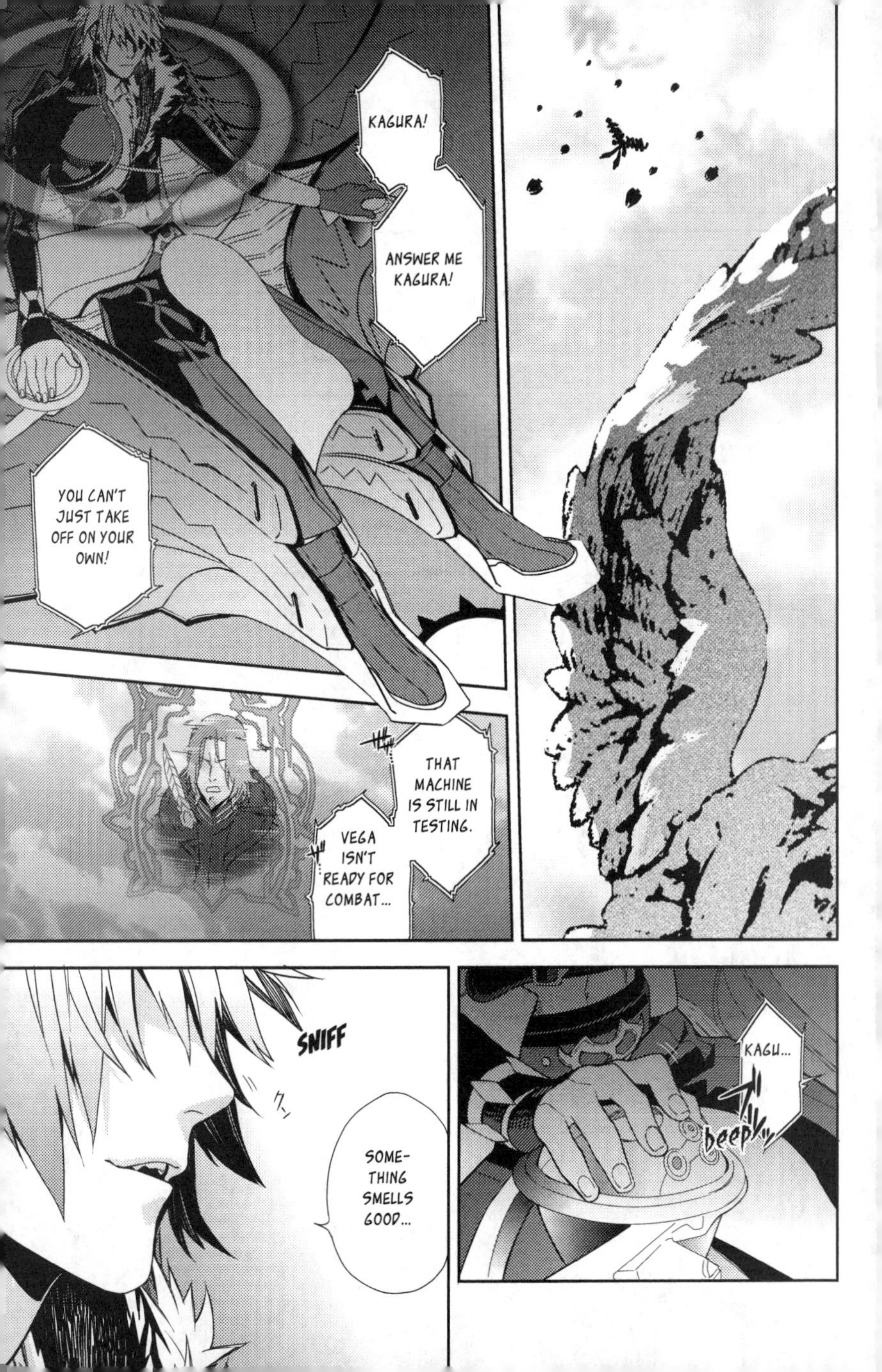
KAGURA!
ANSWER ME KAGURA!
YOU CAN'T JUST TAKE OFF ON YOUR OWN!
THAT MACHINE IS STILL IN TESTING.
VEGA ISN'T READY FOR COMBAT...
KAGU...
beep
SNIFF
SOME-THING SMELLS GOOD...

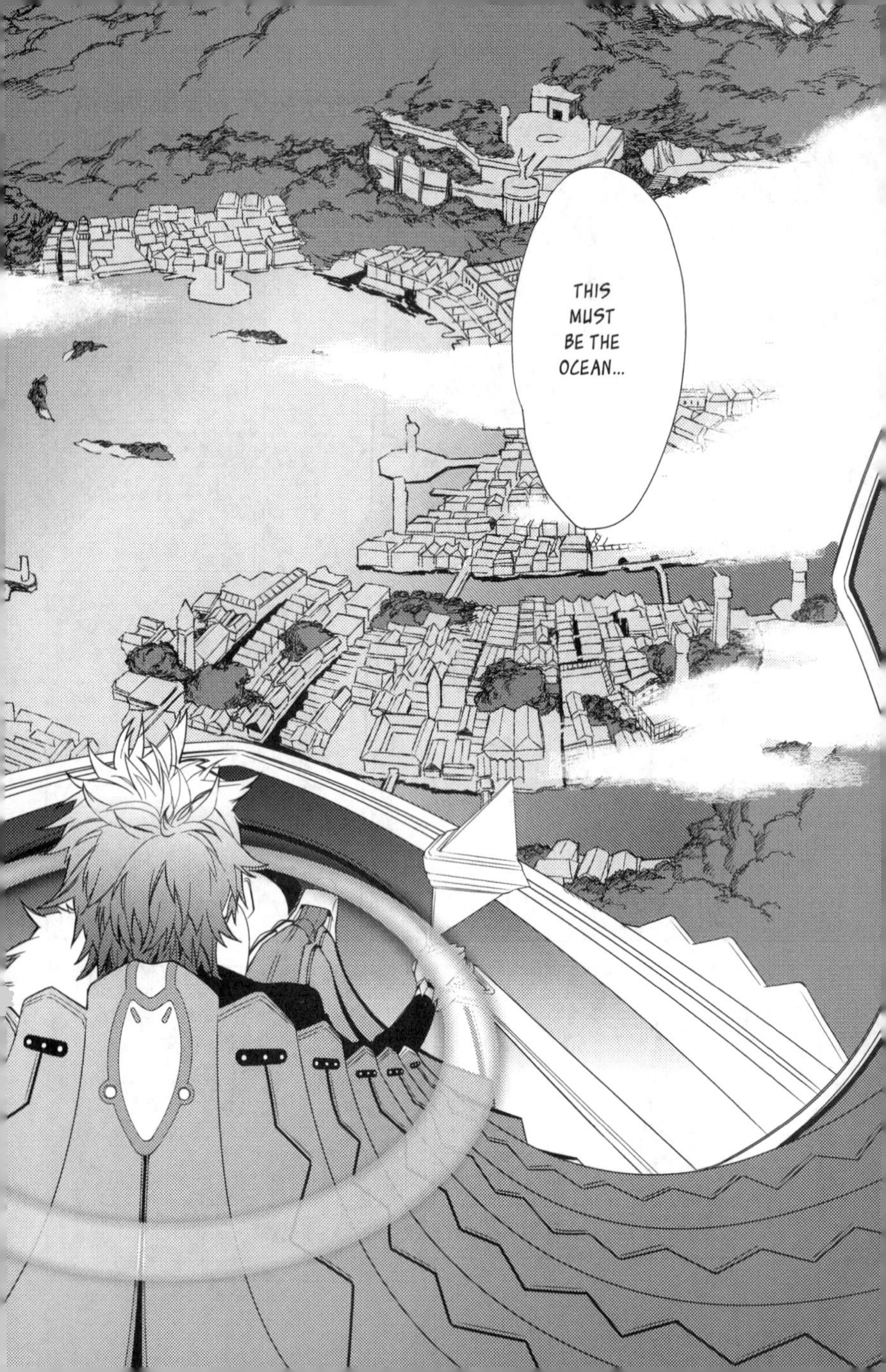
THIS MUST BE THE OCEAN...

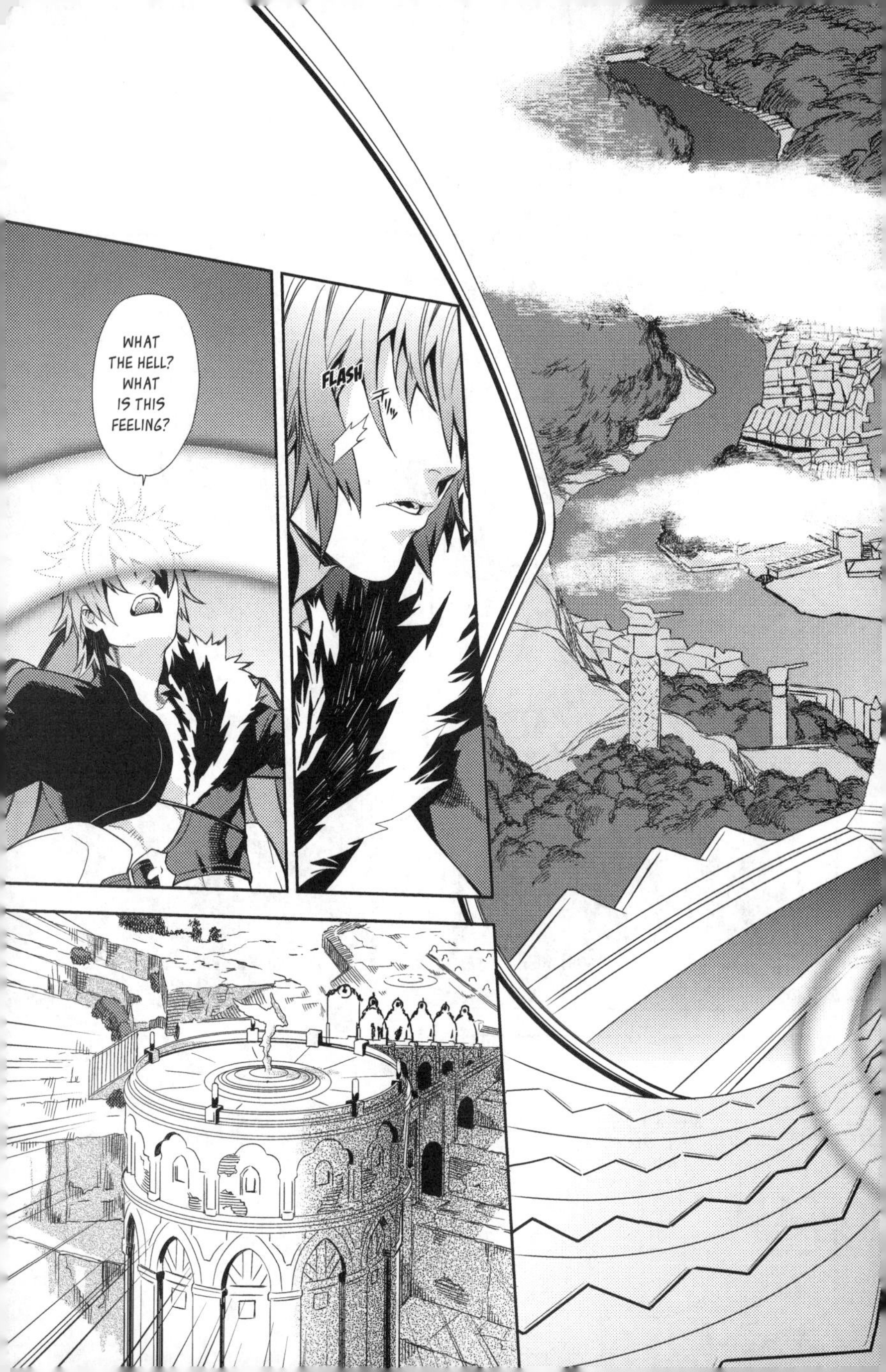
FLASH
WHAT THE HELL? WHAT IS THIS FEELING?

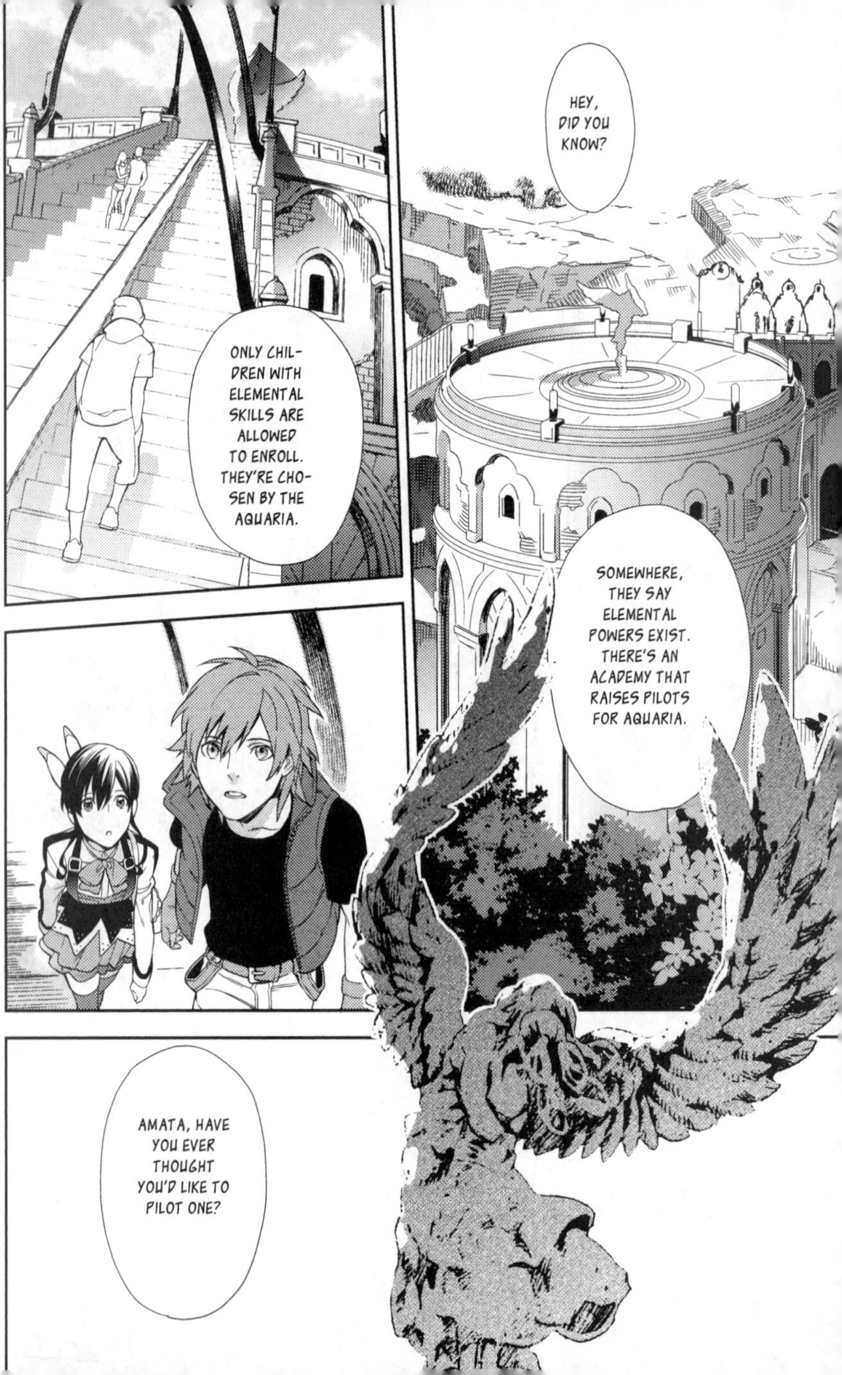
HEY, DID YOU KNOW?
SOMEWHERE, THEY SAY ELEMENTAL POWERS EXIST. THERE'S AN ACADEMY THAT RAISES PILOTS FOR AQUARIA.
ONLY CHILDREN WITH ELEMENTAL SKILLS ARE ALLOWED TO ENROLL. THEY'RE CHOSEN BY THE AQUARIA.
AMATA, HAVE YOU EVER THOUGHT YOU'D LIKE TO PILOT ONE?

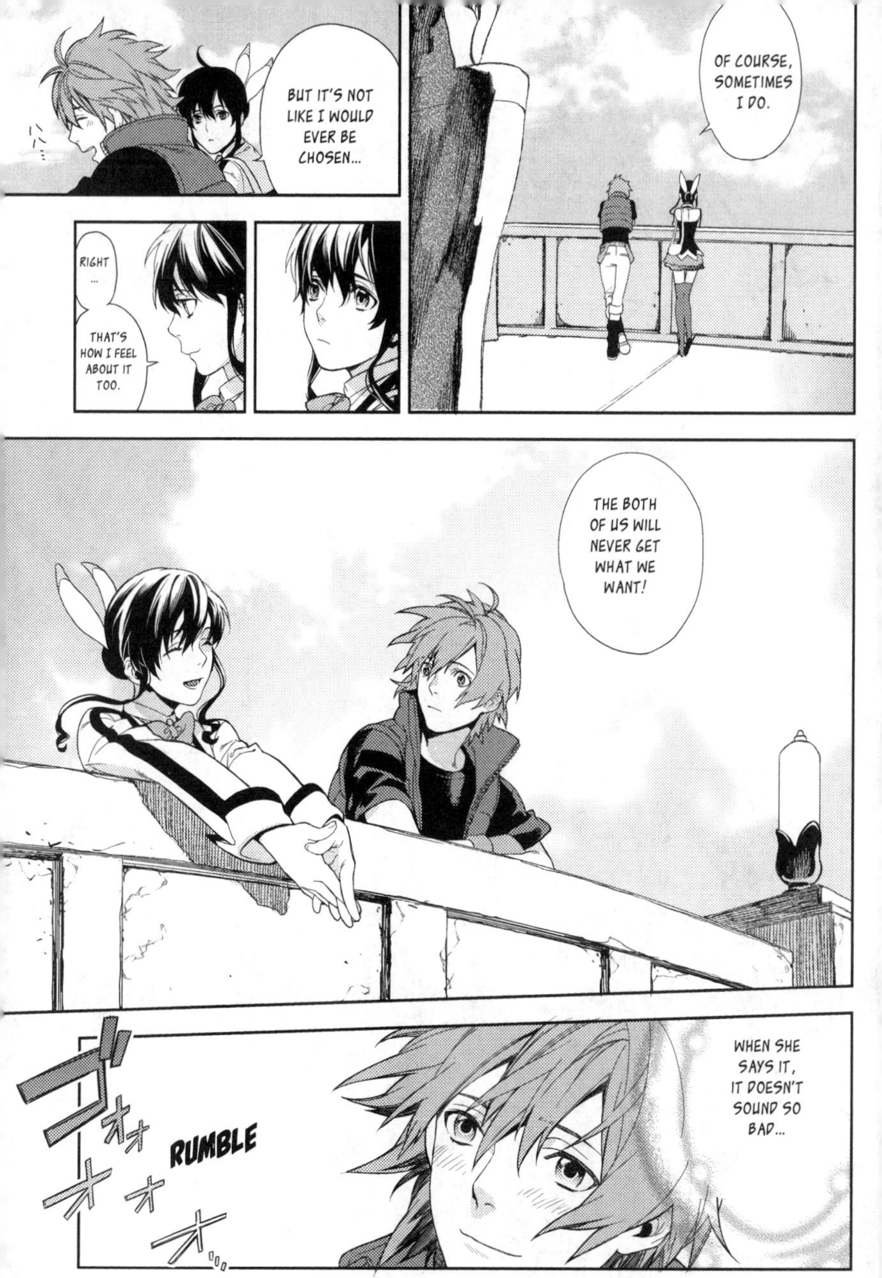
OF COURSE, SOMETIMES I DO.
BUT IT'S NOT LIKE I WOULD EVER BE CHOSEN...
RIGHT ...
THAT'S HOW I FEEL ABOUT IT TOO.
THE BOTH OF US WILL NEVER GET WHAT WE WANT!
WHEN SHE SAYS IT, IT DOESN'T SOUND SO BAD...
RUMBLE

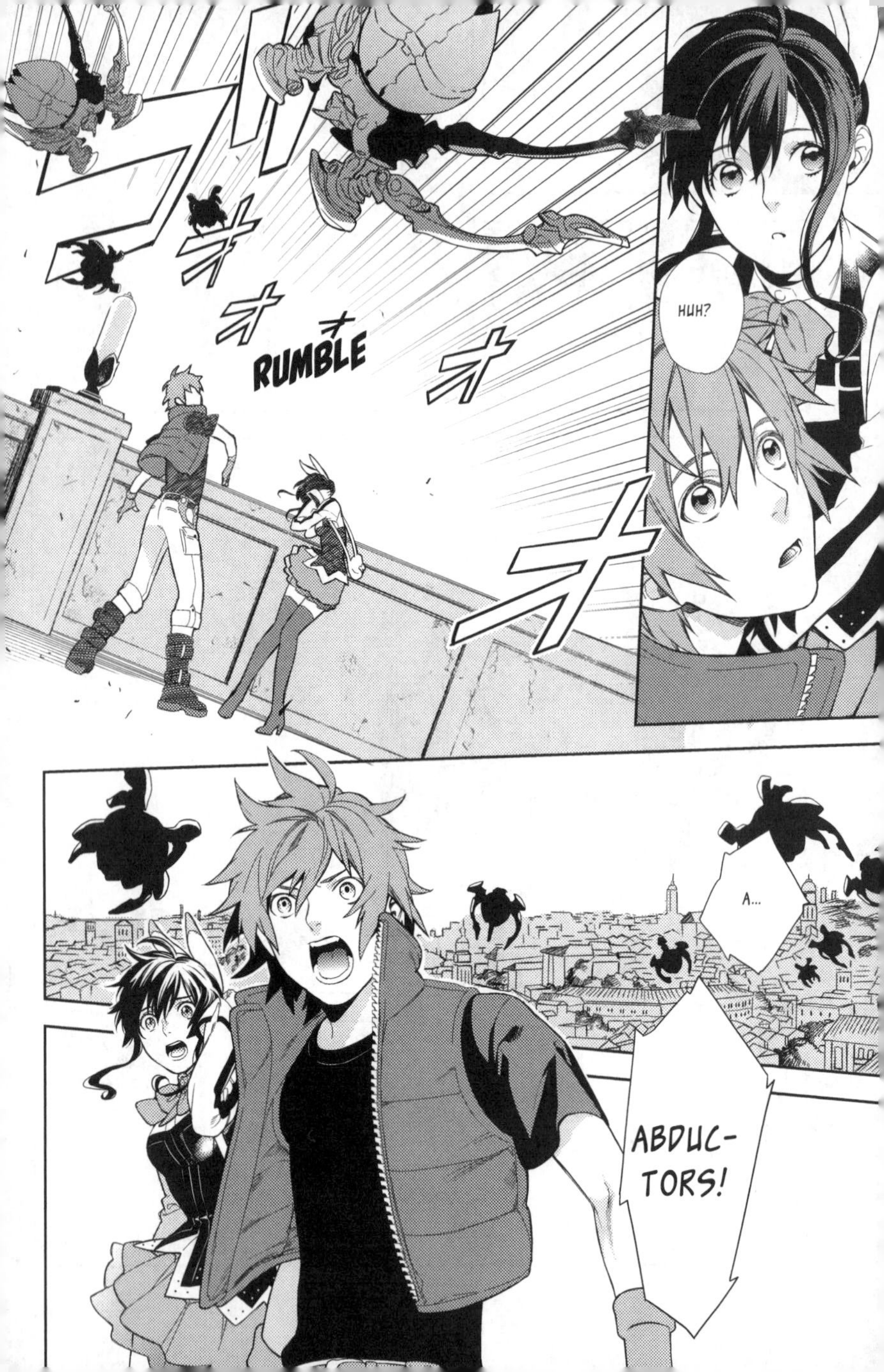
HUH?
RUMBLE
A...
ABDUC-
TORS!

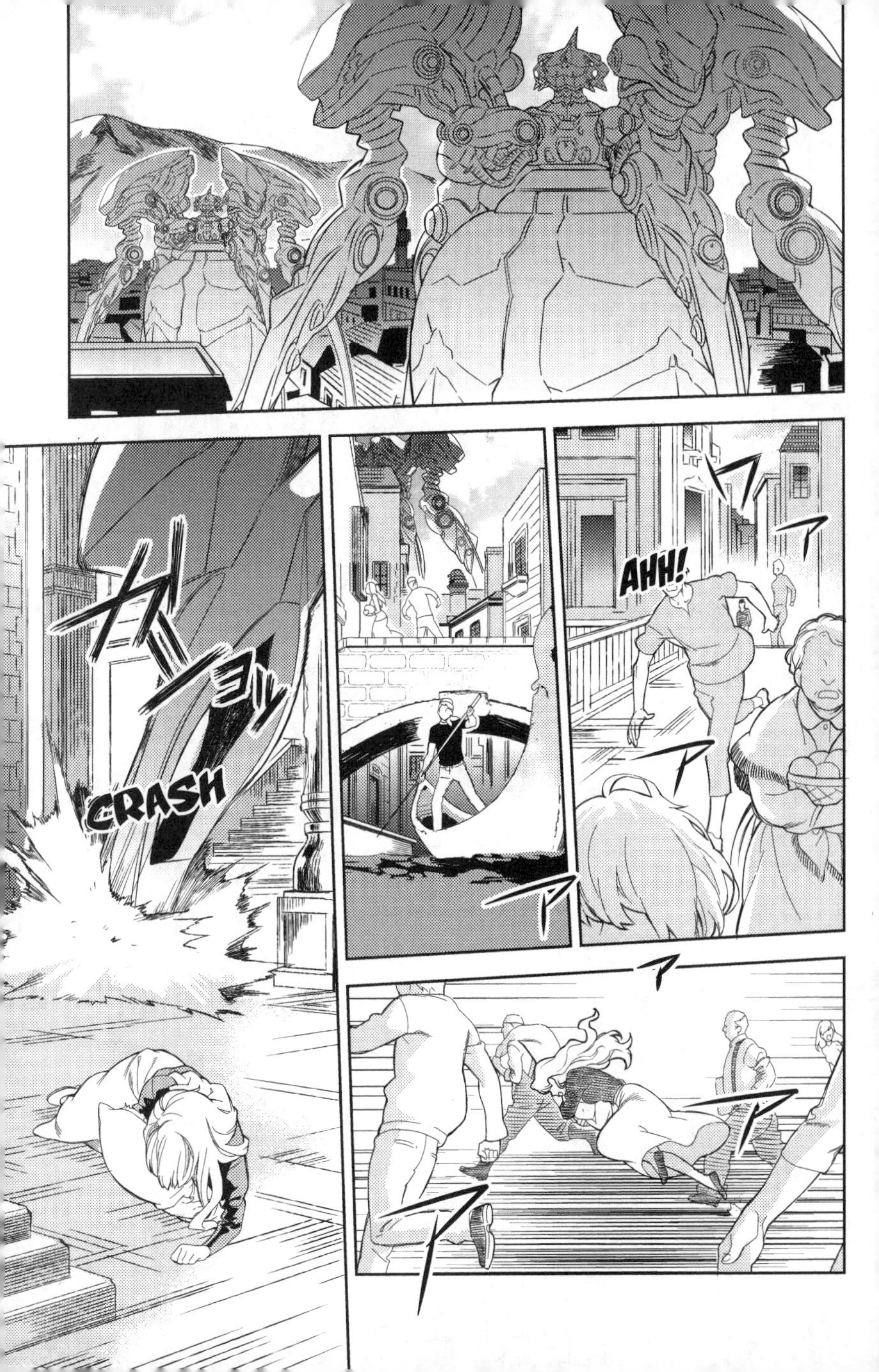
AHH!
CRASH

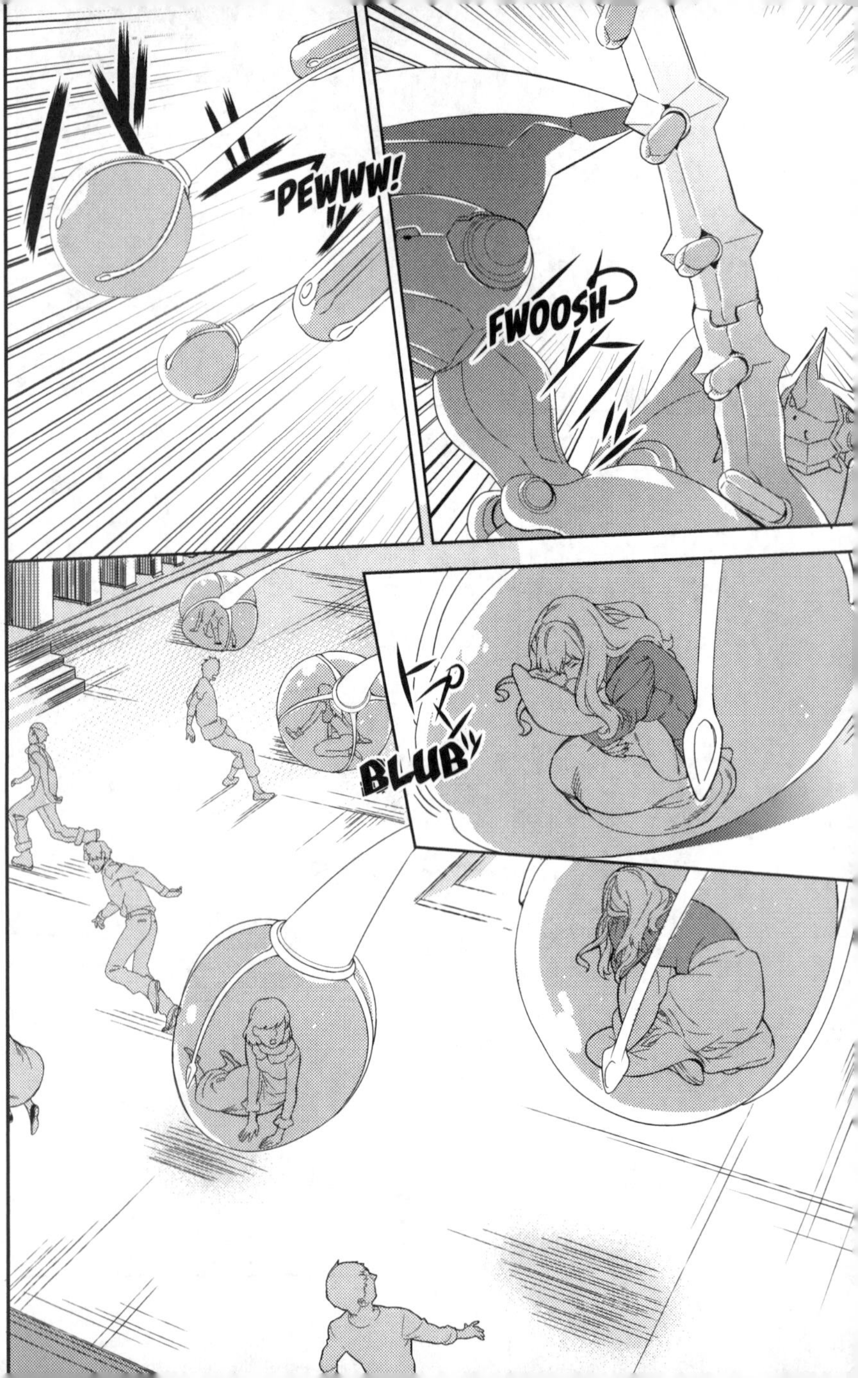
FWOOSH
PEWWW!
BLUB

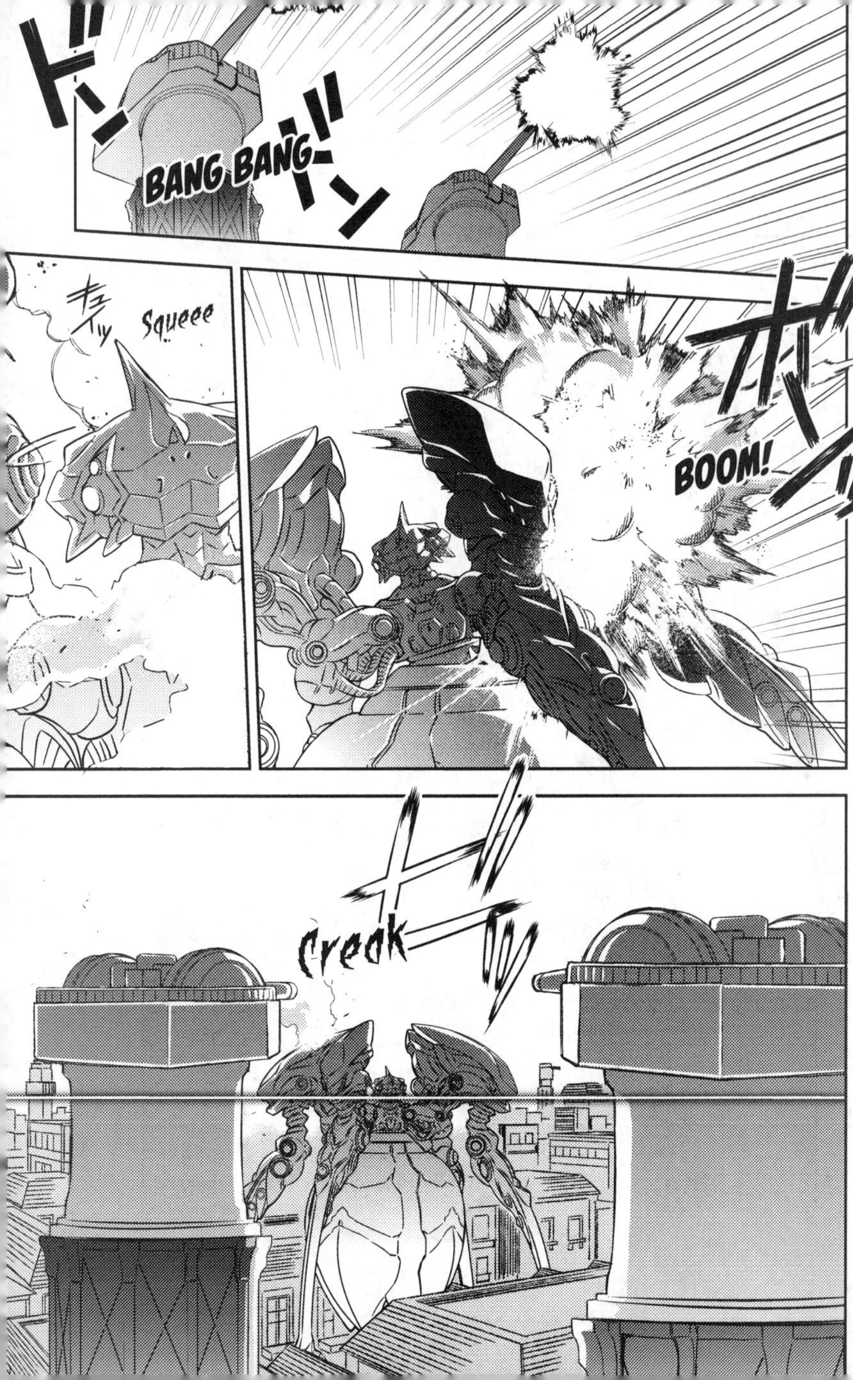
ドン
ドン
BANG BANG
BOOM!
キュイッ
Squeee
Creak

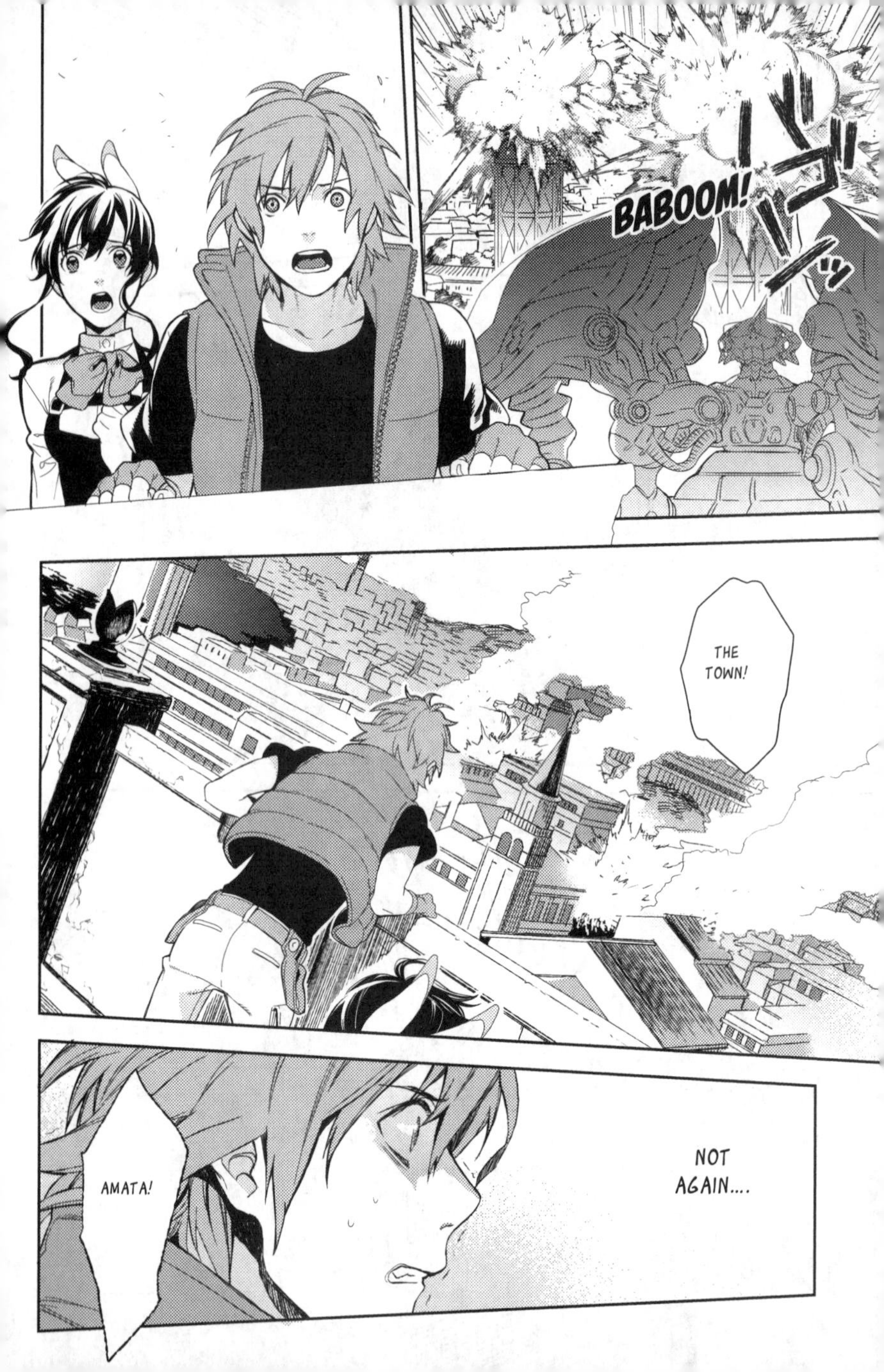
BABOOM!
THE TOWN!
NOT AGAIN....
AMATA!

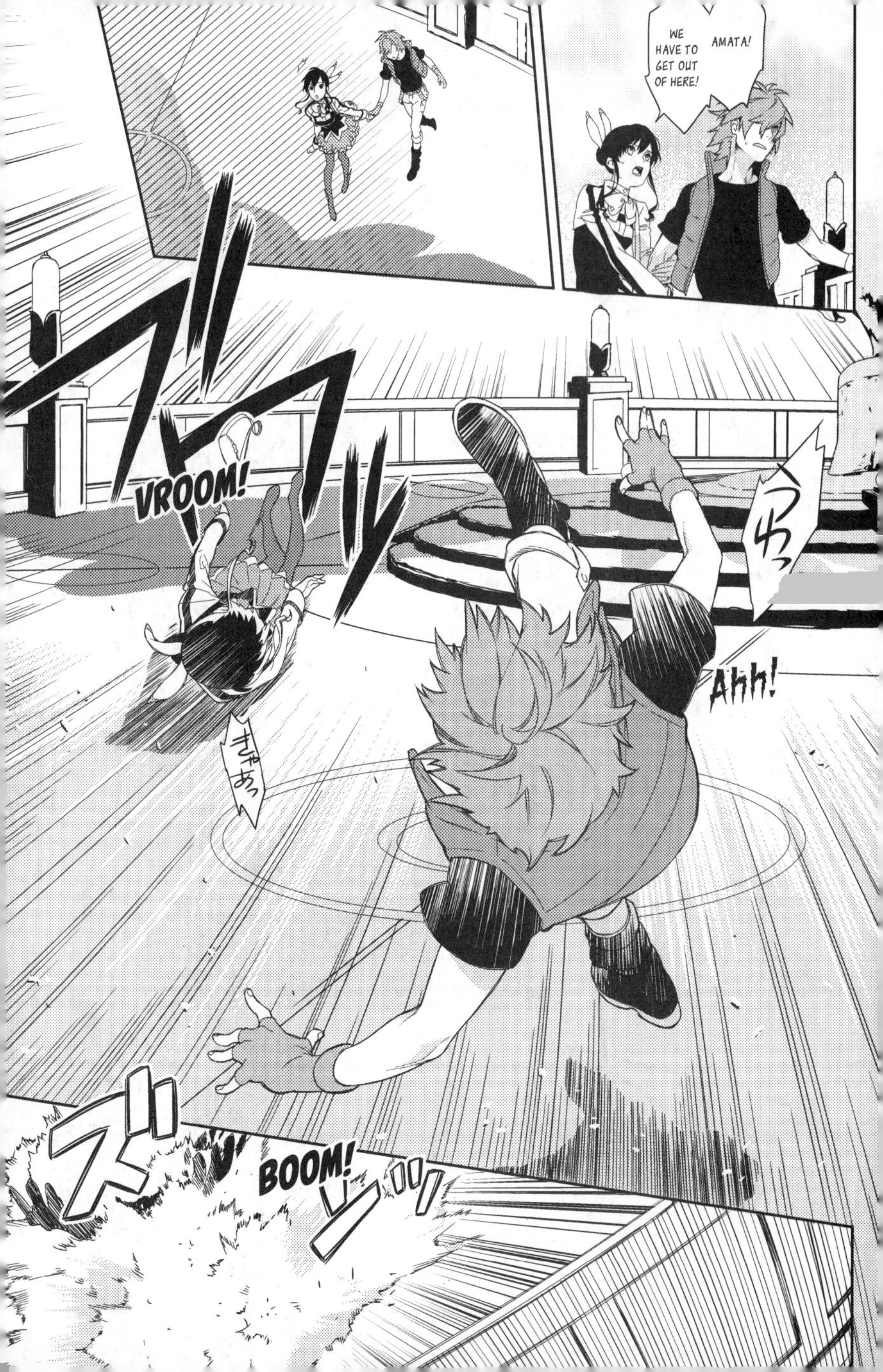
AMATA!
WE HAVE TO GET OUT OF HERE!
VROOM!
うわっ
Ahh!
きゃあっ
BOOM!

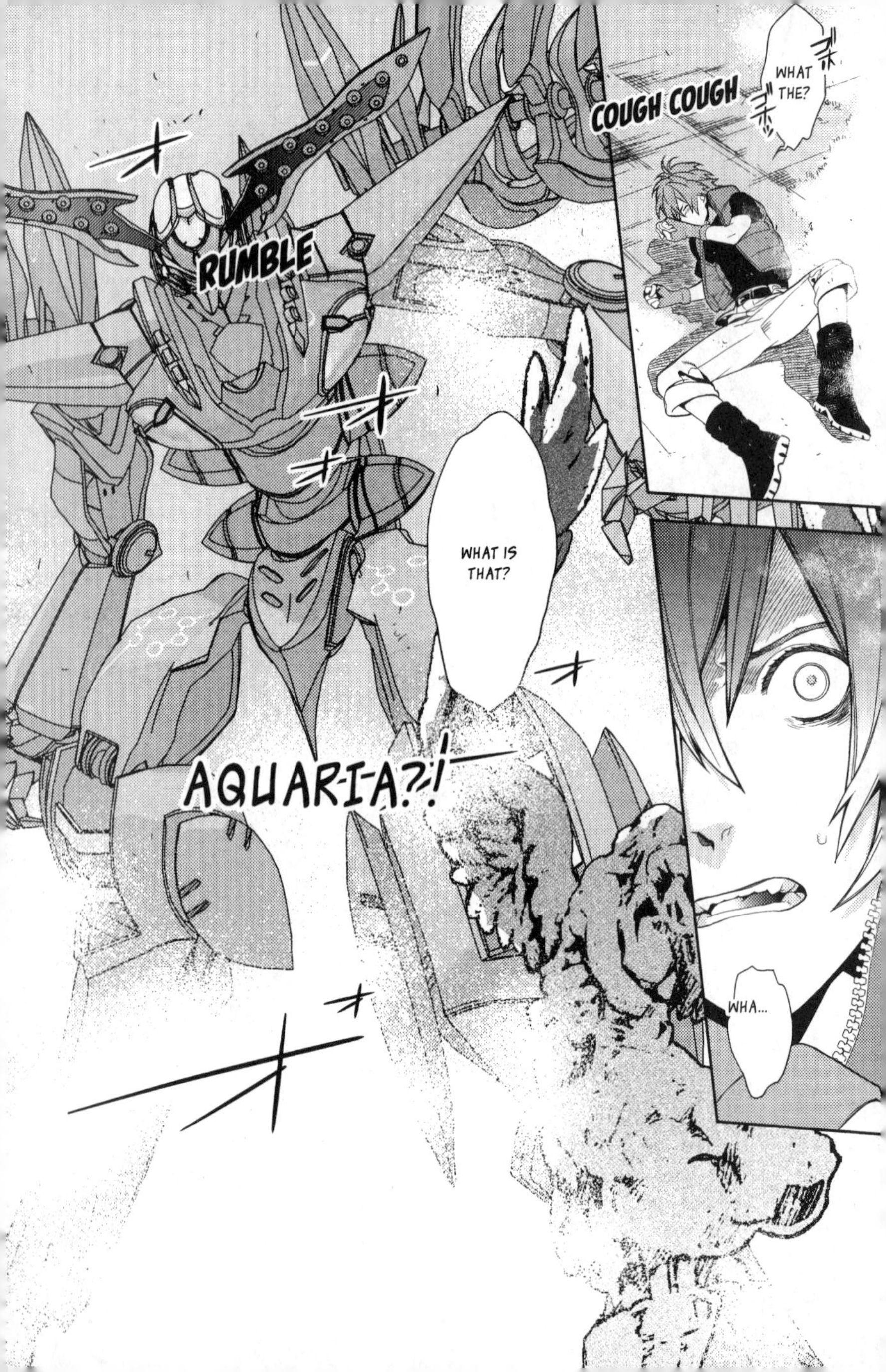
COUGH COUGH
ゴホ
ゴホッ
WHAT THE?
WHA...
RUMBLE
WHAT IS THAT?
AQUARI-A?!

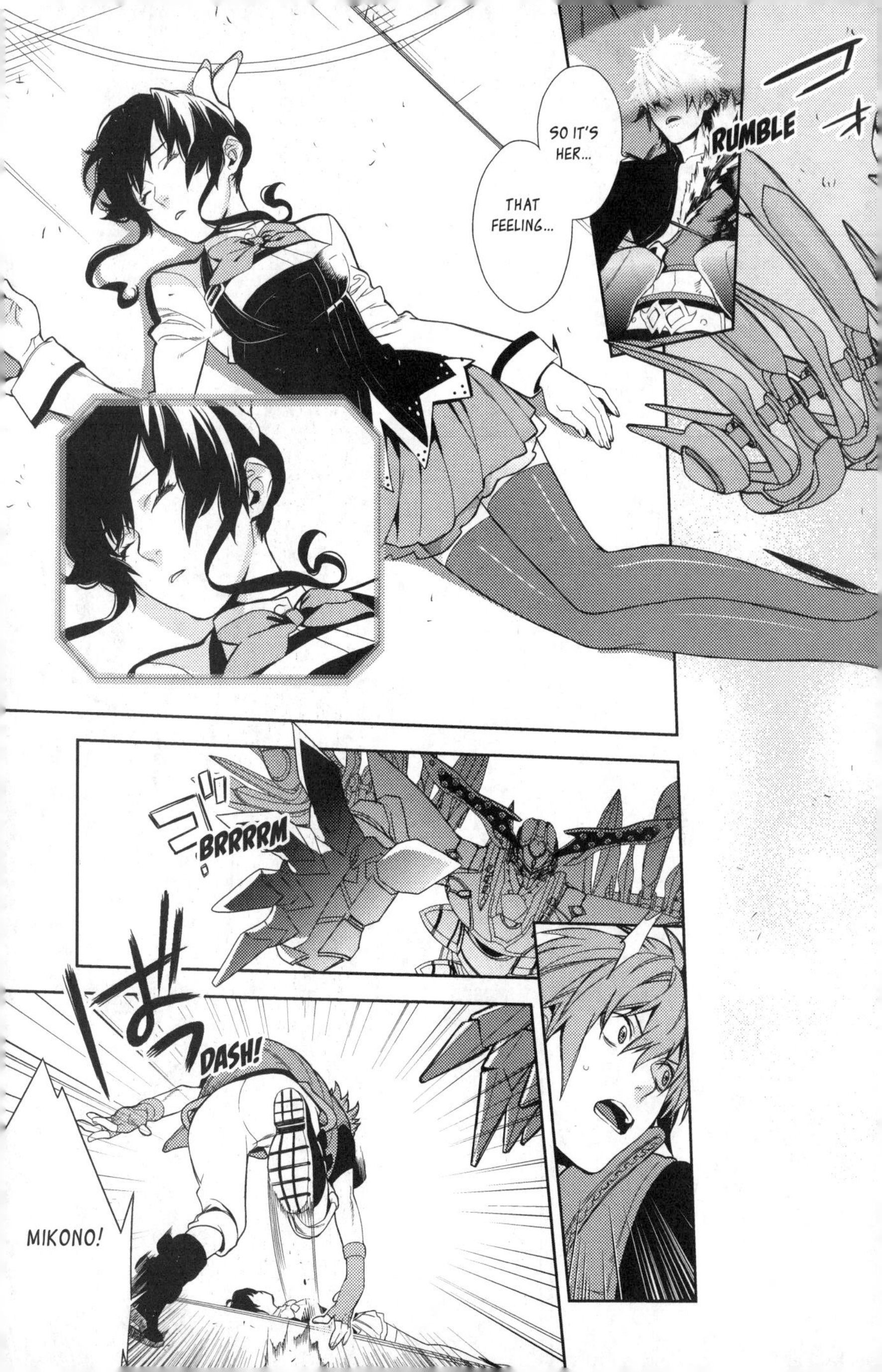
SO IT'S HER...
THAT FEELING...
RUMBLE
BRRRRM
DASH!
MIKONO!

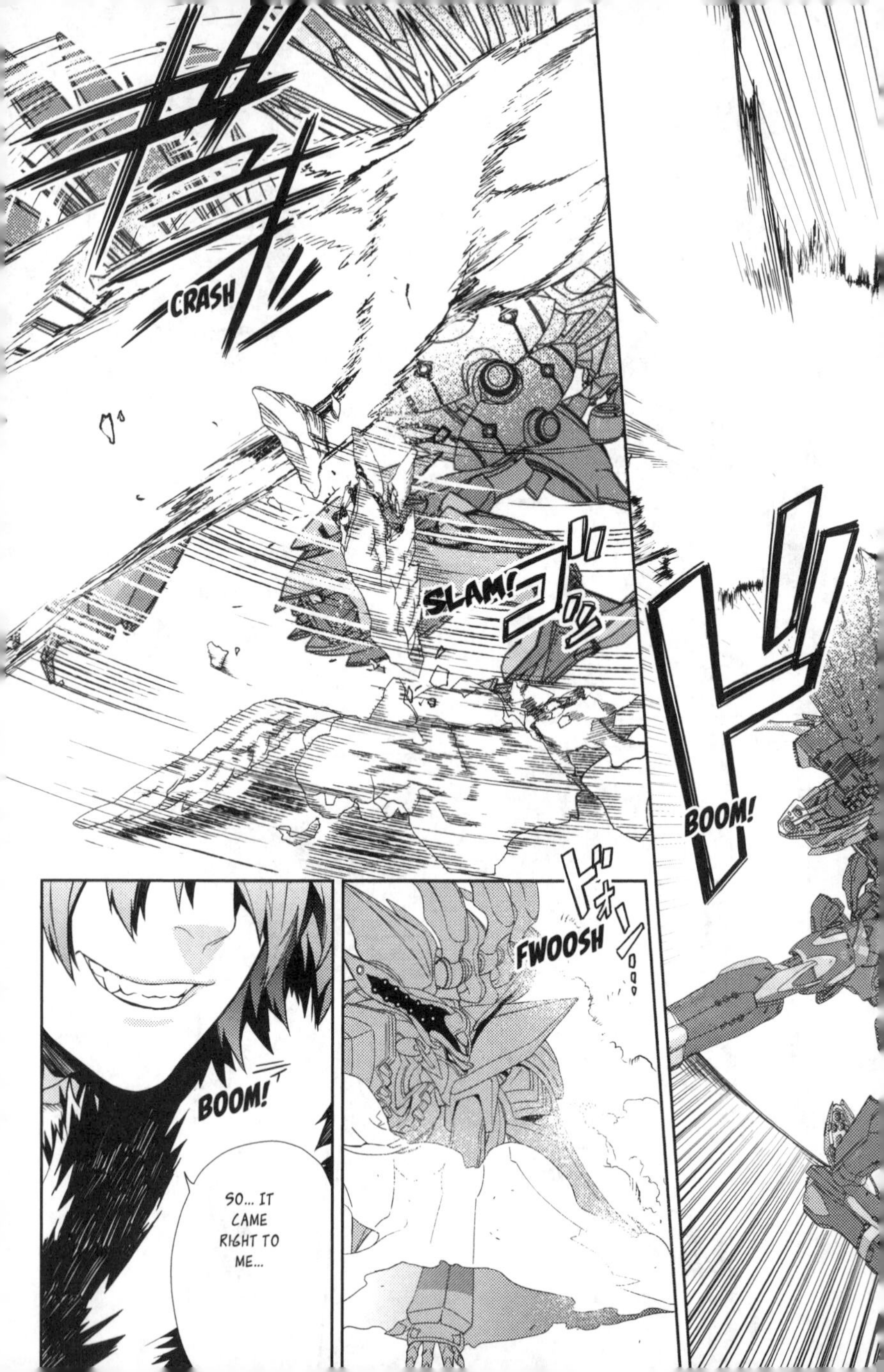
BOOM!
CRASH
SLAM!
FWOOSH
BOOM!
SO... IT CAME RIGHT TO ME...

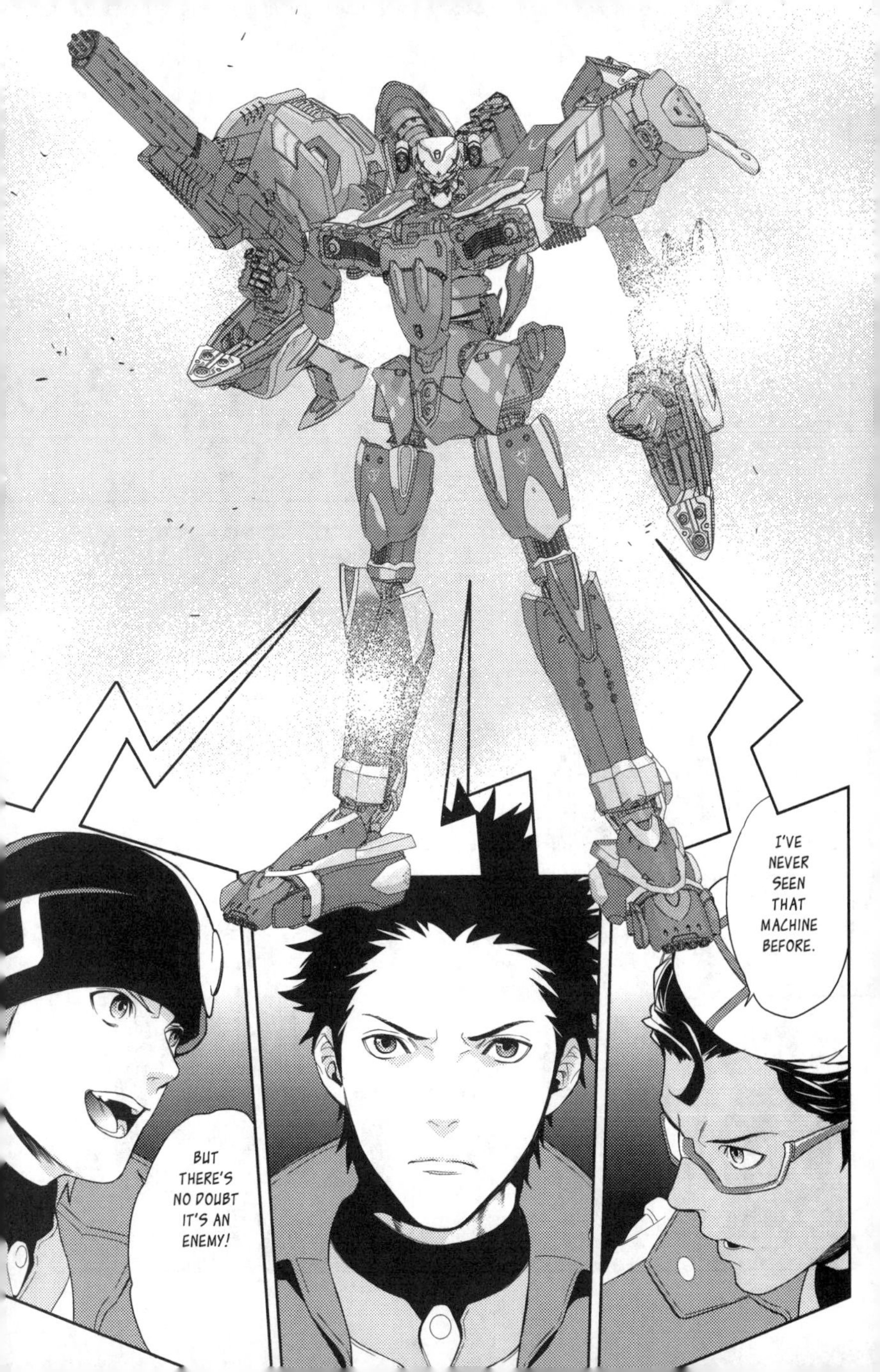
I'VE NEVER SEEN THAT MACHINE BEFORE.
BUT THERE'S NO DOUBT IT'S AN ENEMY!

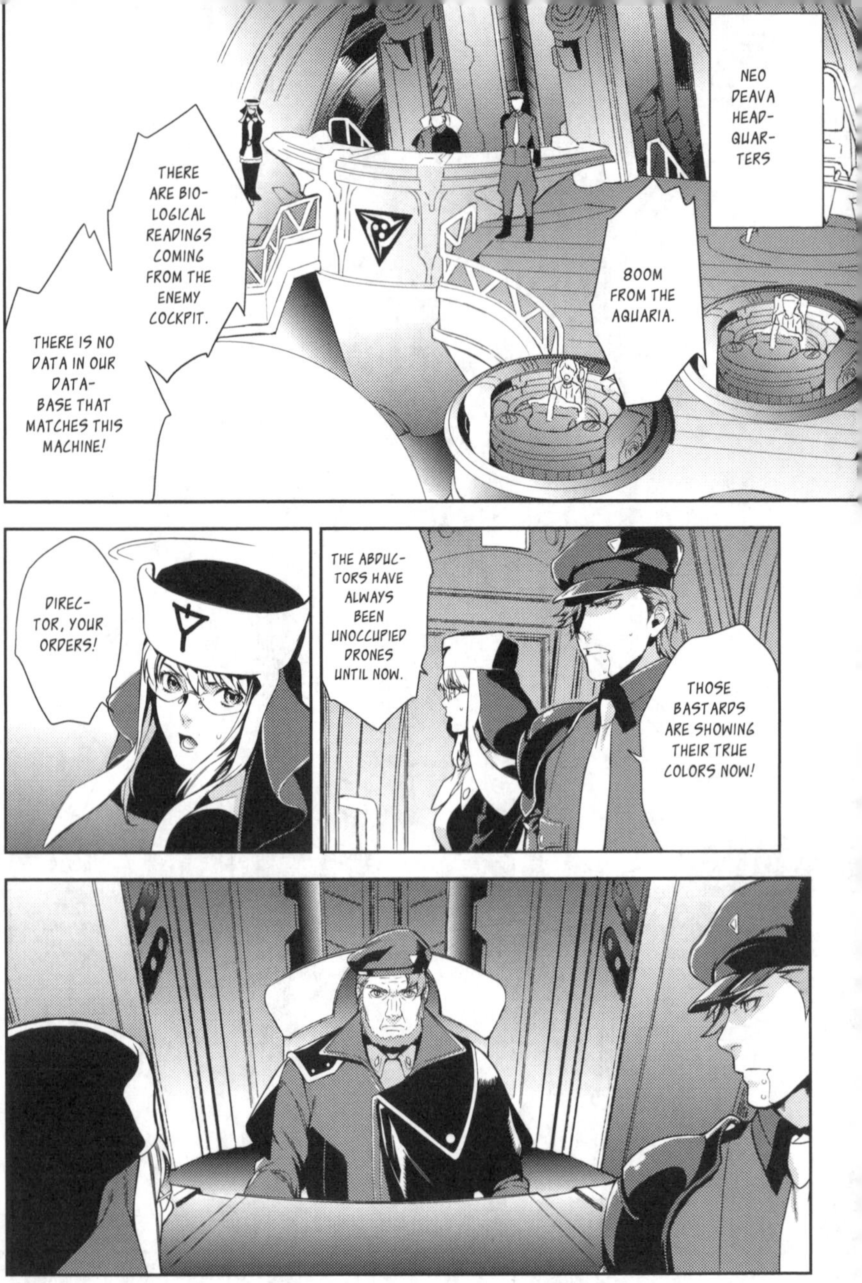
NEO DEAVA HEADQUARTERS
800M FROM THE AQUARIA.
THERE ARE BIOLOGICAL READINGS COMING FROM THE ENEMY COCKPIT.
THERE IS NO DATA IN OUR DATABASE THAT MATCHES THIS MACHINE!
THE ABDUCTORS HAVE ALWAYS BEEN UNOCCUPIED DRONES UNTIL NOW.
THOSE BASTARDS ARE SHOWING THEIR TRUE COLORS NOW!
DIRECTOR, YOUR ORDERS!

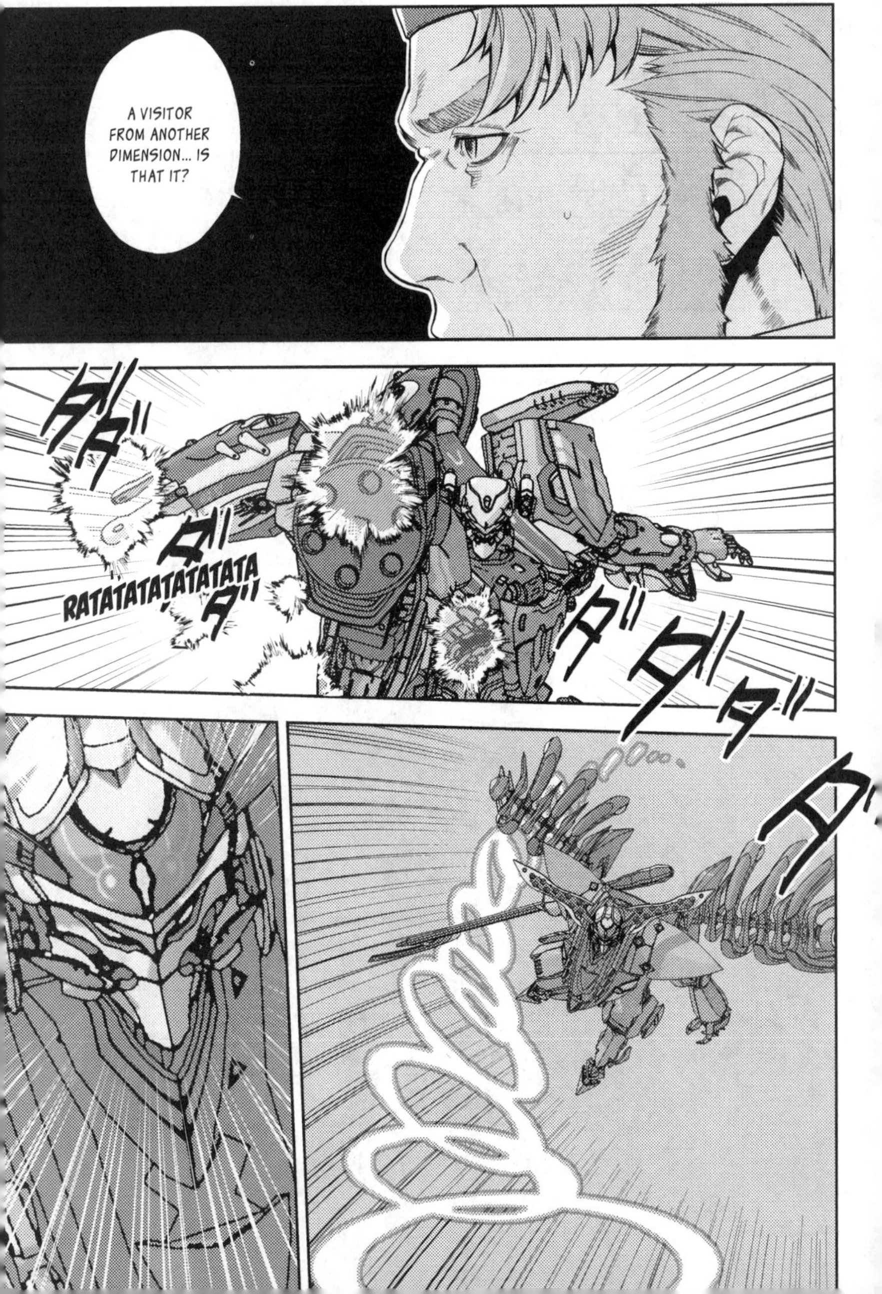
A VISITOR FROM ANOTHER DIMENSION... IS THAT IT?
RATATATATATATATA

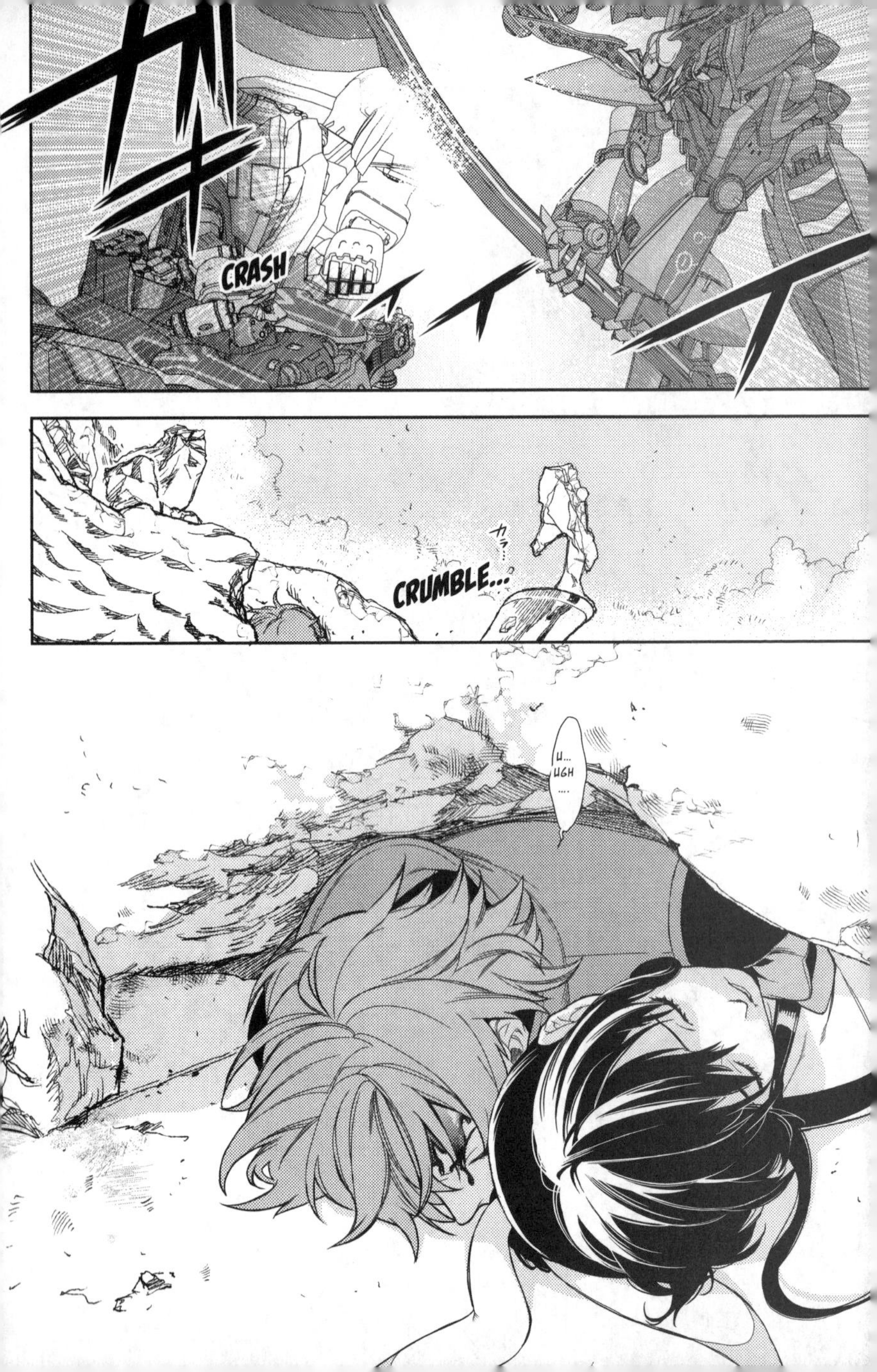
CRASH
カラ…
CRUMBLE...
U... UGH....

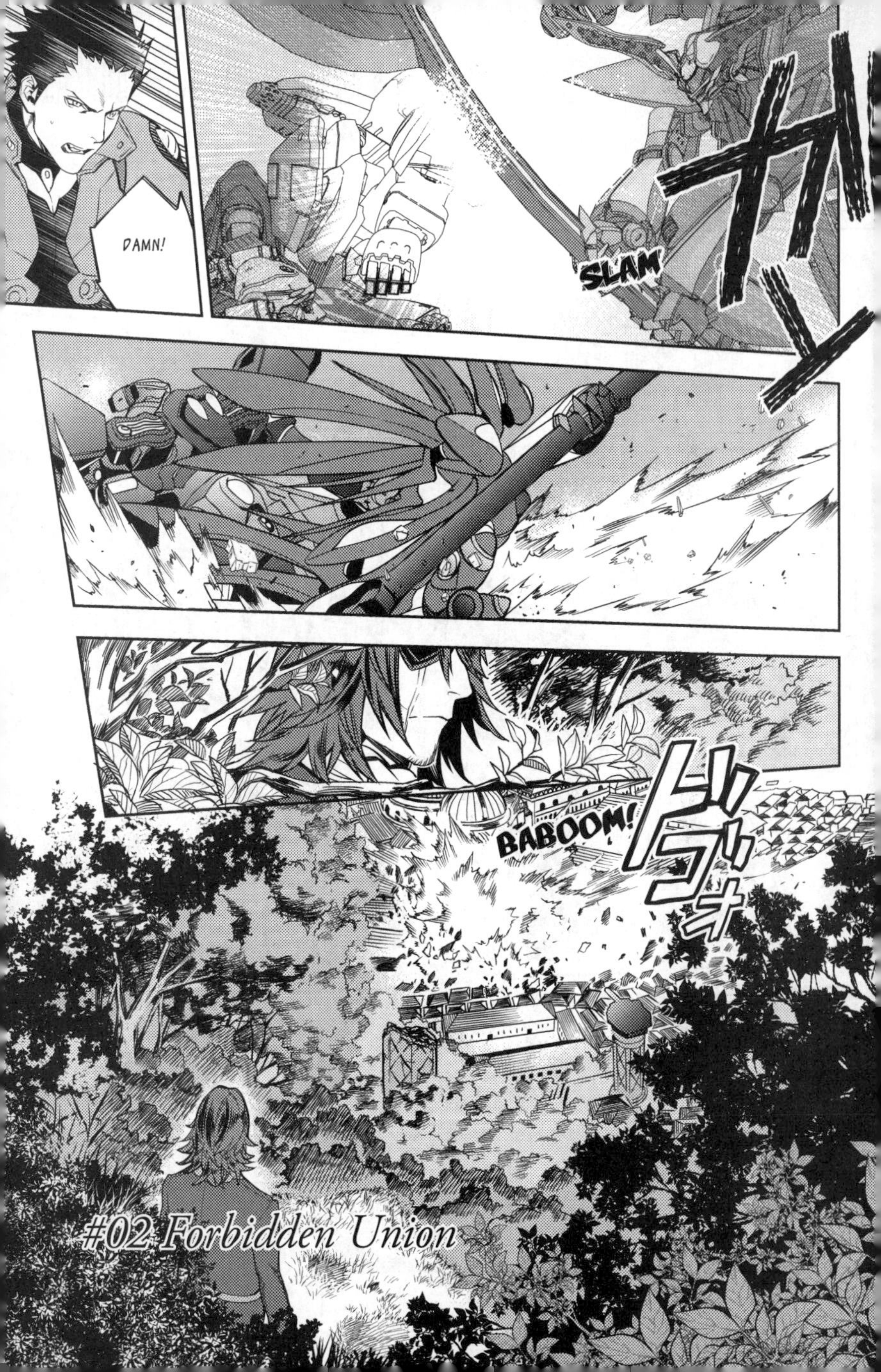

ガッ
SLAM
DAMN!
BABOOM!
ドゴォ
#02 Forbidden Union

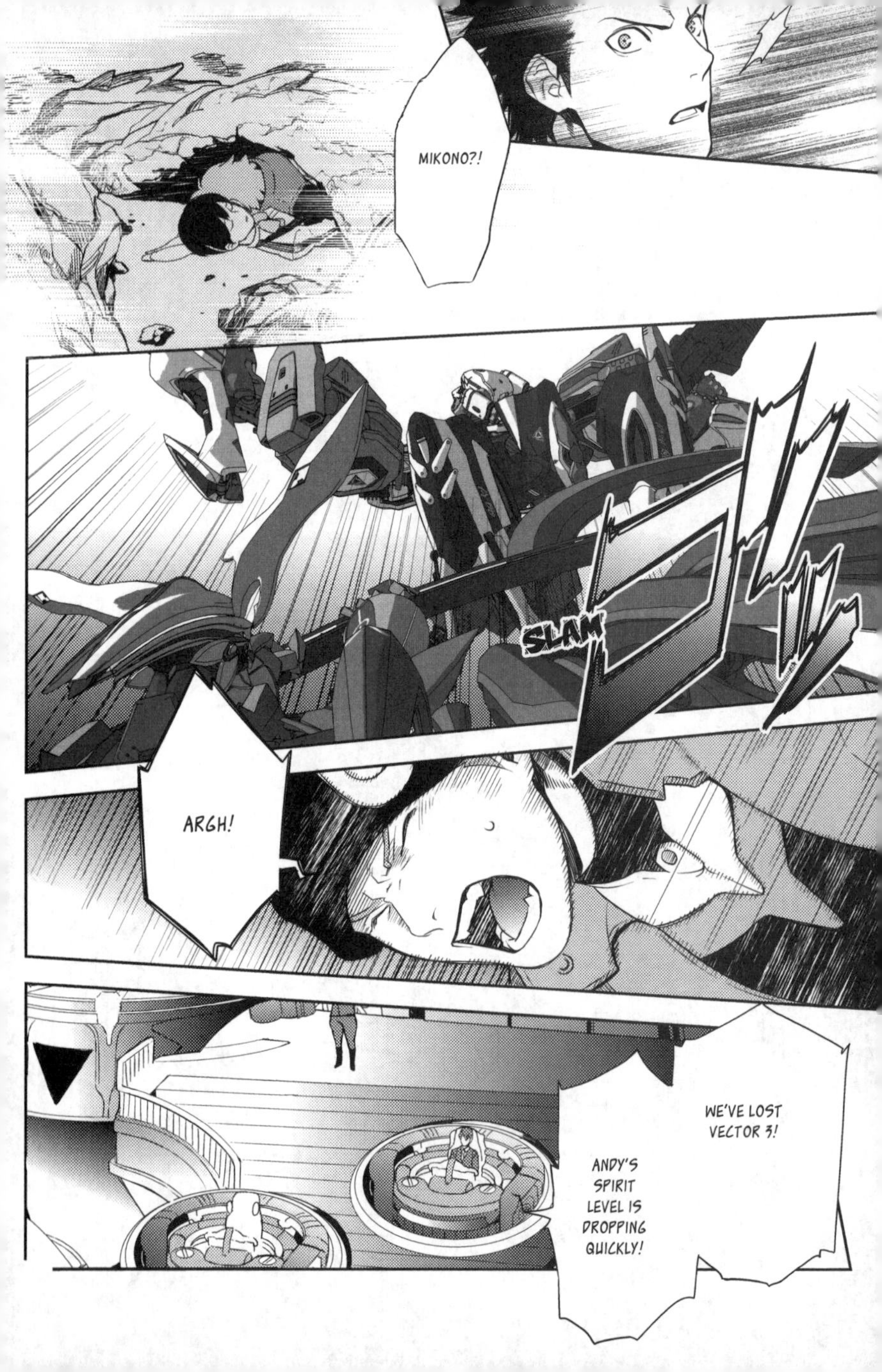
MIKONO?!
SLAM
ARGH!
WE'VE LOST VECTOR 3!
ANDY'S SPIRIT LEVEL IS DROPPING QUICKLY!

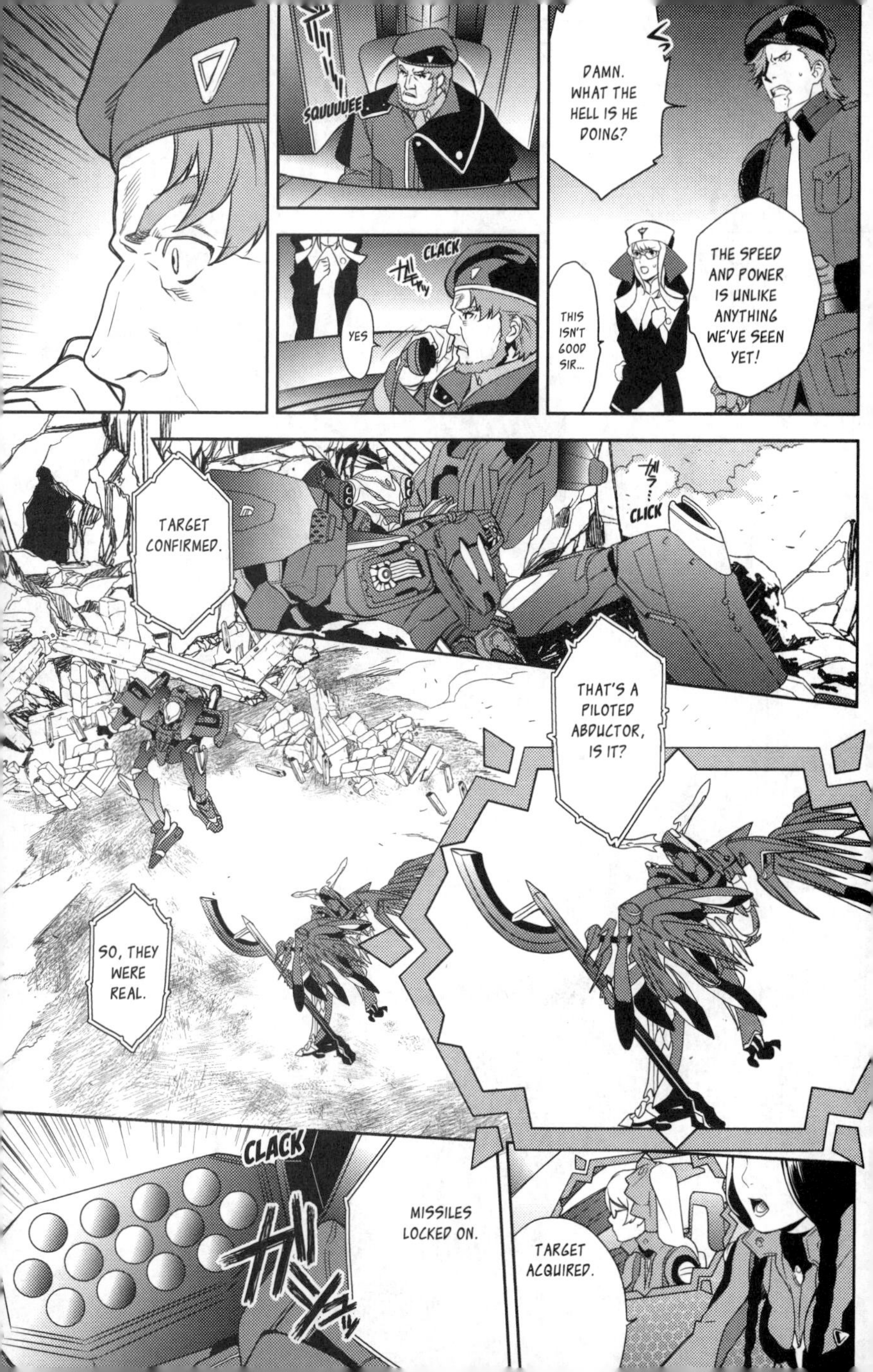
DAMN. WHAT THE HELL IS HE DOING?
THE SPEED AND POWER IS UNLIKE ANYTHING WE'VE SEEN YET!
THIS ISN'T GOOD SIR...
SQUUUUEE
CLACK
YES
CLICK
TARGET CONFIRMED.
THAT'S A PILOTED ABDUCTOR, IS IT?
SO, THEY WERE REAL.
TARGET ACQUIRED.
MISSILES LOCKED ON.
CLACK

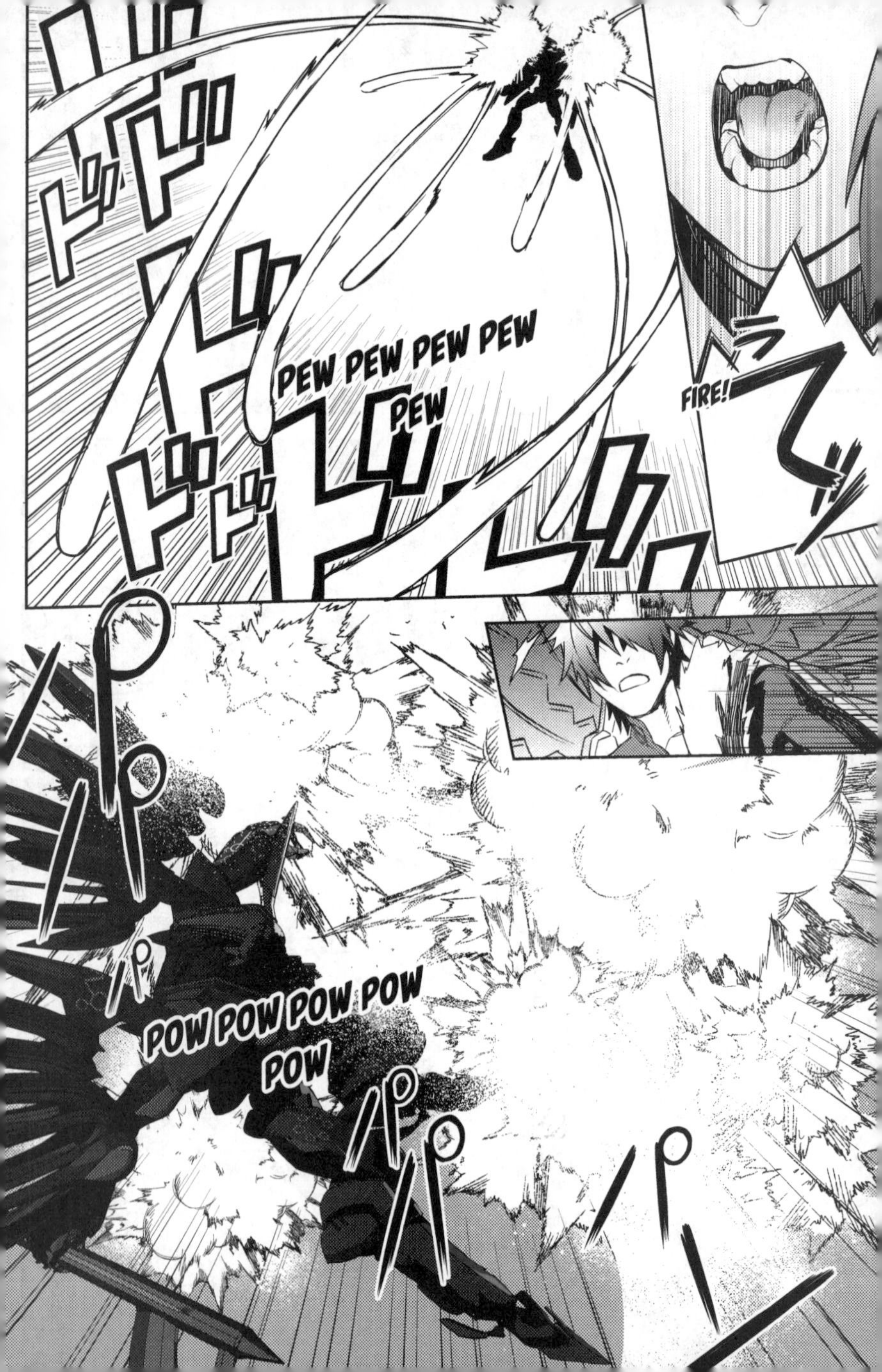
FIRE!
PEW PEW PEW PEW
PEW
POW POW POW POW
POW

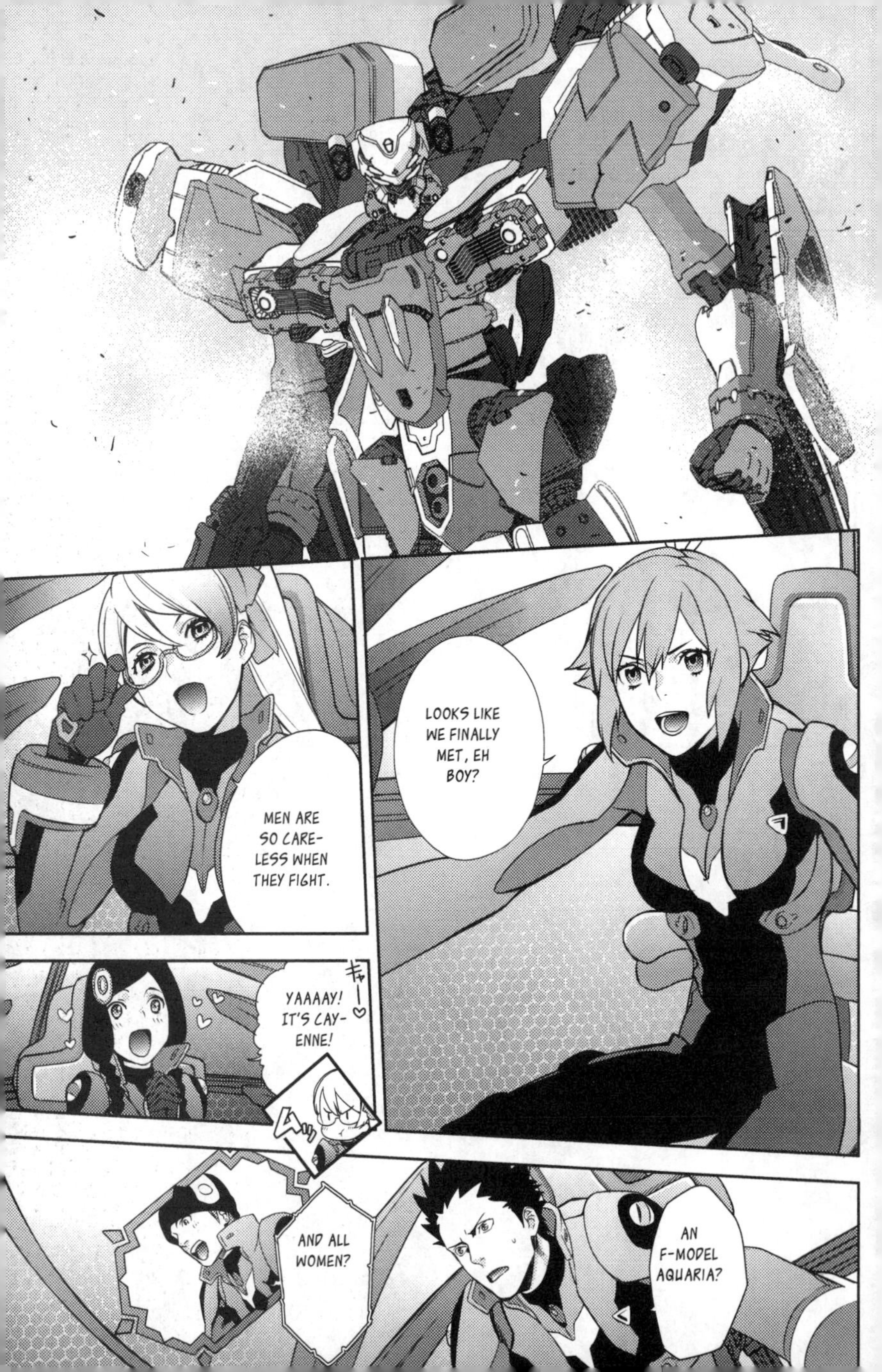
LOOKS LIKE WE FINALLY MET, EH BOY?
MEN ARE SO CARE-LESS WHEN THEY FIGHT.
YAAAAY! IT'S CAY-ENNE!
AN F-MODEL AQUARIA?
AND ALL WOMEN?

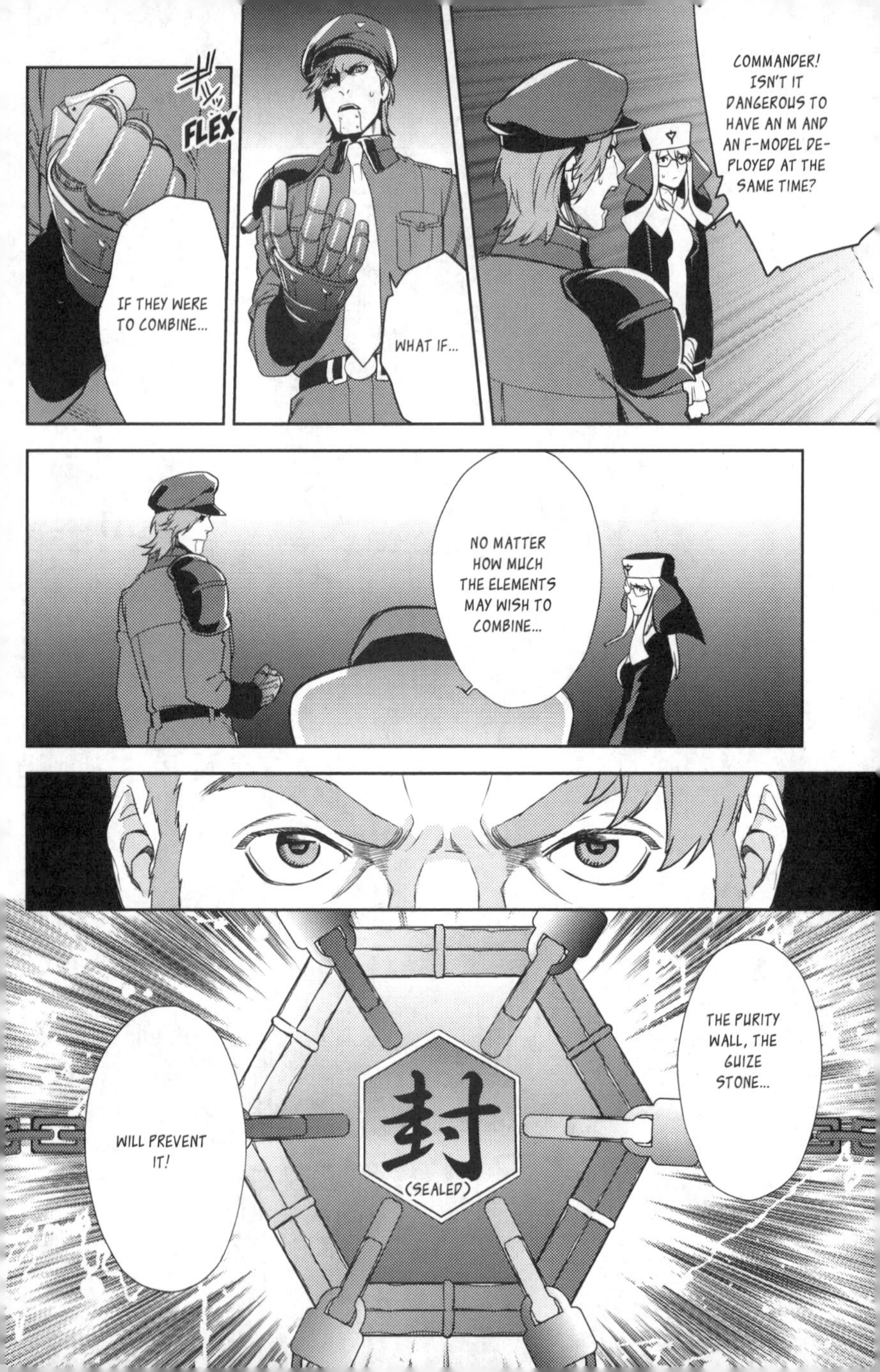
COMMANDER! ISN'T IT DANGEROUS TO HAVE AN M AND AN F-MODEL DE-PLOYED AT THE SAME TIME?
WHAT IF...
FLEX
IF THEY WERE TO COMBINE...
NO MATTER HOW MUCH THE ELEMENTS MAY WISH TO COMBINE...
THE PURITY WALL, THE GUIZE STONE...
封
(SEALED)
WILL PREVENT IT!

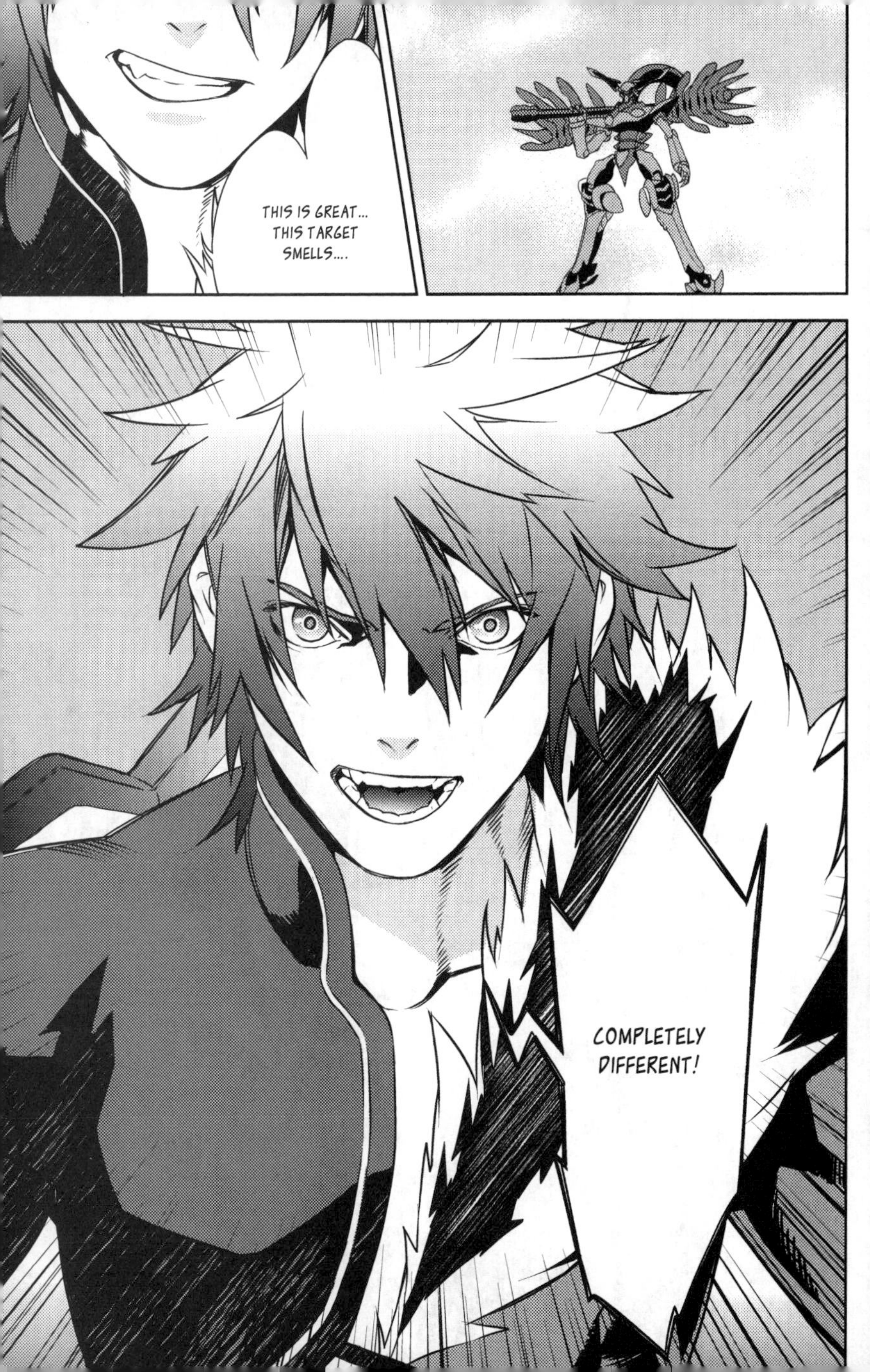
THIS IS GREAT... THIS TARGET SMELLS....
COMPLETELY DIFFERENT!

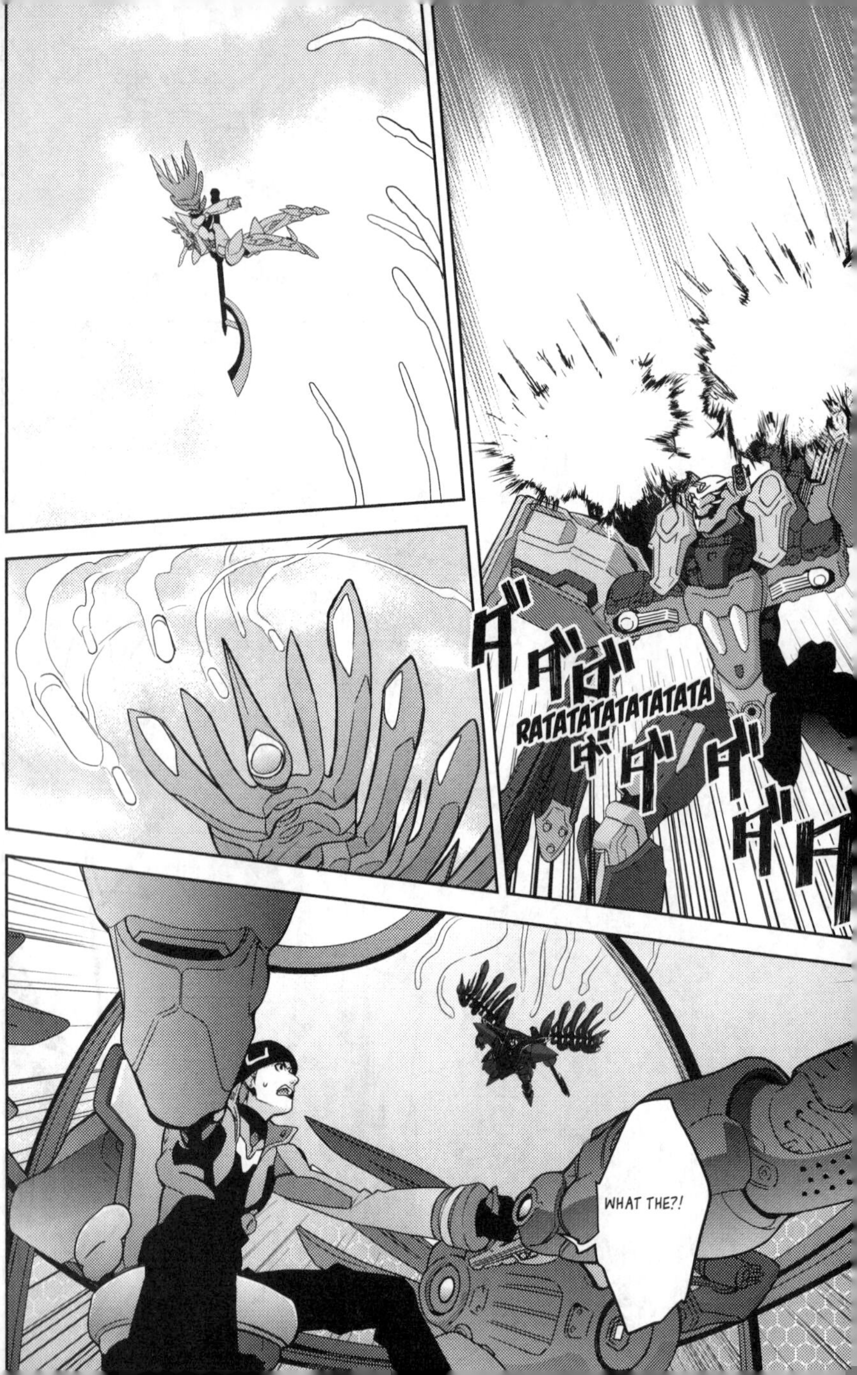

ダダダ
RATATATATATATATA
ダダダダダ
WHAT THE?!

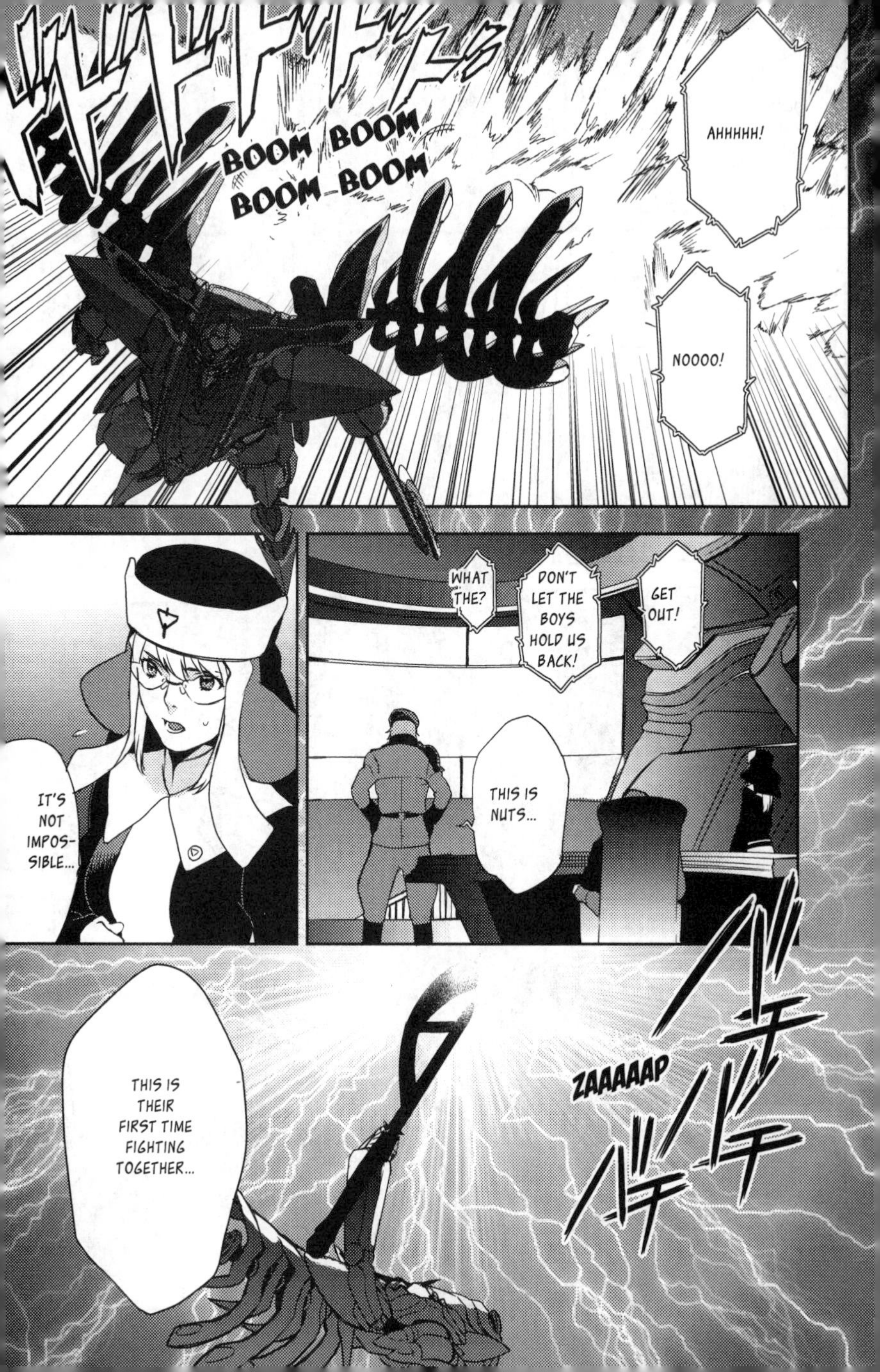
AHHHHH!
NOOOO!
BOOM BOOM
BOOM BOOM
GET OUT!
DON'T LET THE BOYS HOLD US BACK!
WHAT THE?
THIS IS NUTS...
IT'S NOT IMPOSSIBLE...
ZAAAAAP
THIS IS THEIR FIRST TIME FIGHTING TOGETHER...

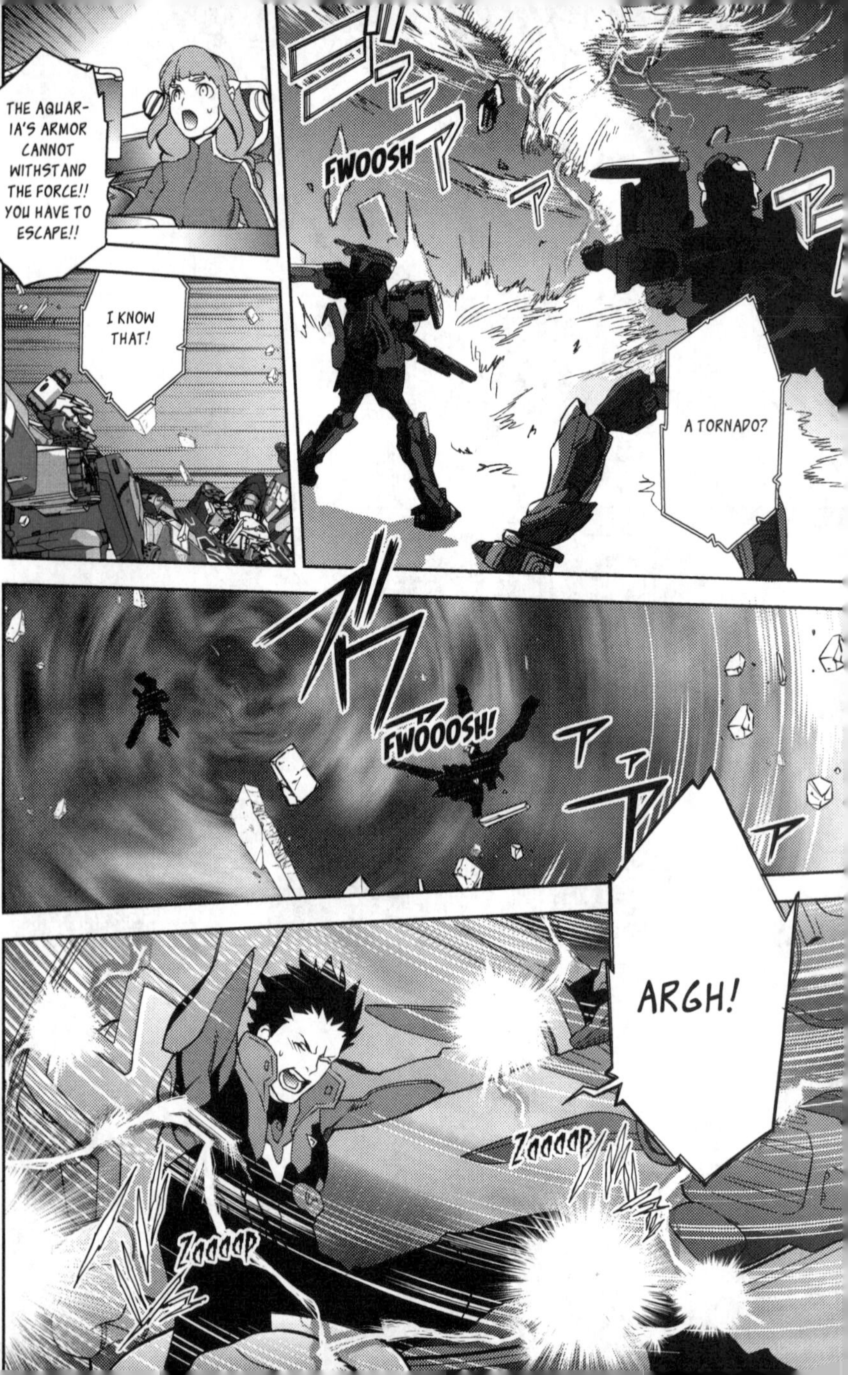
FWOOSH
A TORNADO?
THE AQUARIA'S ARMOR CANNOT WITHSTAND THE FORCE!! YOU HAVE TO ESCAPE!!
I KNOW THAT!
FWOOOSH!
ARGH!
Zaaaap
Zaaaap

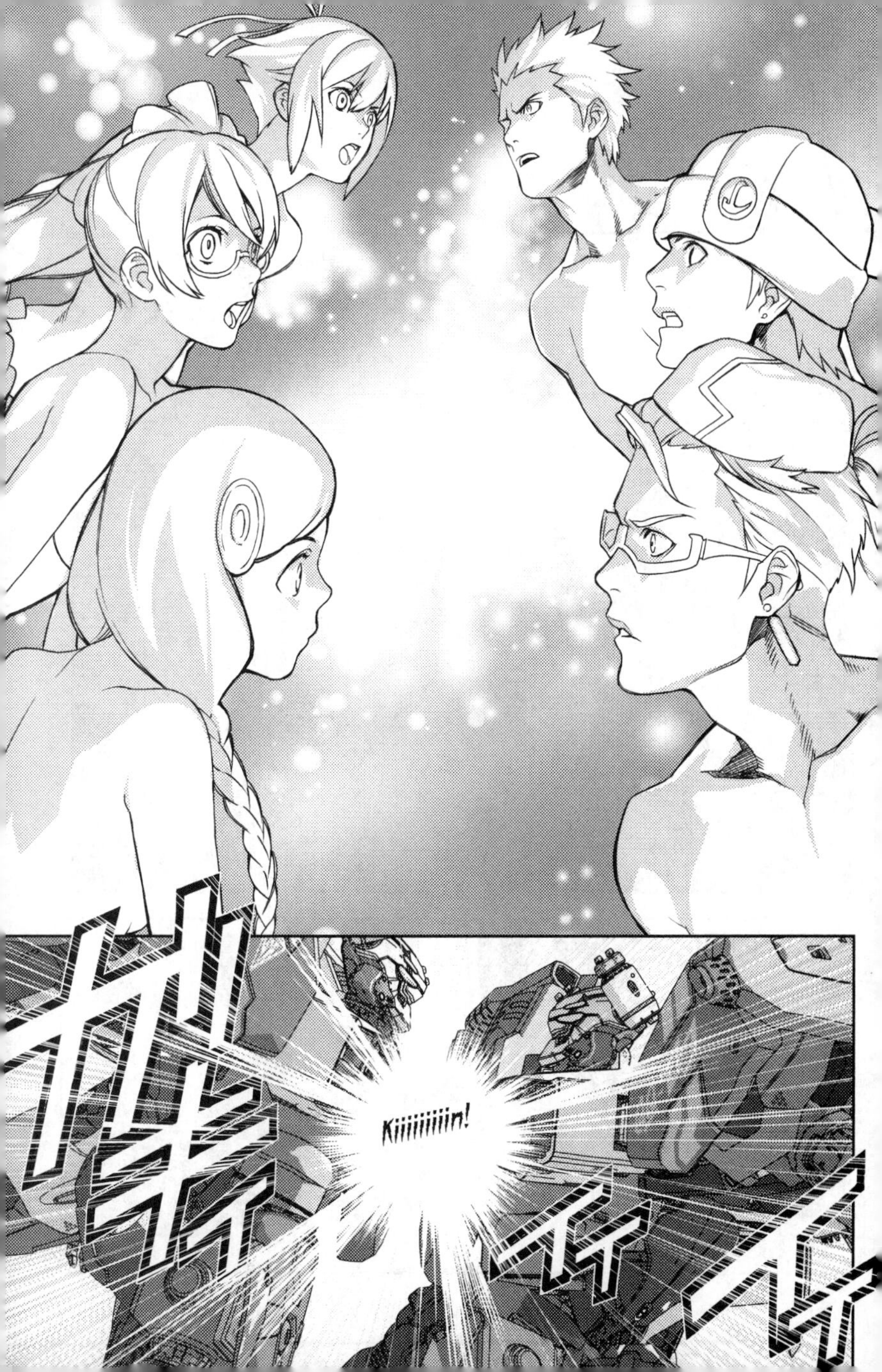
Kiiiiiiiiin!

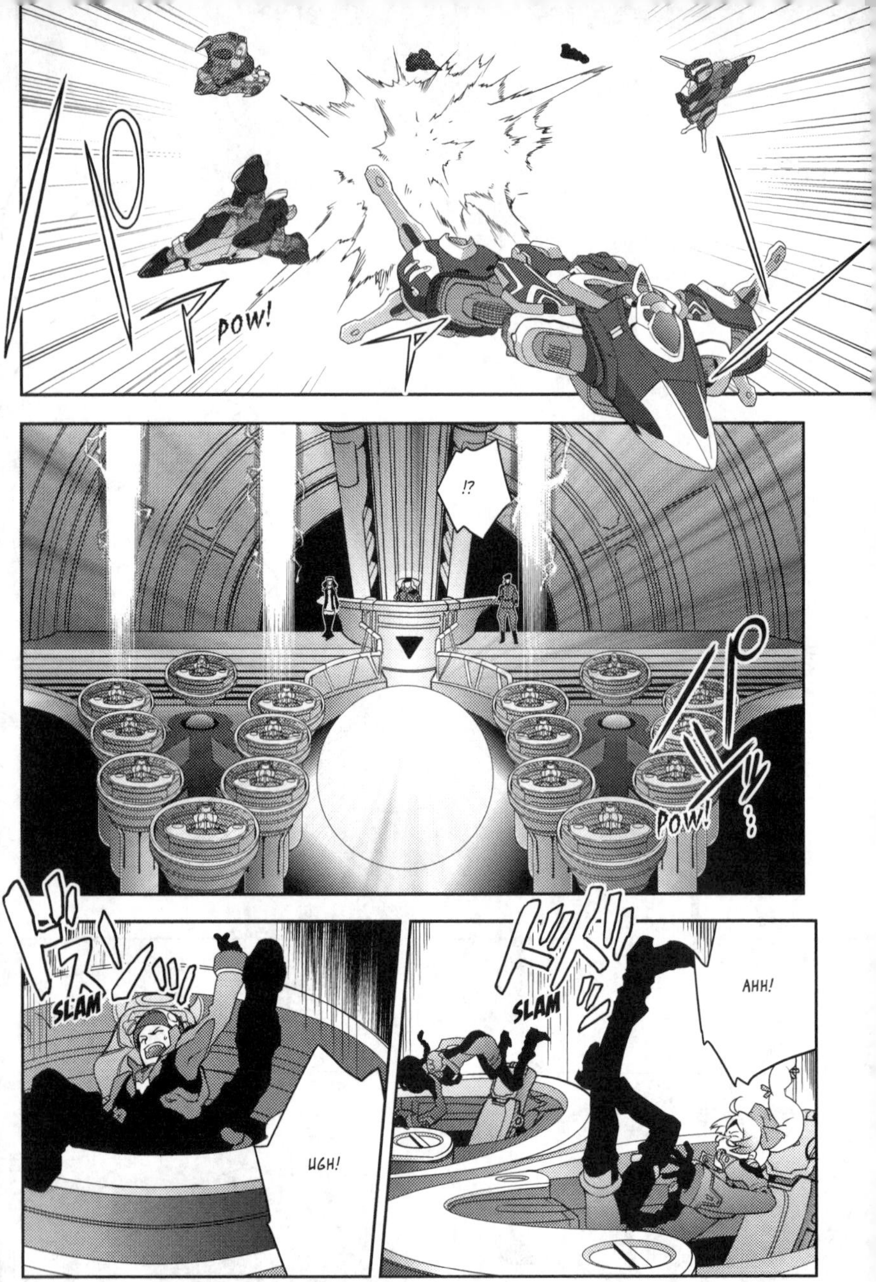
POW!
!?
POW!
SLAM
AHH!
SLAM
UGH!

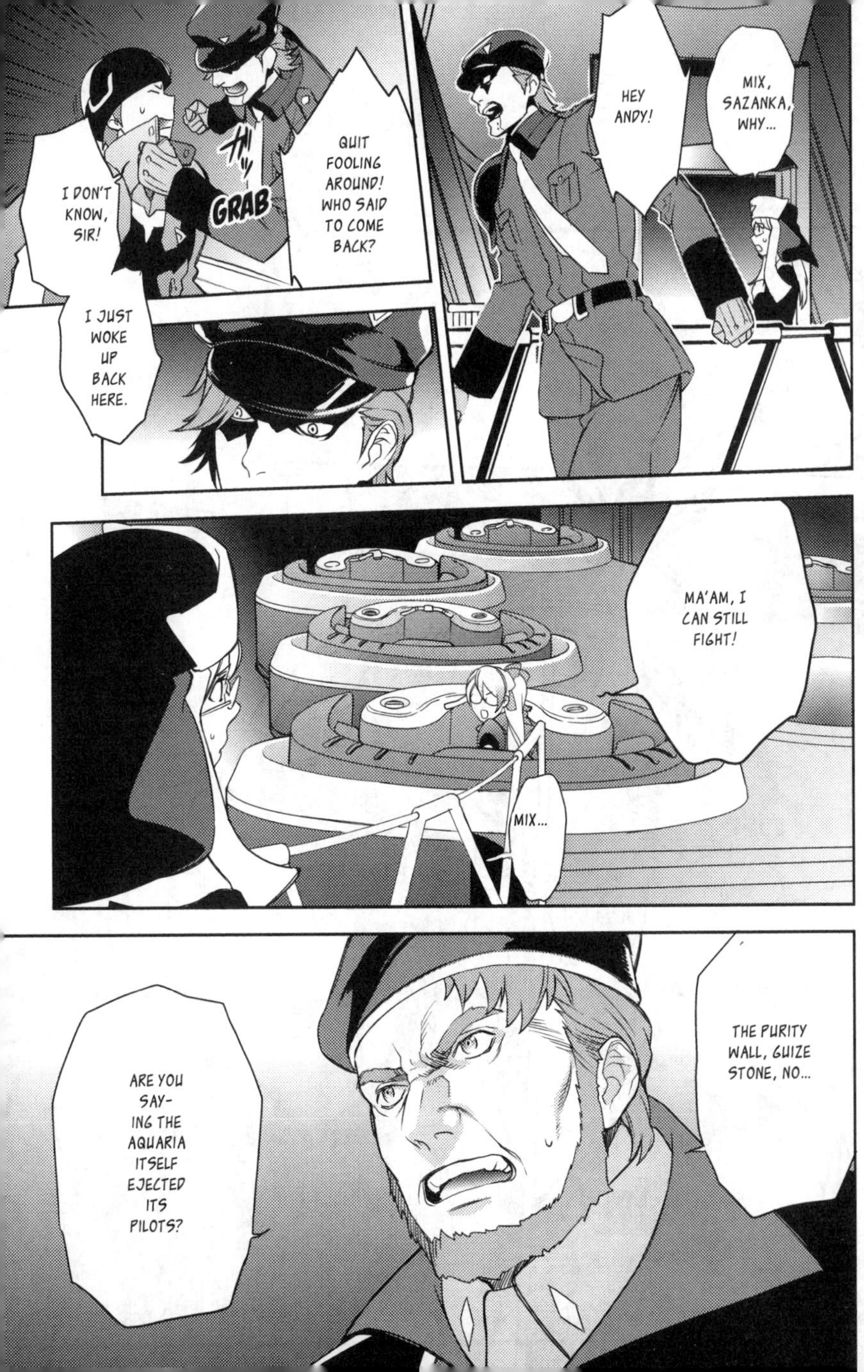
MIX, SAZANKA, WHY...
HEY ANDY!
QUIT FOOLING AROUND! WHO SAID TO COME BACK?
GRAB
I DON'T KNOW, SIR!
I JUST WOKE UP BACK HERE.
MA'AM, I CAN STILL FIGHT!
MIX...
THE PURITY WALL, GUIZE STONE, NO...
ARE YOU SAY-ING THE AQUARIA ITSELF EJECTED ITS PILOTS?

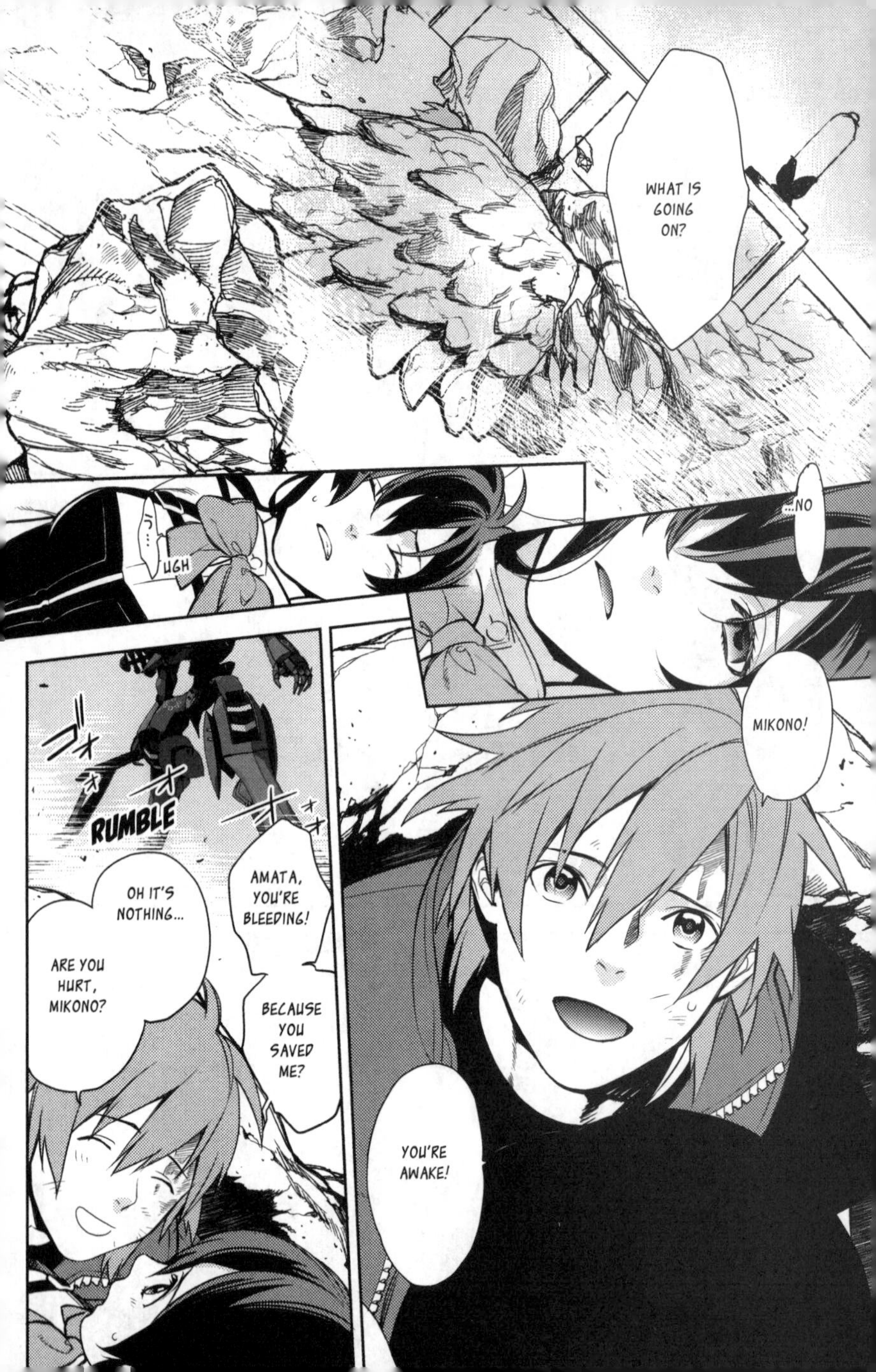
WHAT IS GOING ON?
...NO
UGH
MIKONO!
YOU'RE AWAKE!
RUMBLE
AMATA, YOU'RE BLEEDING!
OH IT'S NOTHING...
ARE YOU HURT, MIKONO?
BECAUSE YOU SAVED ME?

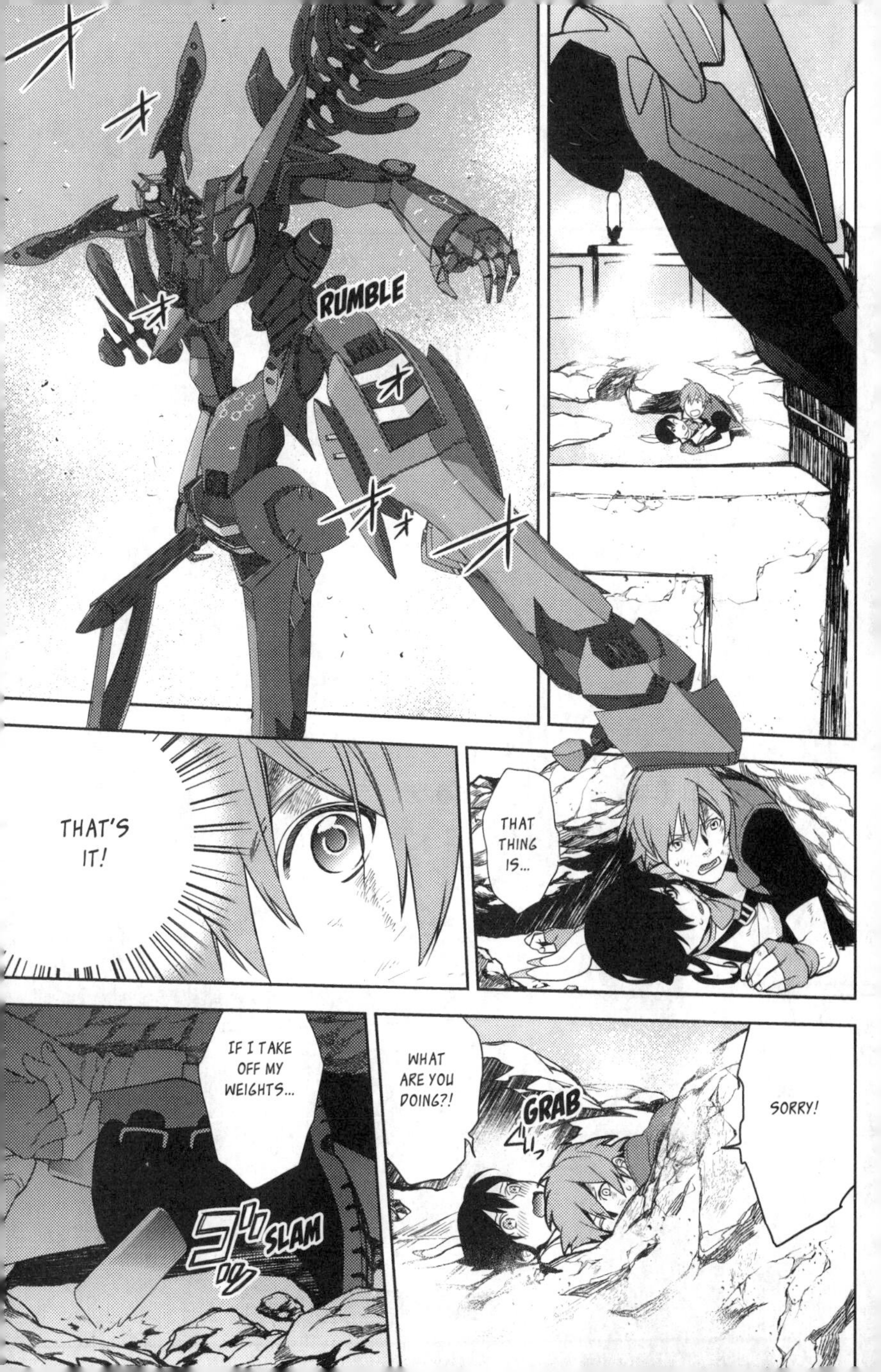
RUMBLE
THAT THING IS...
THAT'S IT!
WHAT ARE YOU DOING?!
GRAB
SORRY!
IF I TAKE OFF MY WEIGHTS...
SLAM

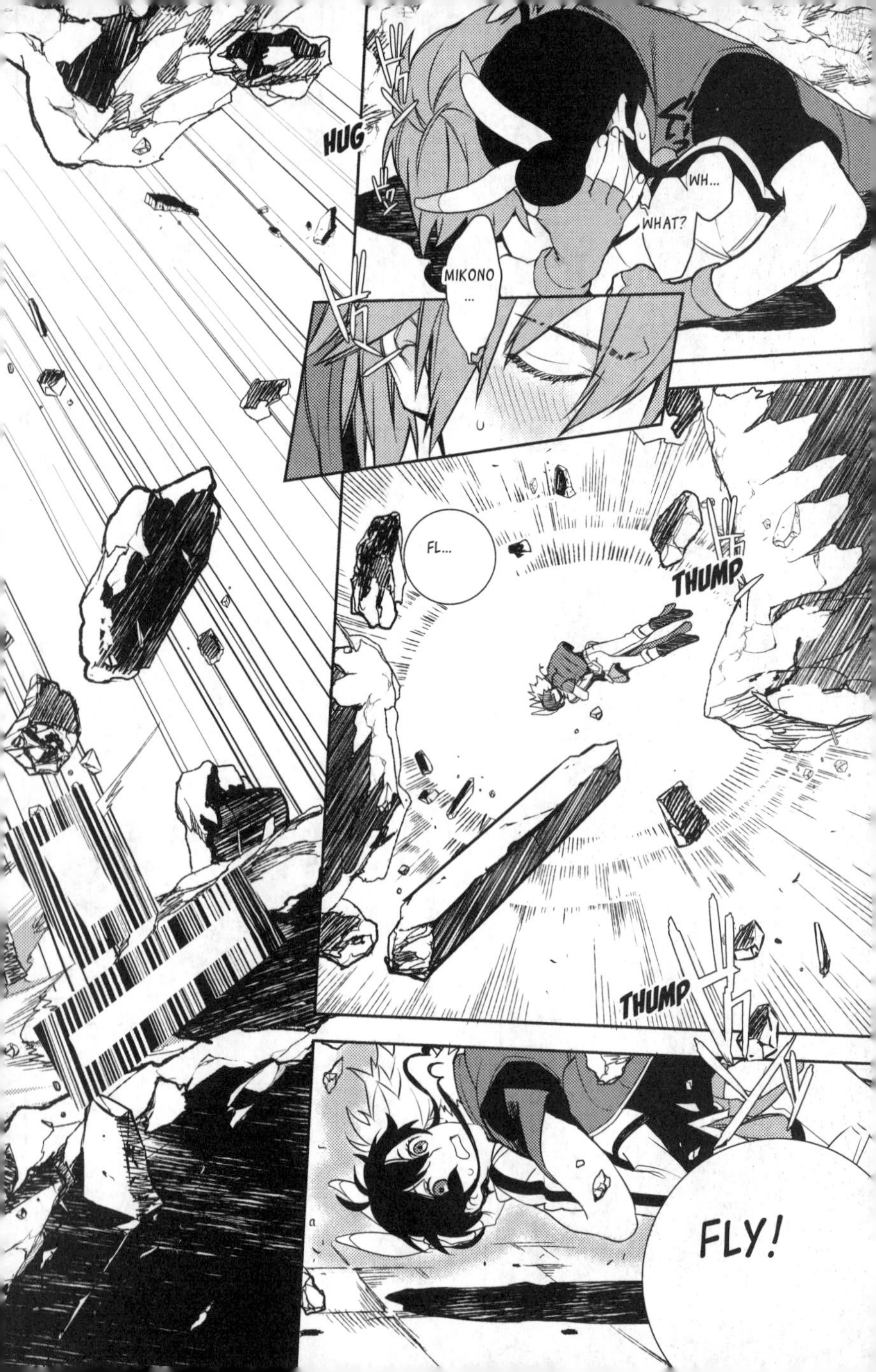
WH...
WHAT?
HUG
MIKONO ...
THUMP
FL...
THUMP
FLY!

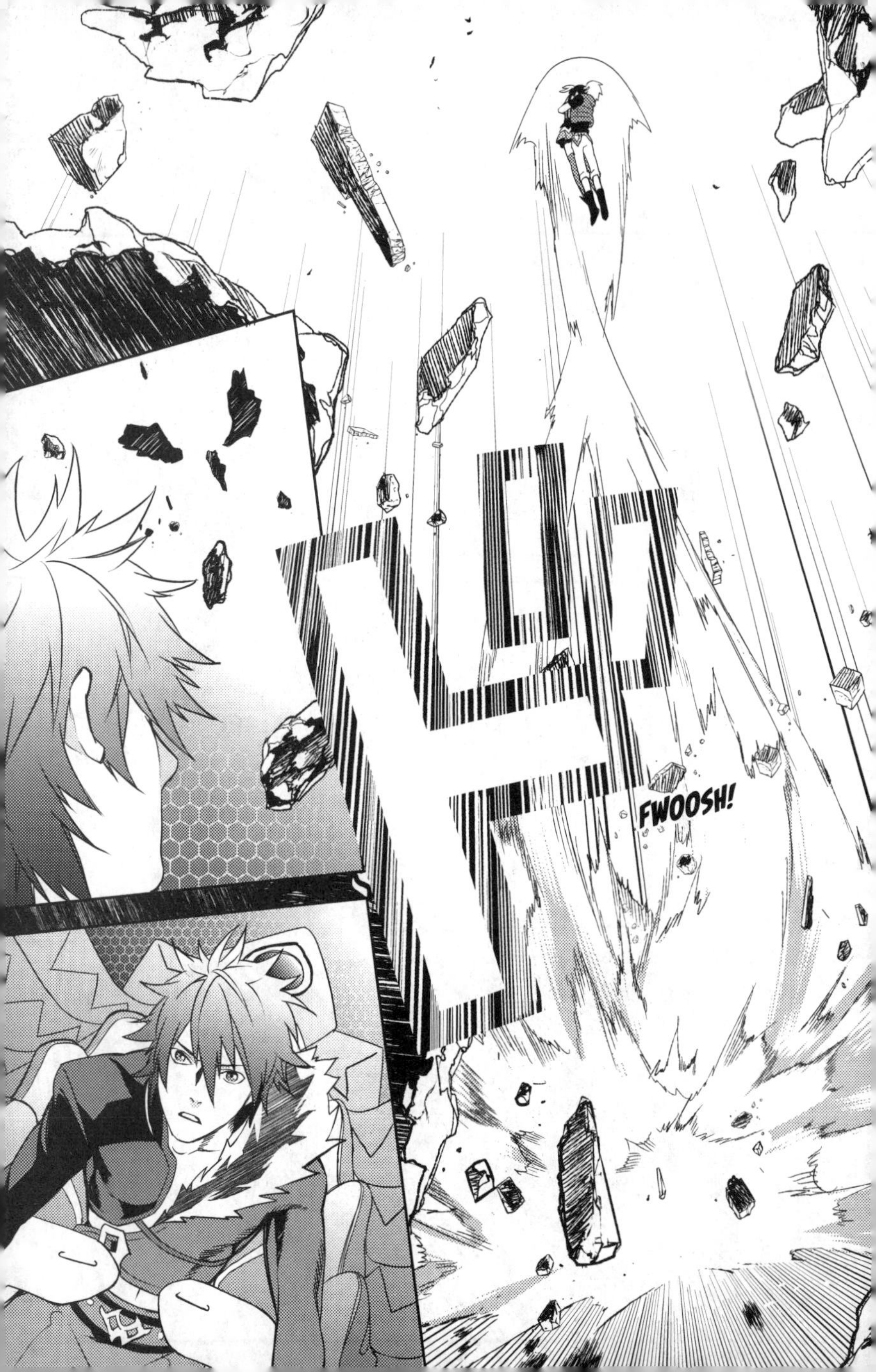
FWOOSH!

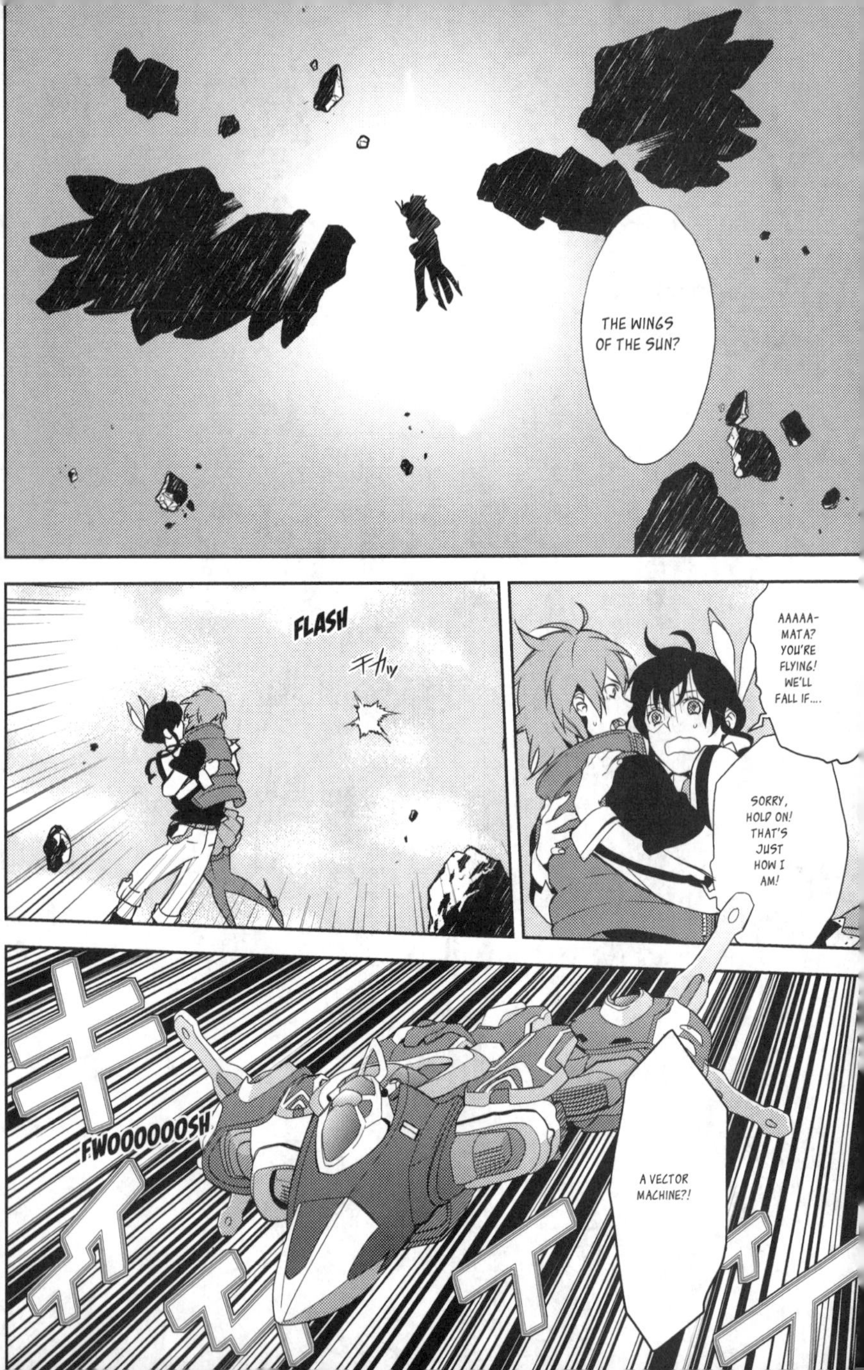
THE WINGS OF THE SUN?
AAAAA-MATA? YOU'RE FLYING! WE'LL FALL IF....
SORRY, HOLD ON! THAT'S JUST HOW I AM!
FLASH
チカッ
キィィィィ
FWOOOOOOSH
A VECTOR MACHINE?!

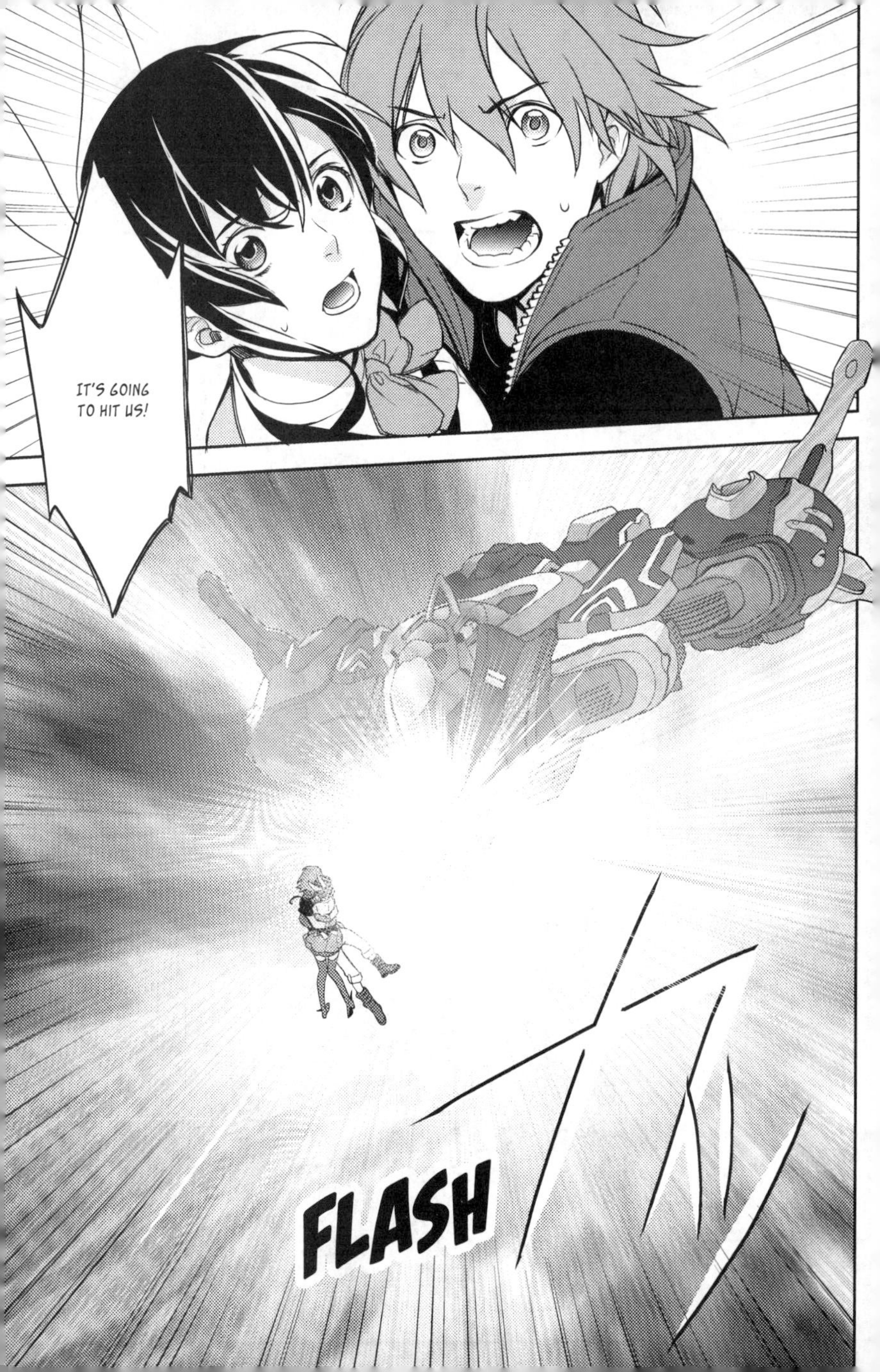
IT'S GOING TO HIT US!
FLASH

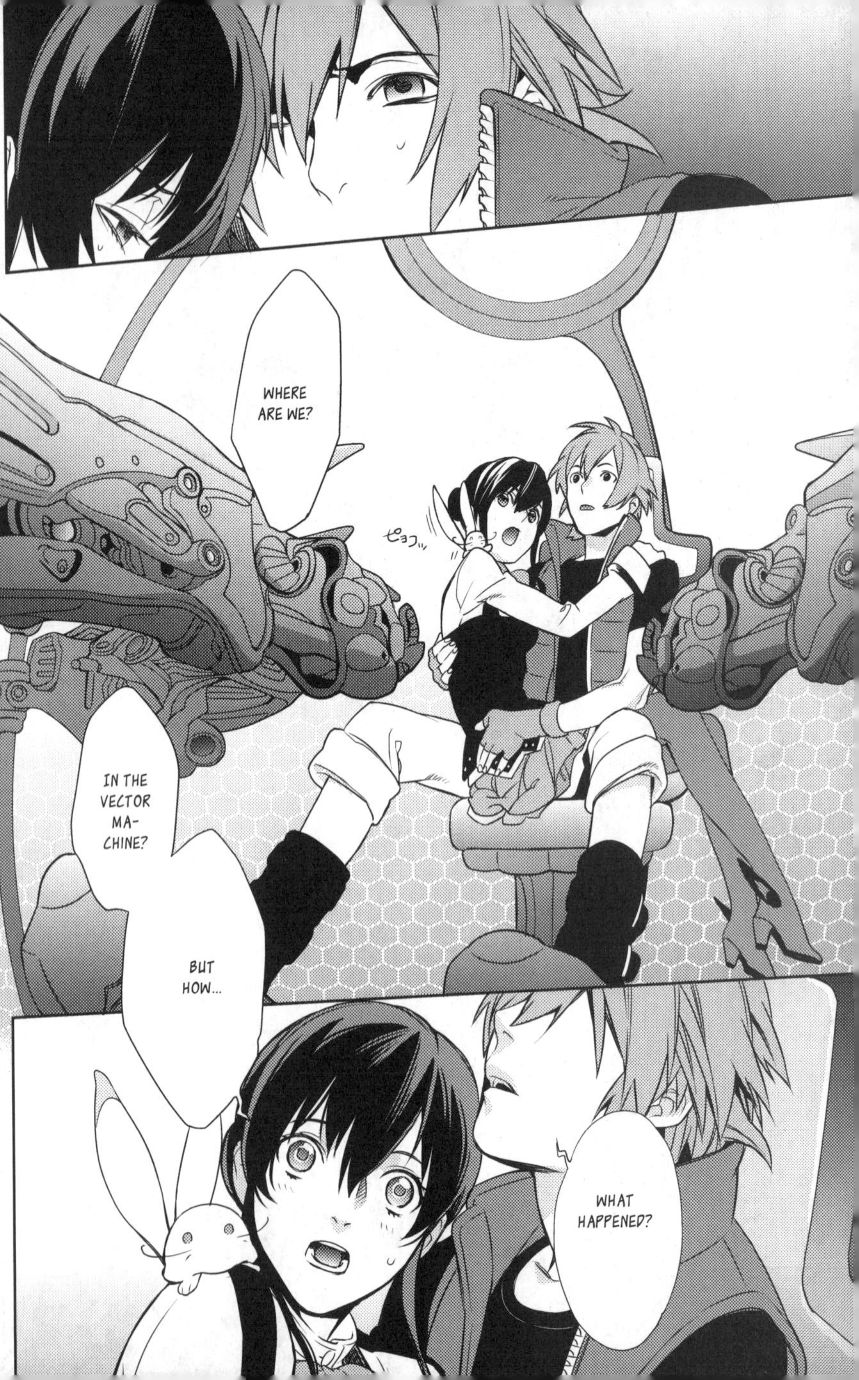
WHERE ARE WE?
ピョコッ
IN THE VECTOR MA-CHINE?
BUT HOW...
WHAT HAPPENED?

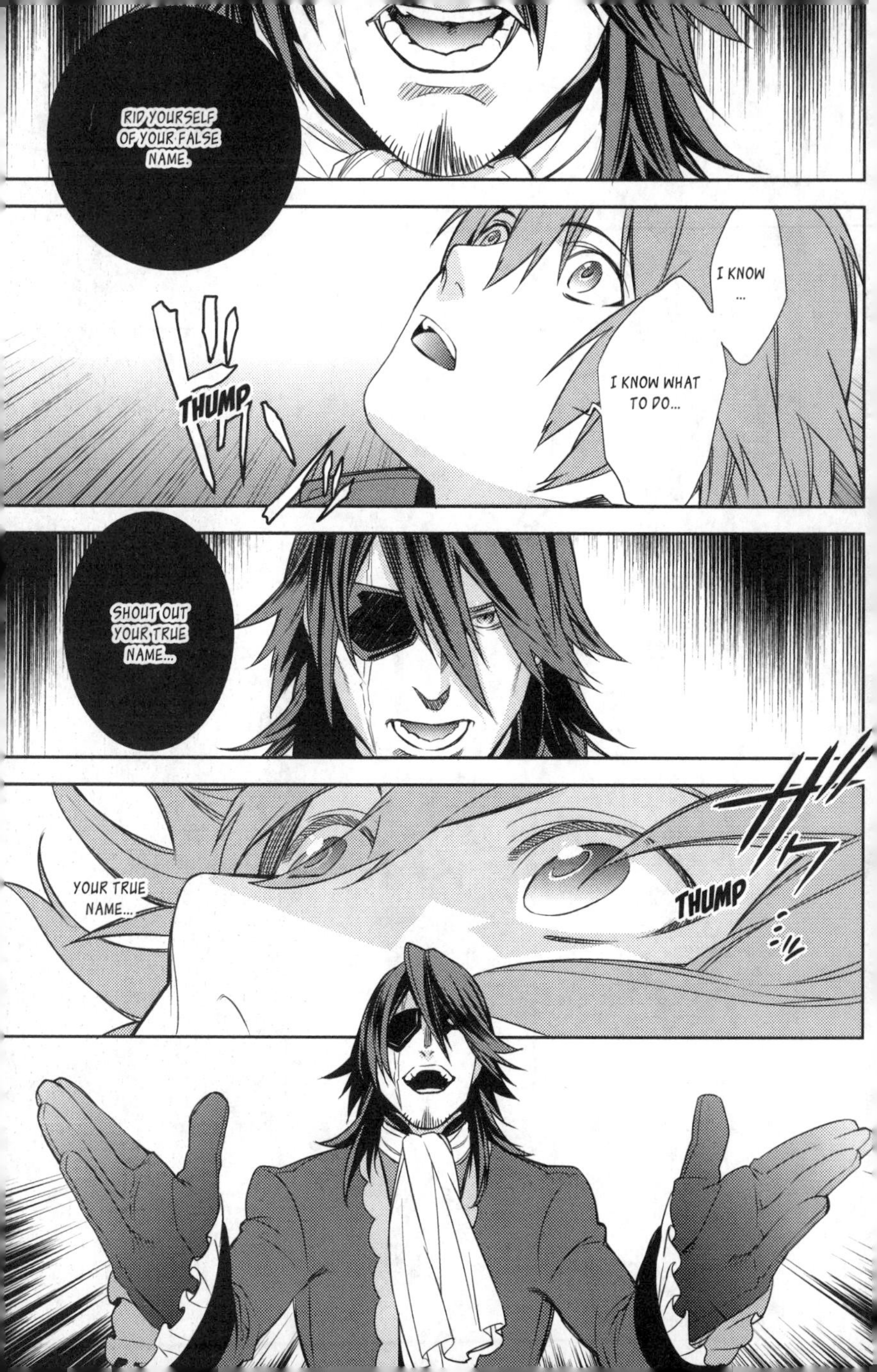
RID YOURSELF OF YOUR FALSE NAME.
I KNOW ...
I KNOW WHAT TO DO...
THUMP
SHOUT OUT YOUR TRUE NAME...
THUMP
YOUR TRUE NAME...

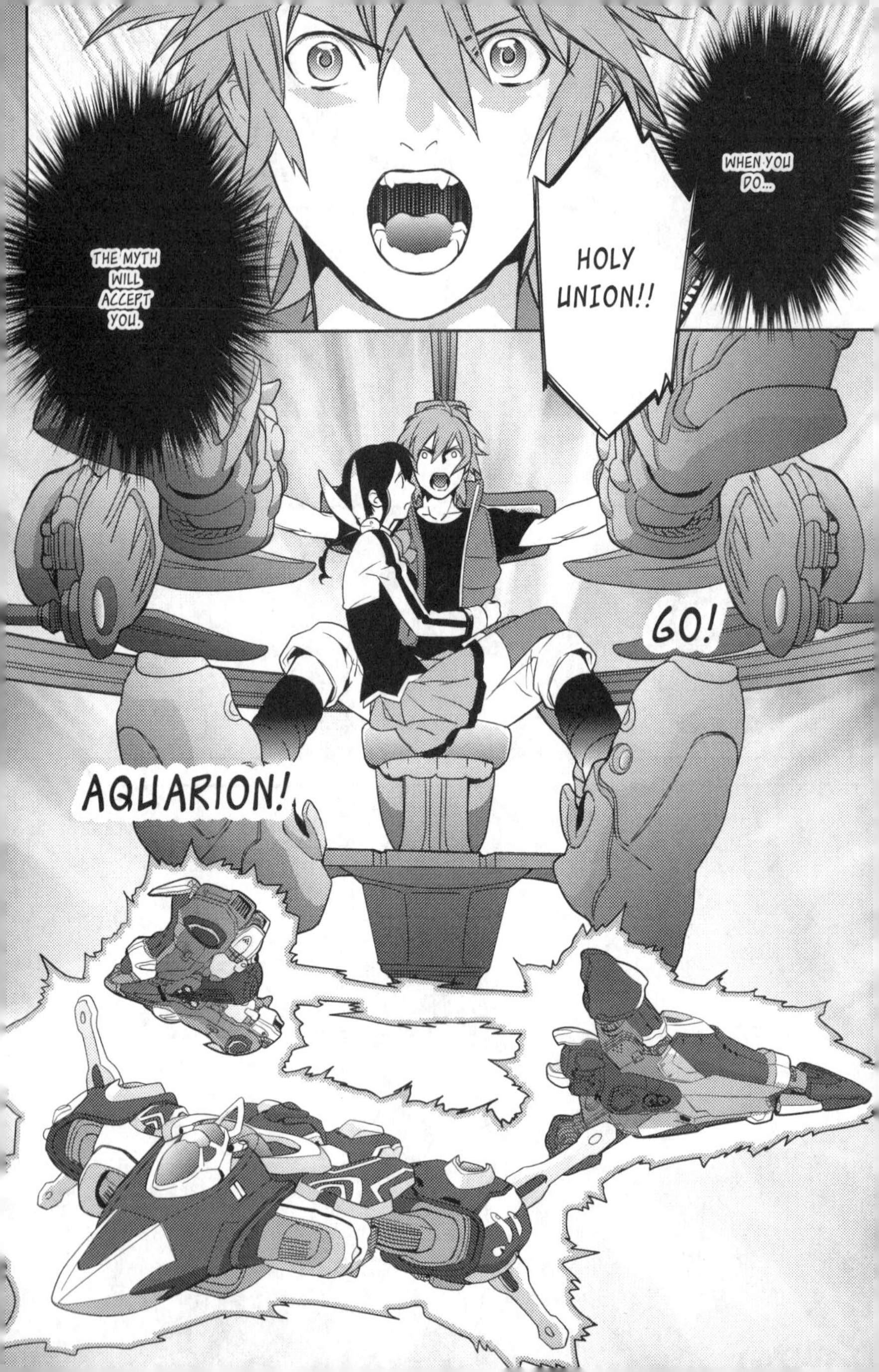
WHEN YOU DO...
HOLY UNION!!
THE MYTH WILL ACCEPT YOU.
GO!
AQUARION!

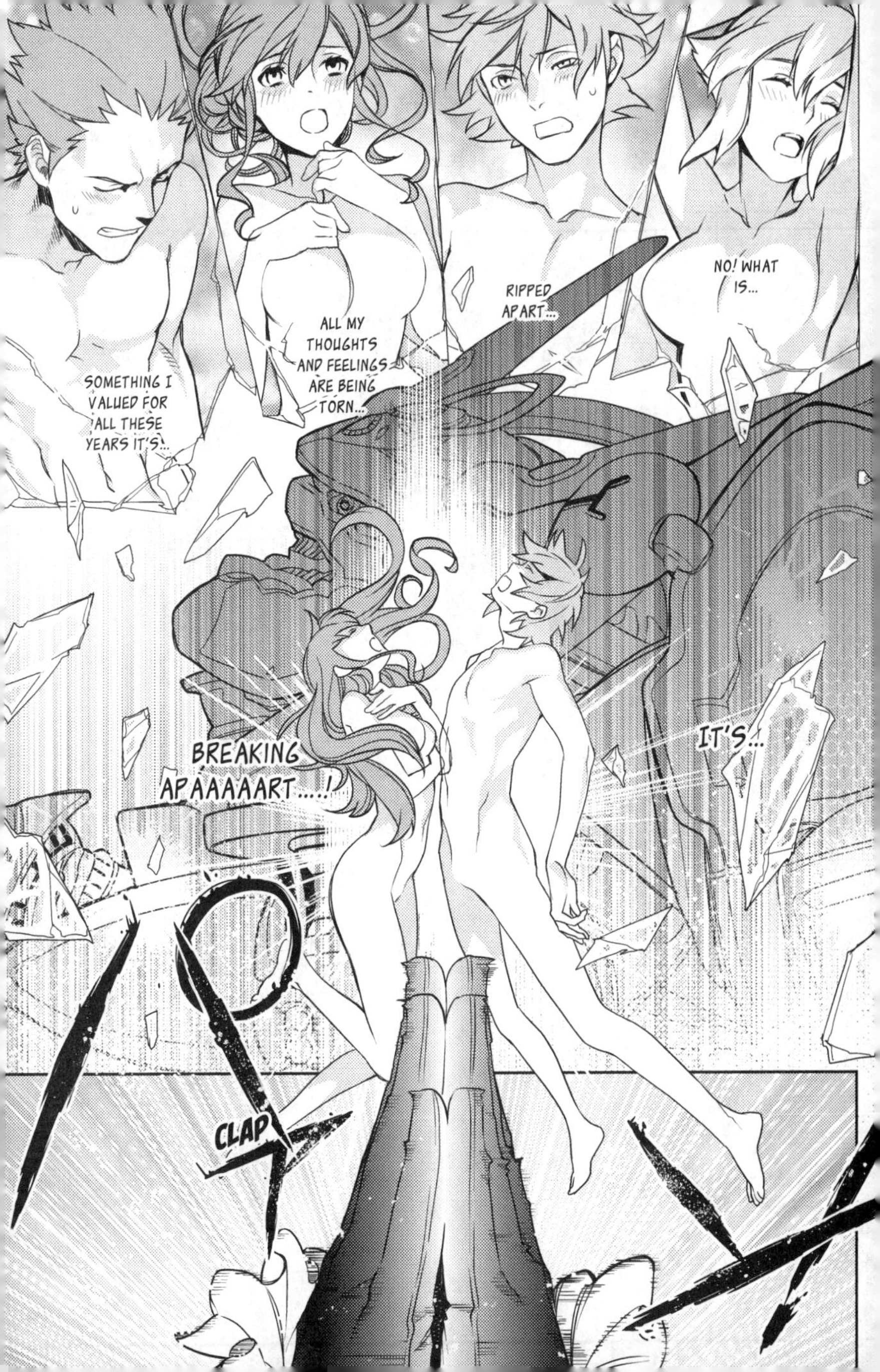
NO! WHAT IS...
RIPPED APART...
ALL MY THOUGHTS AND FEELINGS ARE BEING TORN...
SOMETHING I VALUED FOR ALL THESE YEARS IT'S...
IT'S...
BREAKING APAAAART....!
CLAP

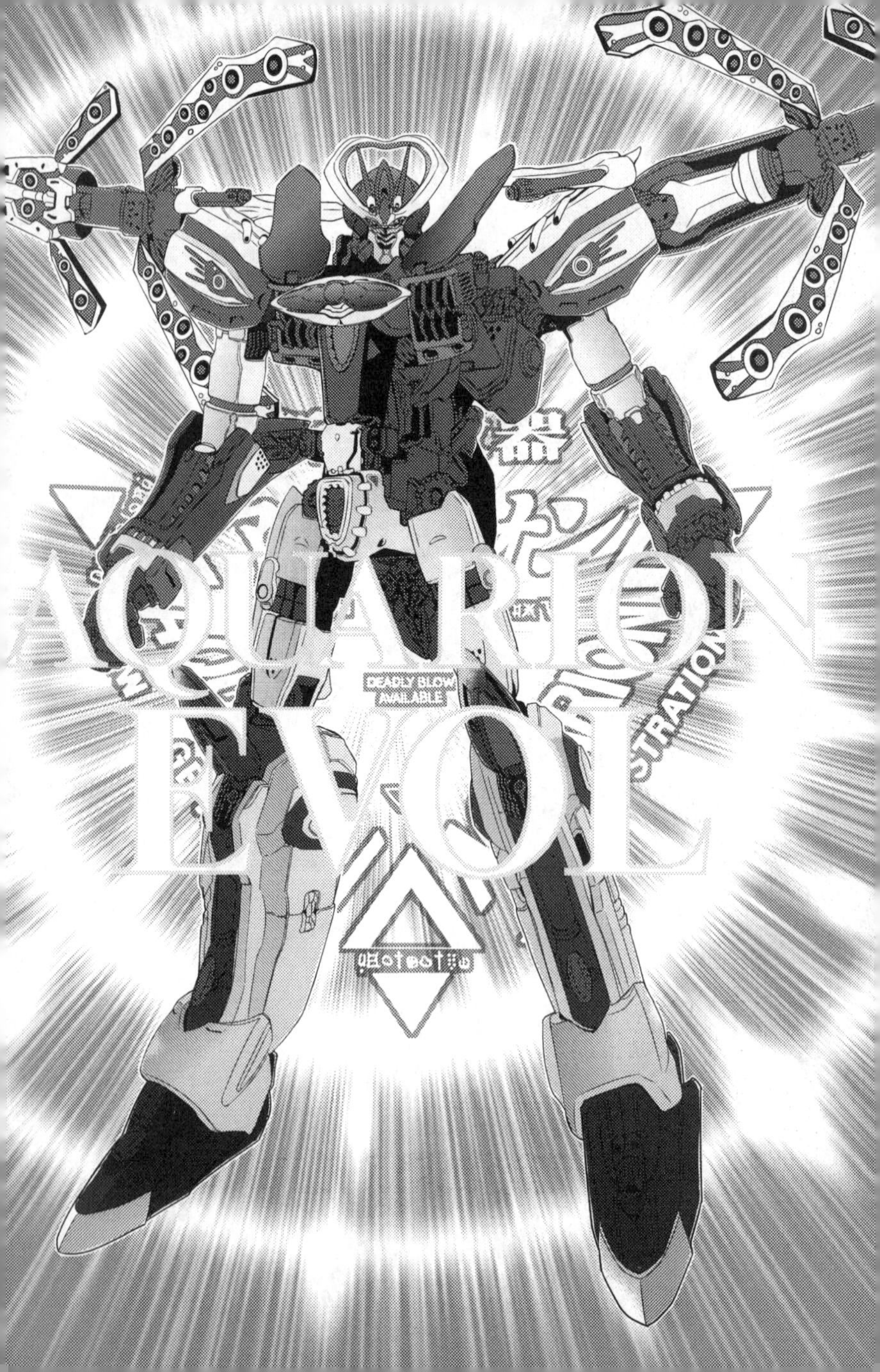
AQUARION
EVOL
DEADLY BLOW
AVAILABLE

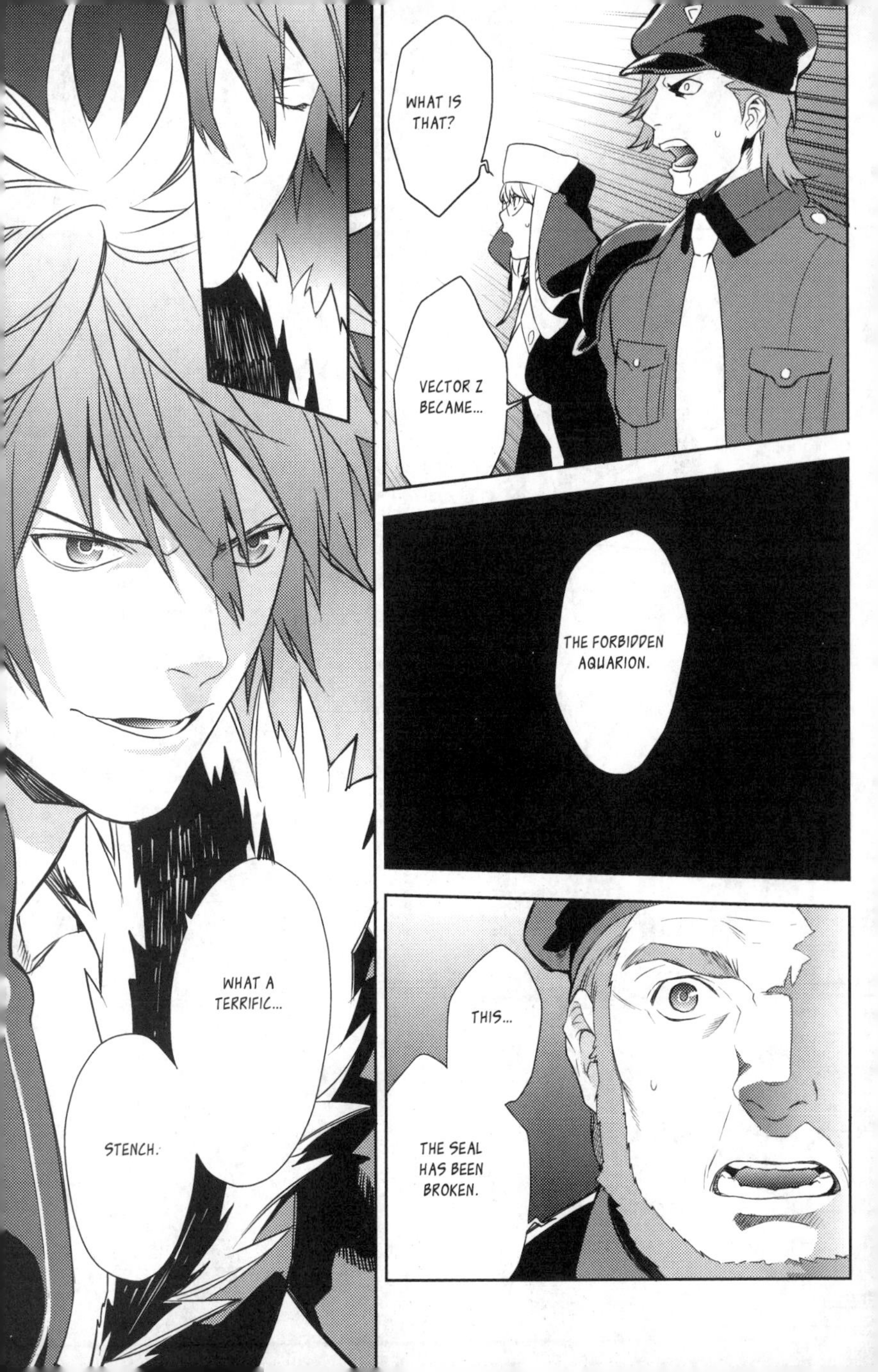
WHAT IS THAT?
VECTOR Z BECAME...
THE FORBIDDEN AQUARION.
THIS...
THE SEAL HAS BEEN BROKEN.
WHAT A TERRIFIC...
STENCH.

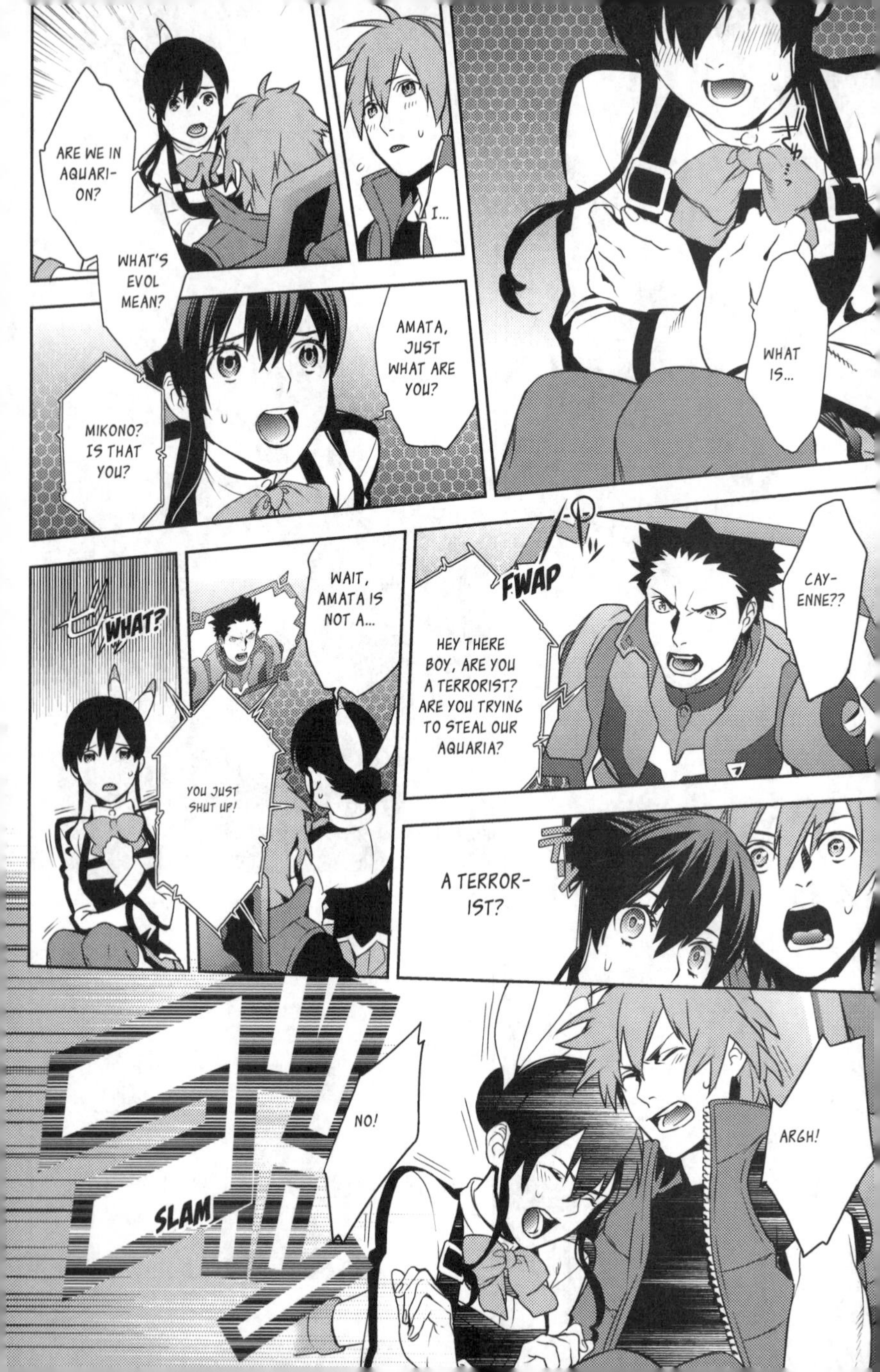

WHAT IS...
I...
ARE WE IN AQUARI-ON?
WHAT'S EVOL MEAN?
AMATA, JUST WHAT ARE YOU?
MIKONO? IS THAT YOU?
FWAP
CAY-ENNE??
HEY THERE BOY, ARE YOU A TERRORIST? ARE YOU TRYING TO STEAL OUR AQUARIA?
A TERROR-IST?
WAIT, AMATA IS NOT A...
WHAT?
YOU JUST SHUT UP!
ARGH!
NO!
SLAM

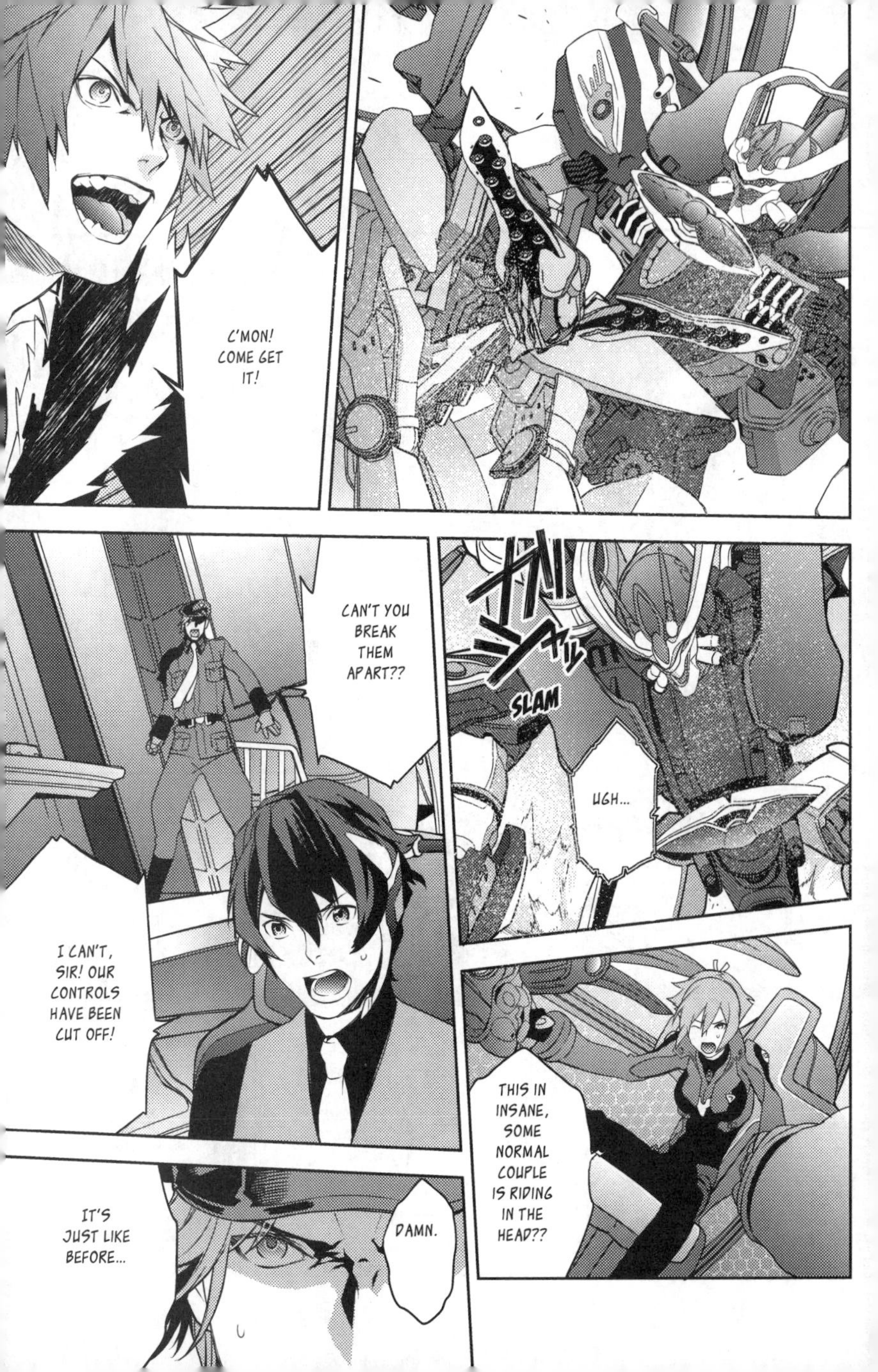
C'MON! COME GET IT!
SLAM
UGH...
THIS IN INSANE, SOME NORMAL COUPLE IS RIDING IN THE HEAD??
CAN'T YOU BREAK THEM APART??
I CAN'T, SIR! OUR CONTROLS HAVE BEEN CUT OFF!
DAMN.
IT'S JUST LIKE BEFORE...

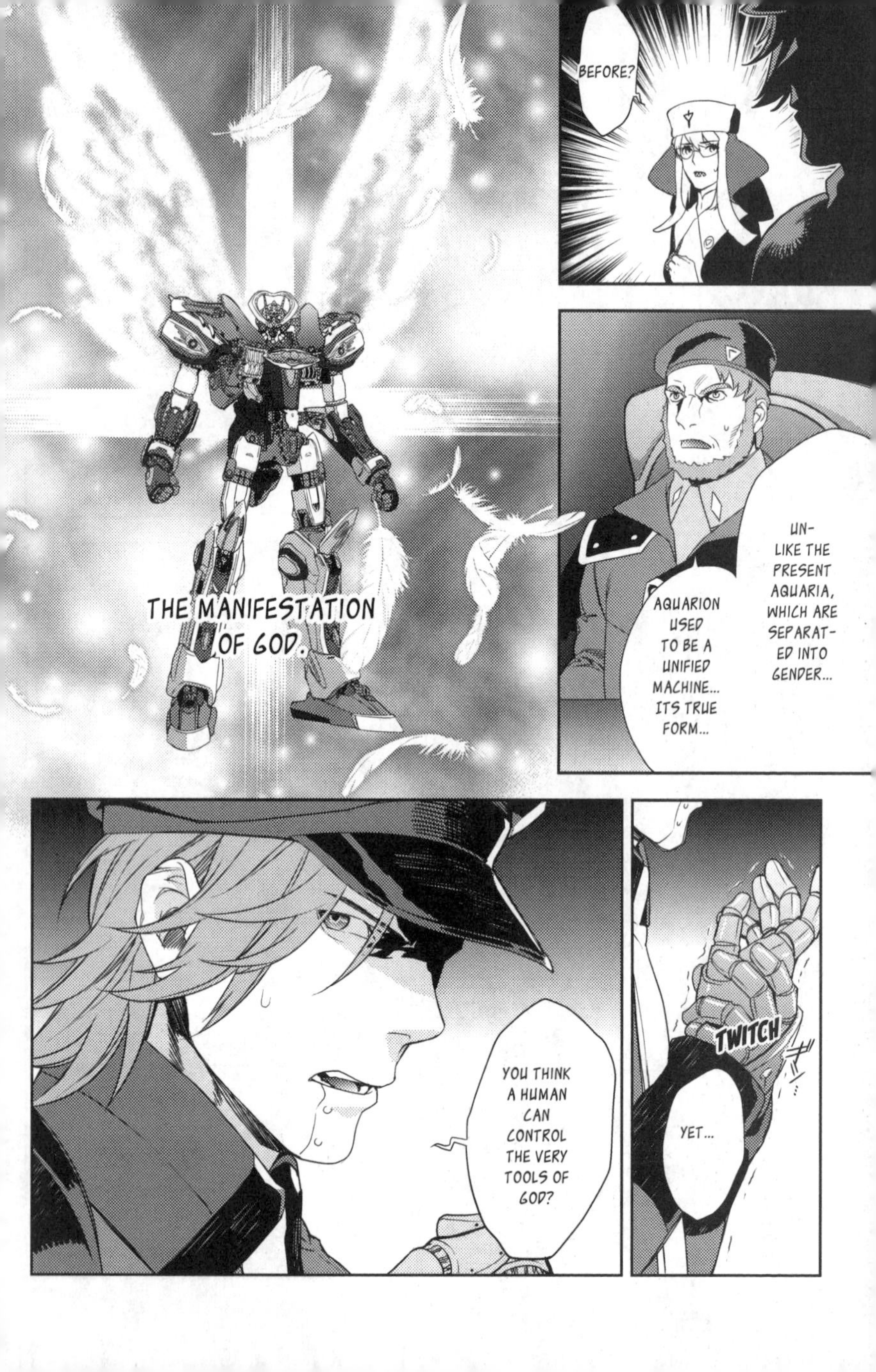
BEFORE?
UN-LIKE THE PRESENT AQUARIA, WHICH ARE SEPARAT-ED INTO GENDER...
AQUARION USED TO BE A UNIFIED MACHINE... ITS TRUE FORM...
THE MANIFESTATION OF GOD.
TWITCH
YET...
YOU THINK A HUMAN CAN CONTROL THE VERY TOOLS OF GOD?

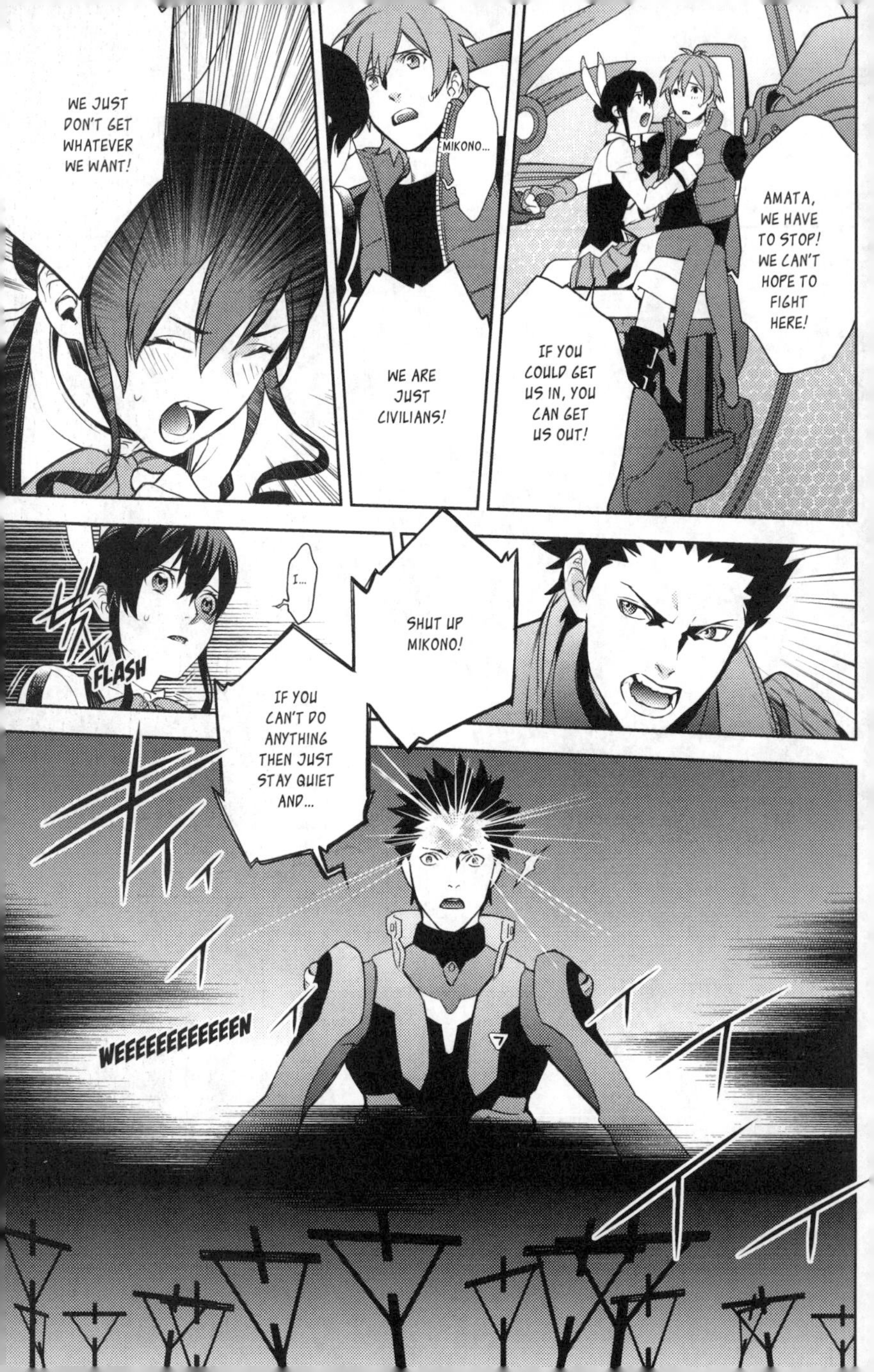
AMATA, WE HAVE TO STOP! WE CAN'T HOPE TO FIGHT HERE!
IF YOU COULD GET US IN, YOU CAN GET US OUT!
MIKONO...
WE ARE JUST CIVILIANS!
WE JUST DON'T GET WHATEVER WE WANT!
SHUT UP MIKONO!
I...
FLASH
IF YOU CAN'T DO ANYTHING THEN JUST STAY QUIET AND...
WEEEEEEEEEEEN

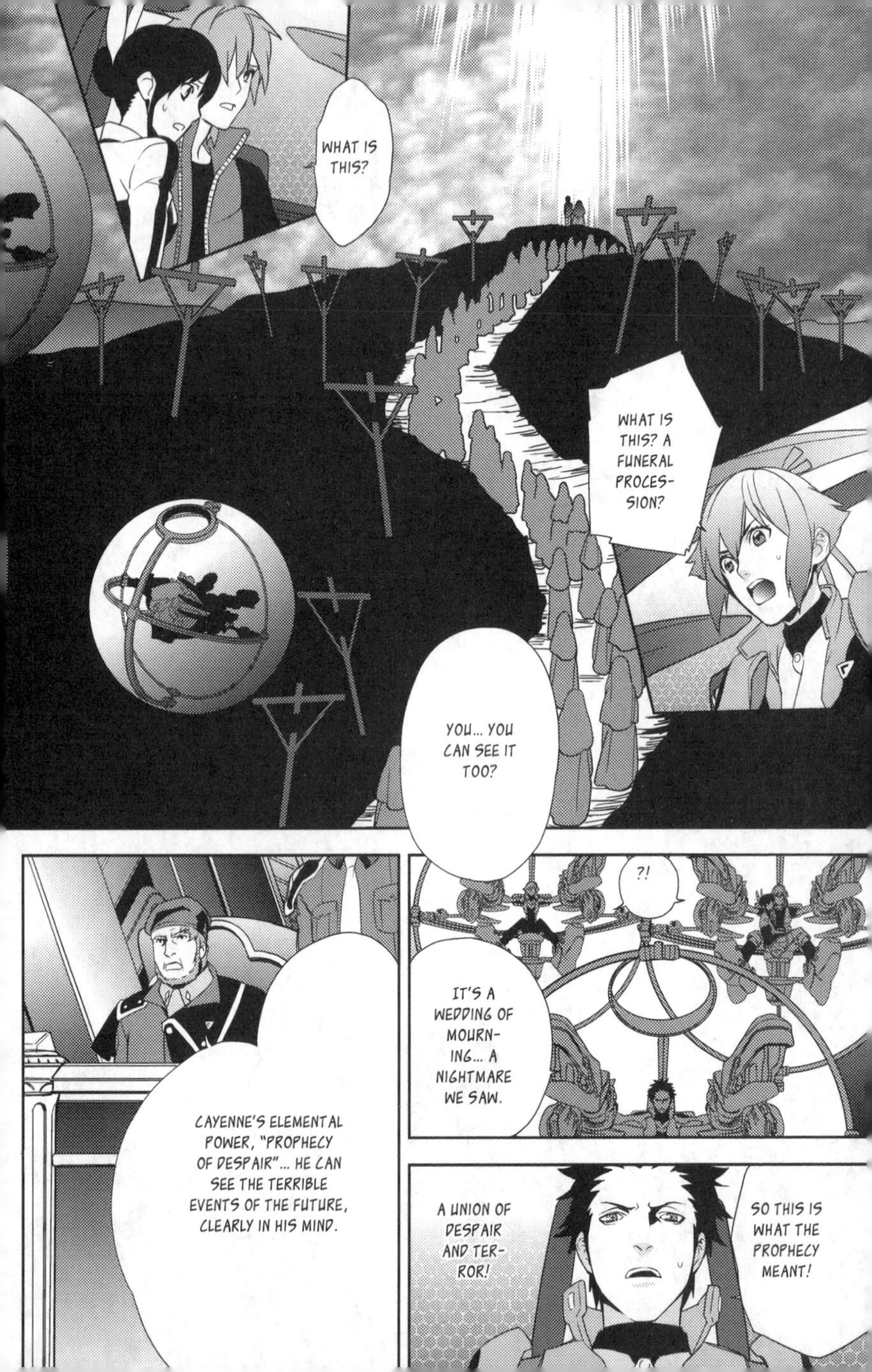
WHAT IS THIS?
WHAT IS THIS? A FUNERAL PROCESSION?
YOU... YOU CAN SEE IT TOO?
?!
IT'S A WEDDING OF MOURNING... A NIGHTMARE WE SAW.
SO THIS IS WHAT THE PROPHECY MEANT!
A UNION OF DESPAIR AND TERROR!
CAYENNE'S ELEMENTAL POWER, "PROPHECY OF DESPAIR"... HE CAN SEE THE TERRIBLE EVENTS OF THE FUTURE, CLEARLY IN HIS MIND.

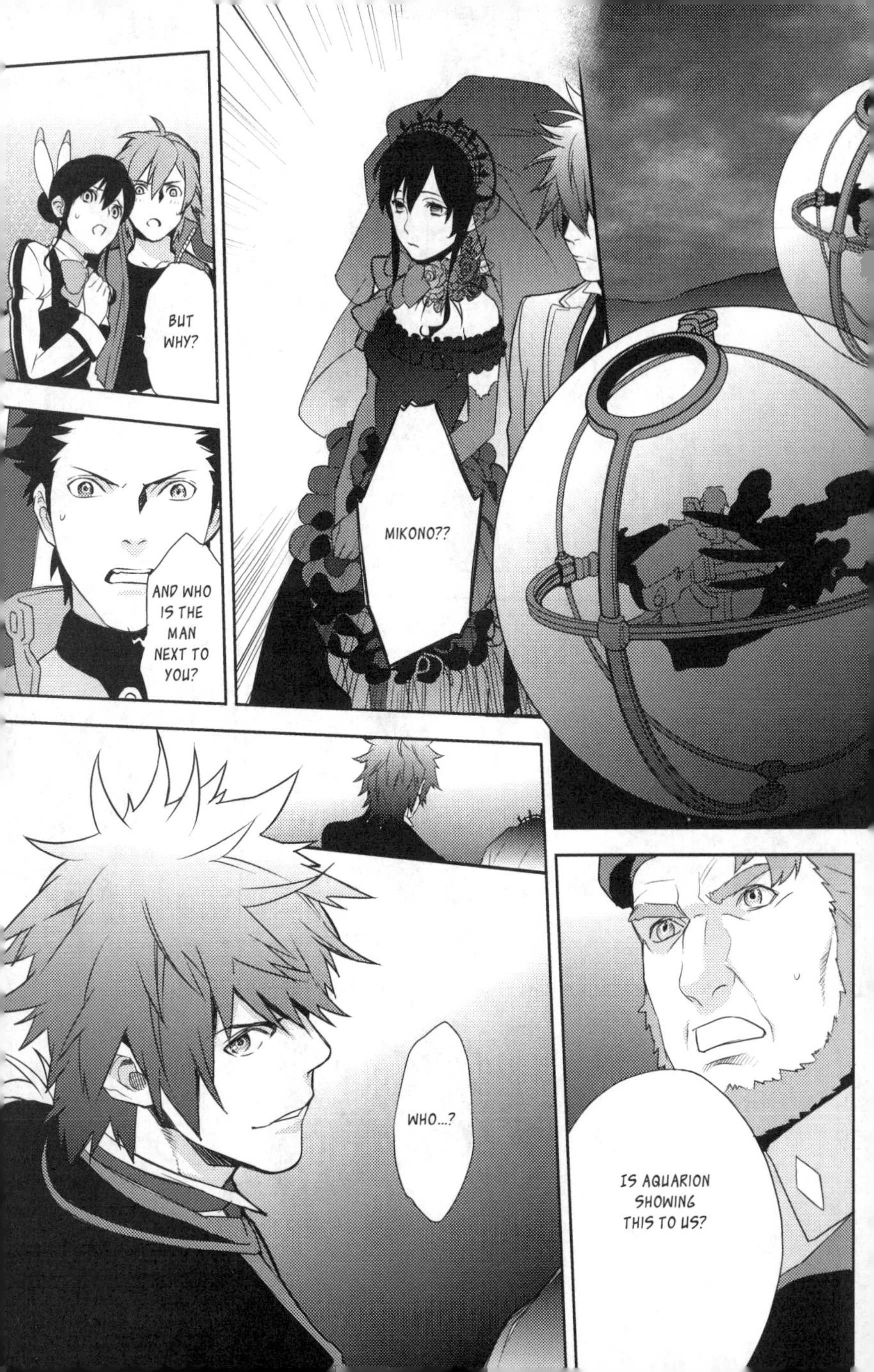
MIKONO??
BUT WHY?
AND WHO IS THE MAN NEXT TO YOU?
IS AQUARION SHOWING THIS TO US?
WHO...?

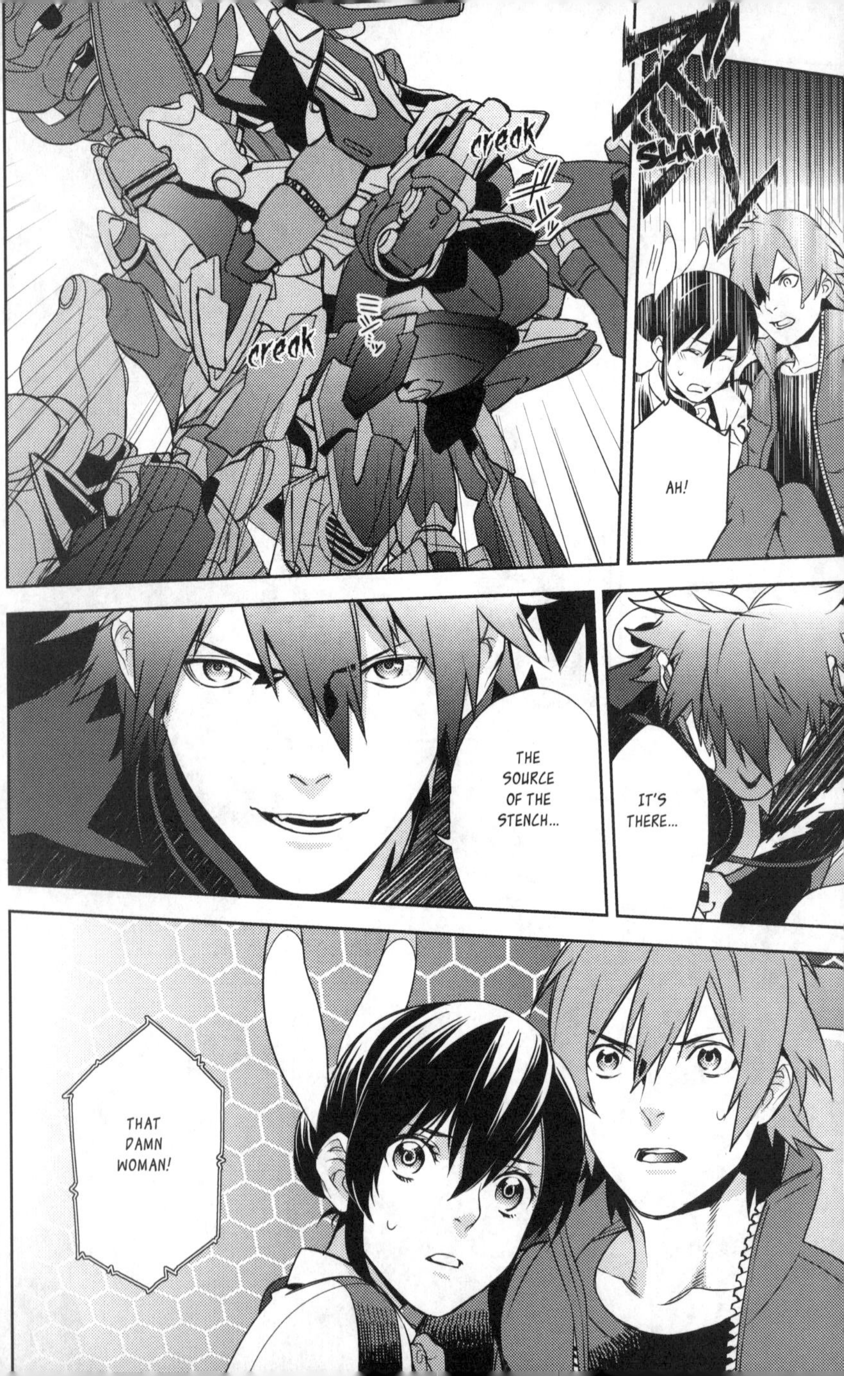
SLAM
AH!
creak
creak
IT'S THERE...
THE SOURCE OF THE STENCH...
THAT DAMN WOMAN!

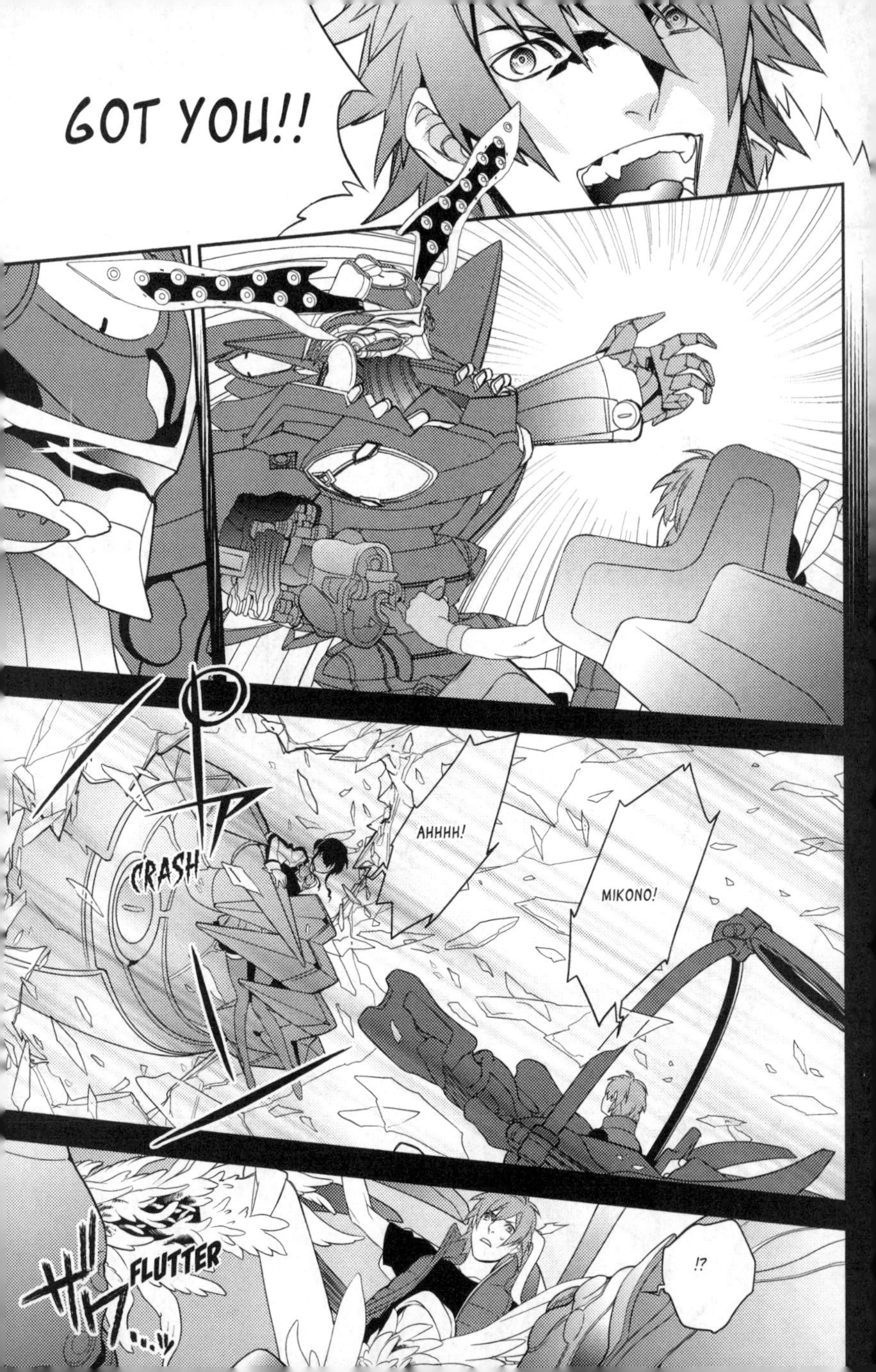
GOT YOU!!
MIKONO!
AHHHH!
CRASH
!?
FLUTTER

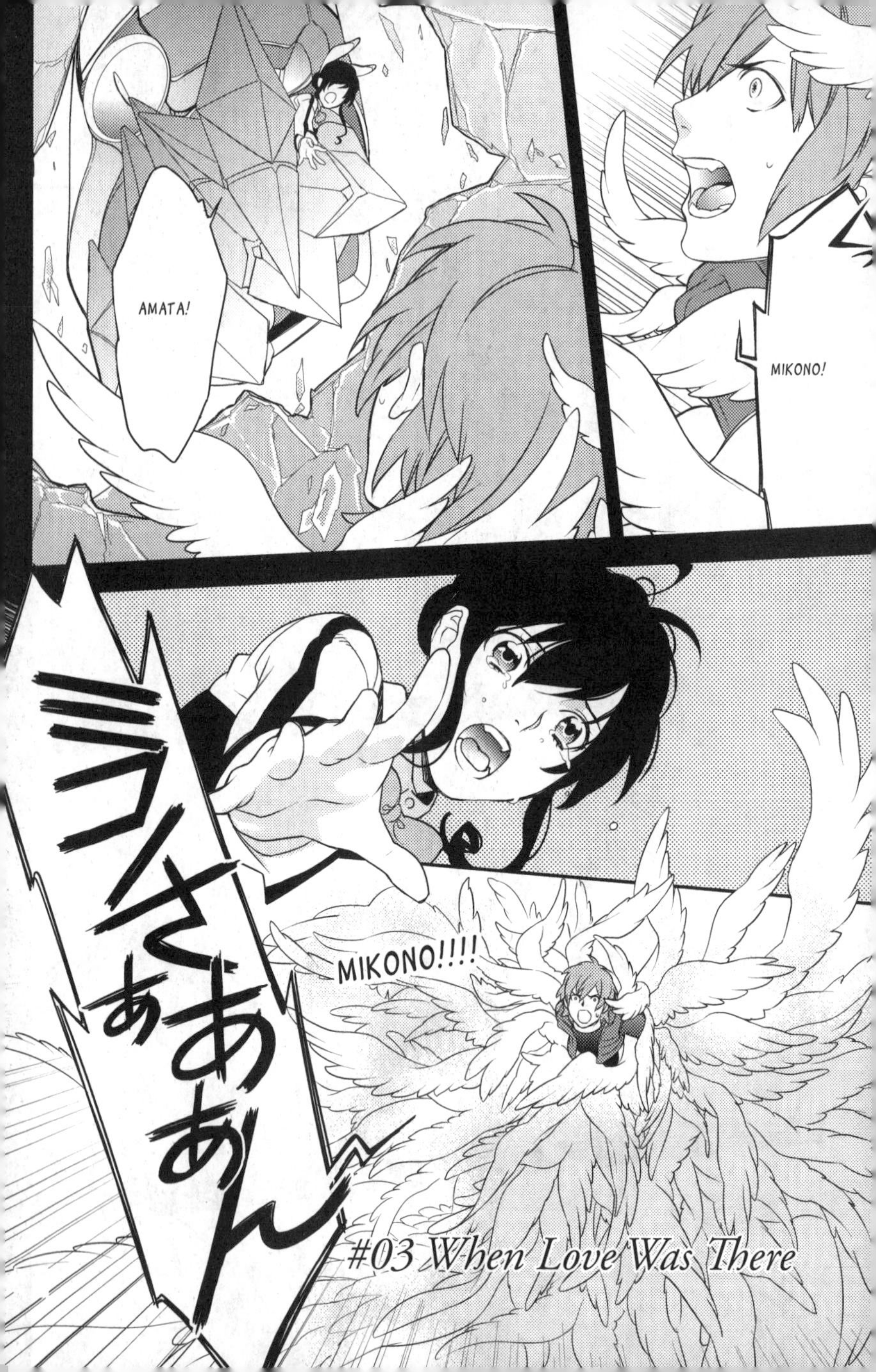
MIKONO!
AMATA!
ミコノさぁぁぁん
MIKONO!!!!
#03 When Love Was There

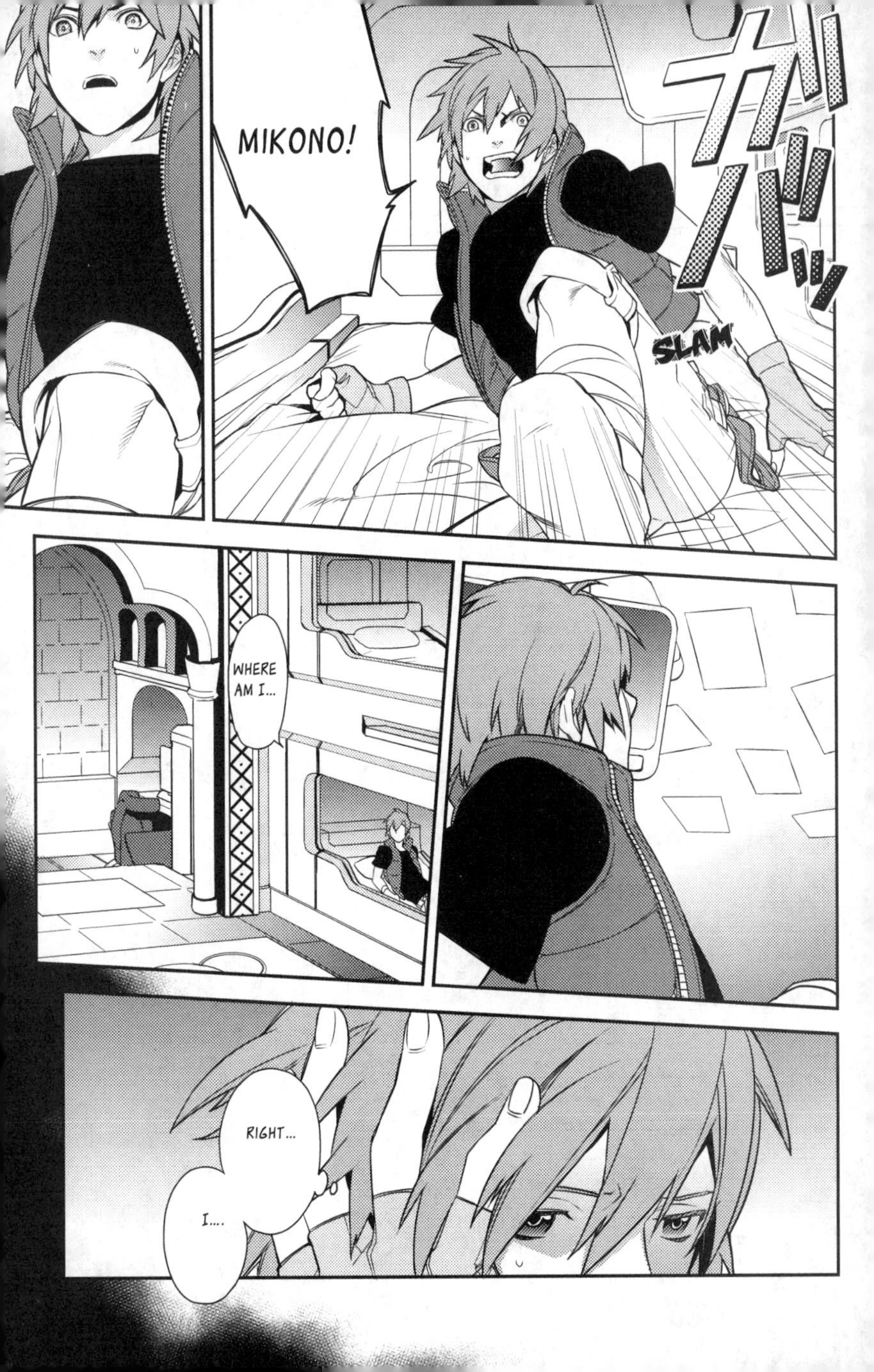
MIKONO!
SLAM
WHERE AM I...
RIGHT...
I....

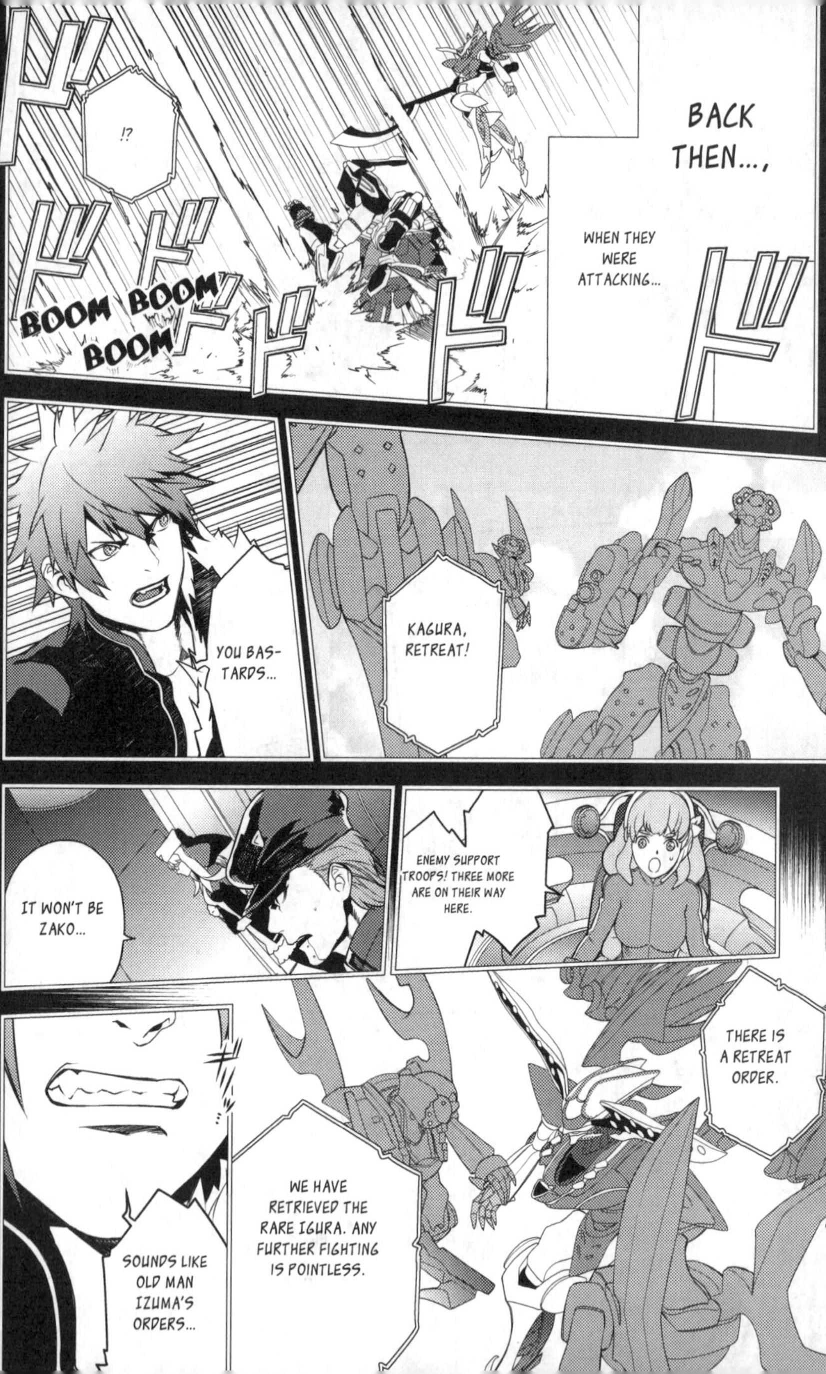
BACK THEN...,
WHEN THEY WERE ATTACKING...
ドドドドド
!?
BOOM BOOM BOOM
KAGURA, RETREAT!
YOU BAS-TARDS...
ENEMY SUPPORT TROOPS! THREE MORE ARE ON THEIR WAY HERE.
IT WON'T BE ZAKO...
THERE IS A RETREAT ORDER.
WE HAVE RETRIEVED THE RARE IGURA. ANY FURTHER FIGHTING IS POINTLESS.
SOUNDS LIKE OLD MAN IZUMA'S ORDERS...

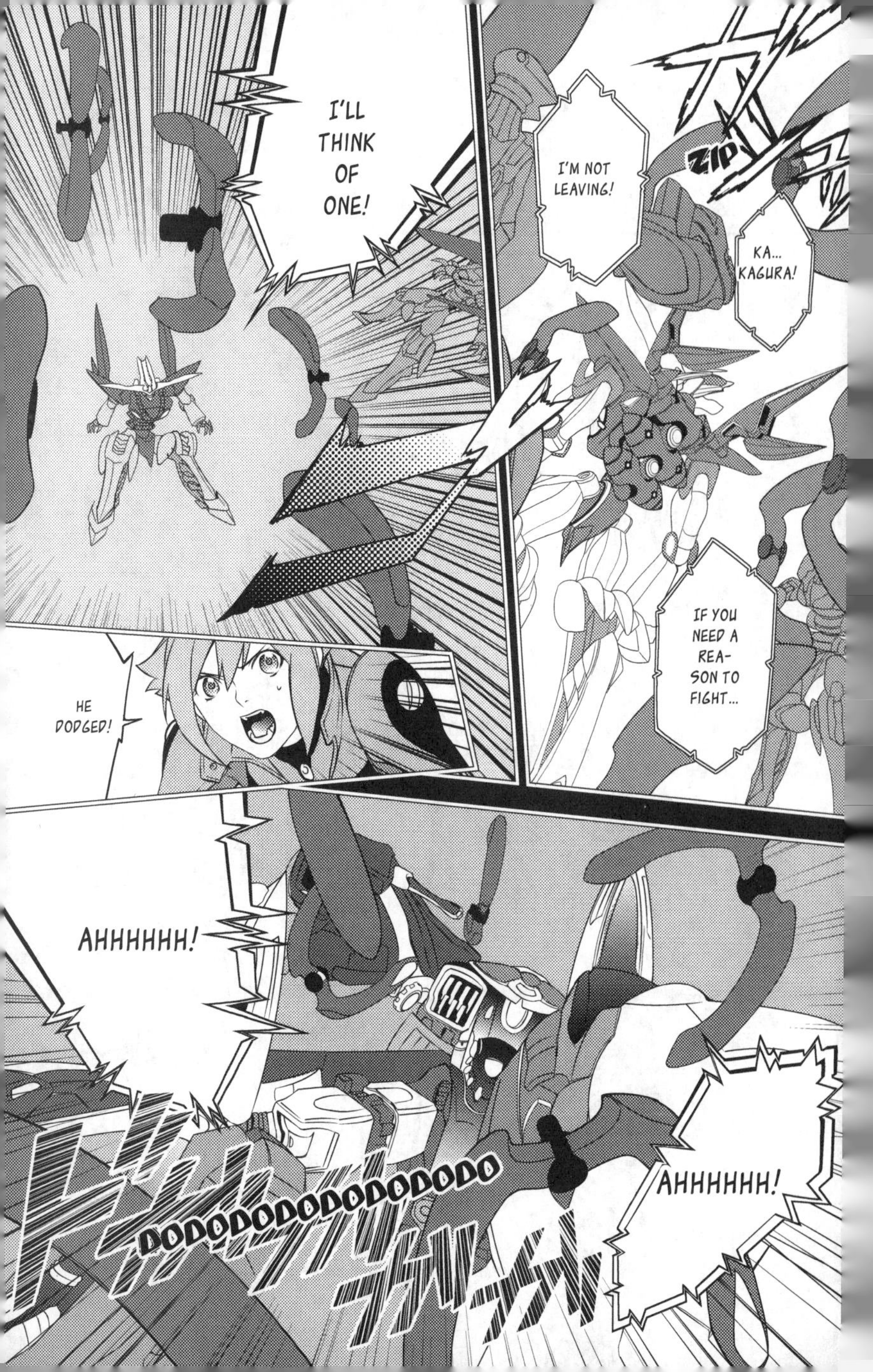

ZIP
KA... KAGURA!
I'M NOT LEAVING!
IF YOU NEED A REA-SON TO FIGHT...
I'LL THINK OF ONE!
HE DODGED!
AHHHHHH!
AHHHHHH!
DODODODODODODODODODODO

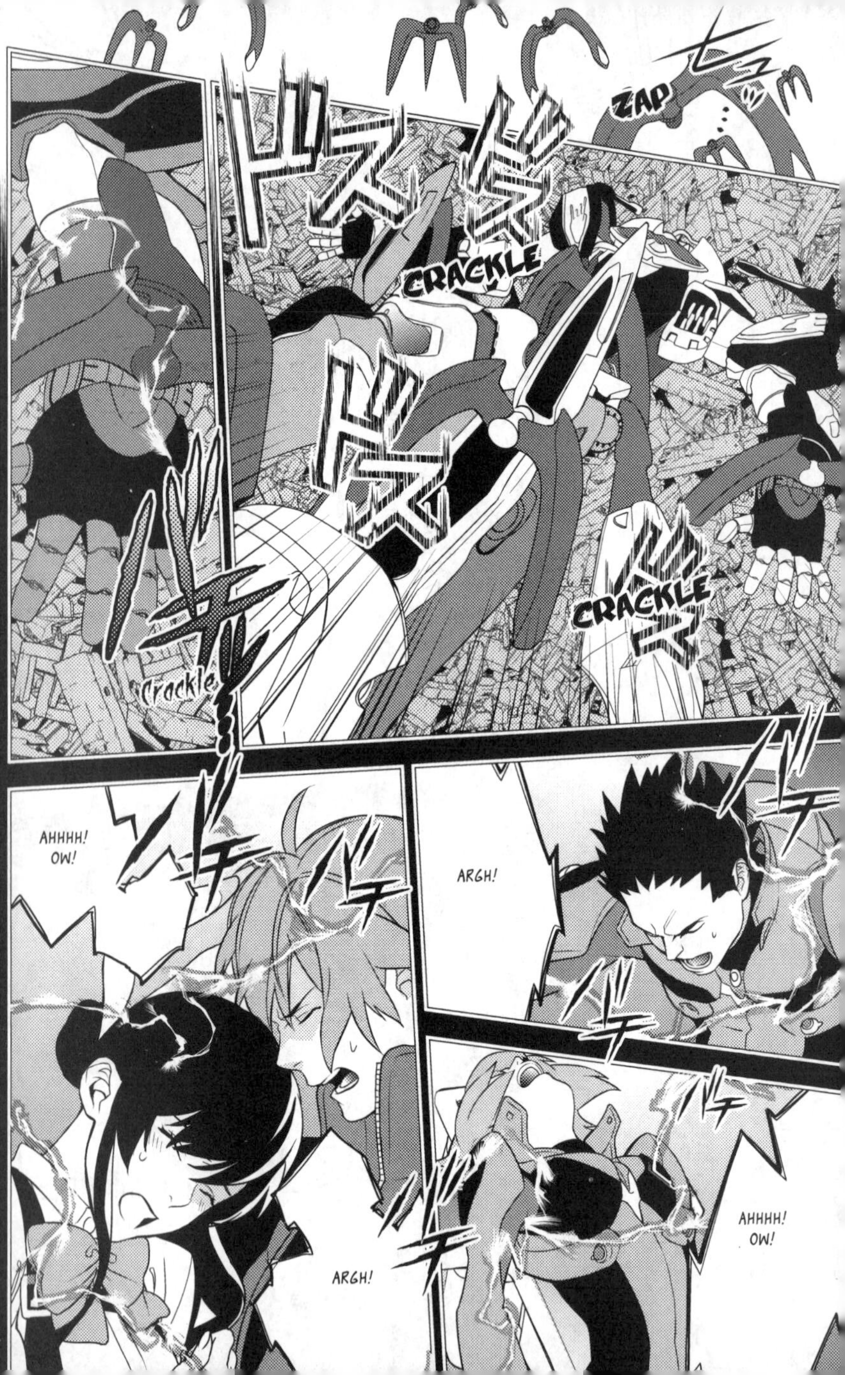
ZAP
CRACKLE
CRACKLE
Crackle
ARGH!
AHHHH! OW!
AHHHH! OW!
ARGH!

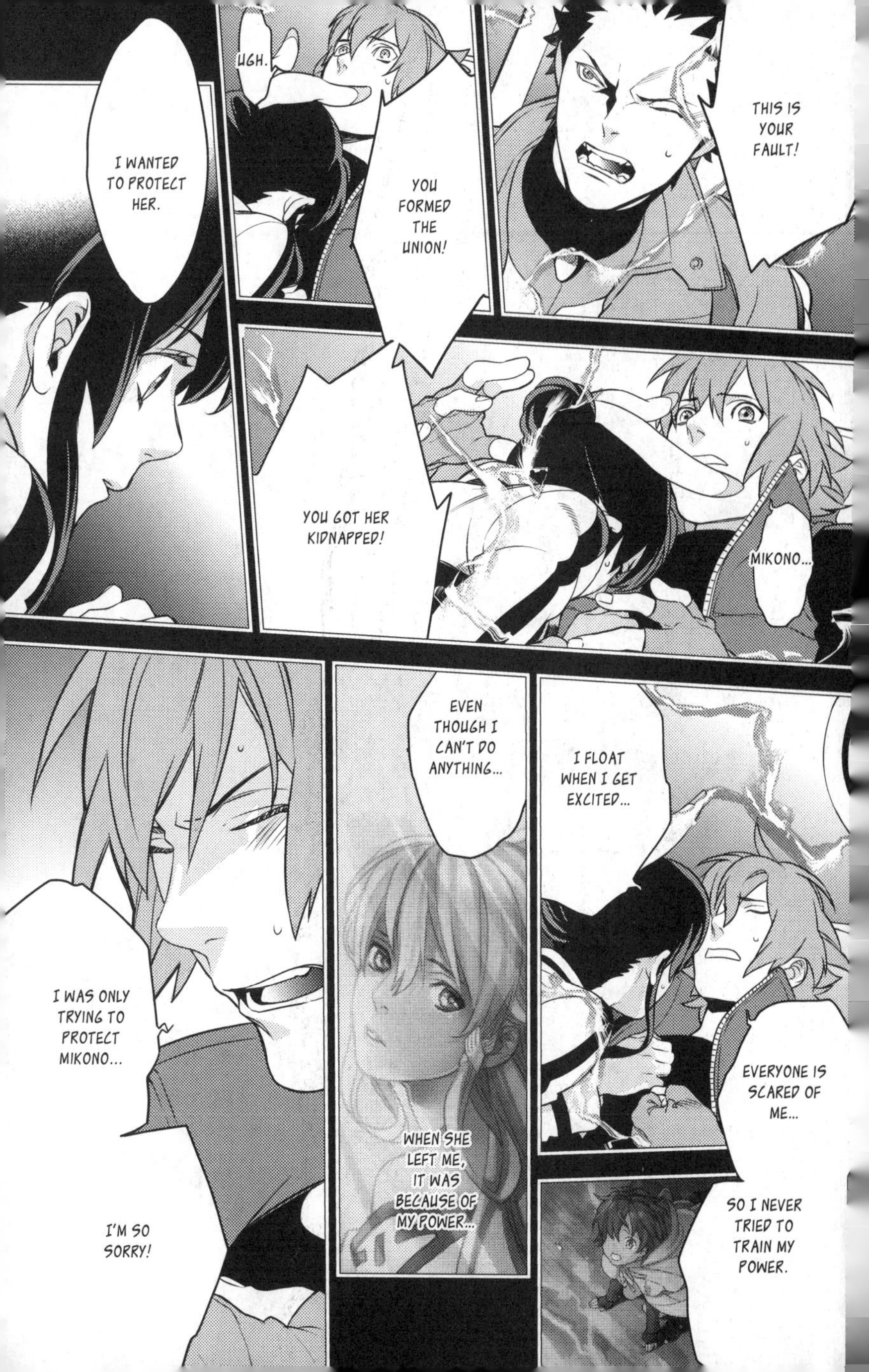
THIS IS YOUR FAULT!
UGH.
YOU FORMED THE UNION!
MIKONO...
YOU GOT HER KIDNAPPED!
I WANTED TO PROTECT HER.
I FLOAT WHEN I GET EXCITED...
EVERYONE IS SCARED OF ME...
SO I NEVER TRIED TO TRAIN MY POWER.
EVEN THOUGH I CAN'T DO ANYTHING...
WHEN SHE LEFT ME, IT WAS BECAUSE OF MY POWER...
I WAS ONLY TRYING TO PROTECT MIKONO...
I'M SO SORRY!

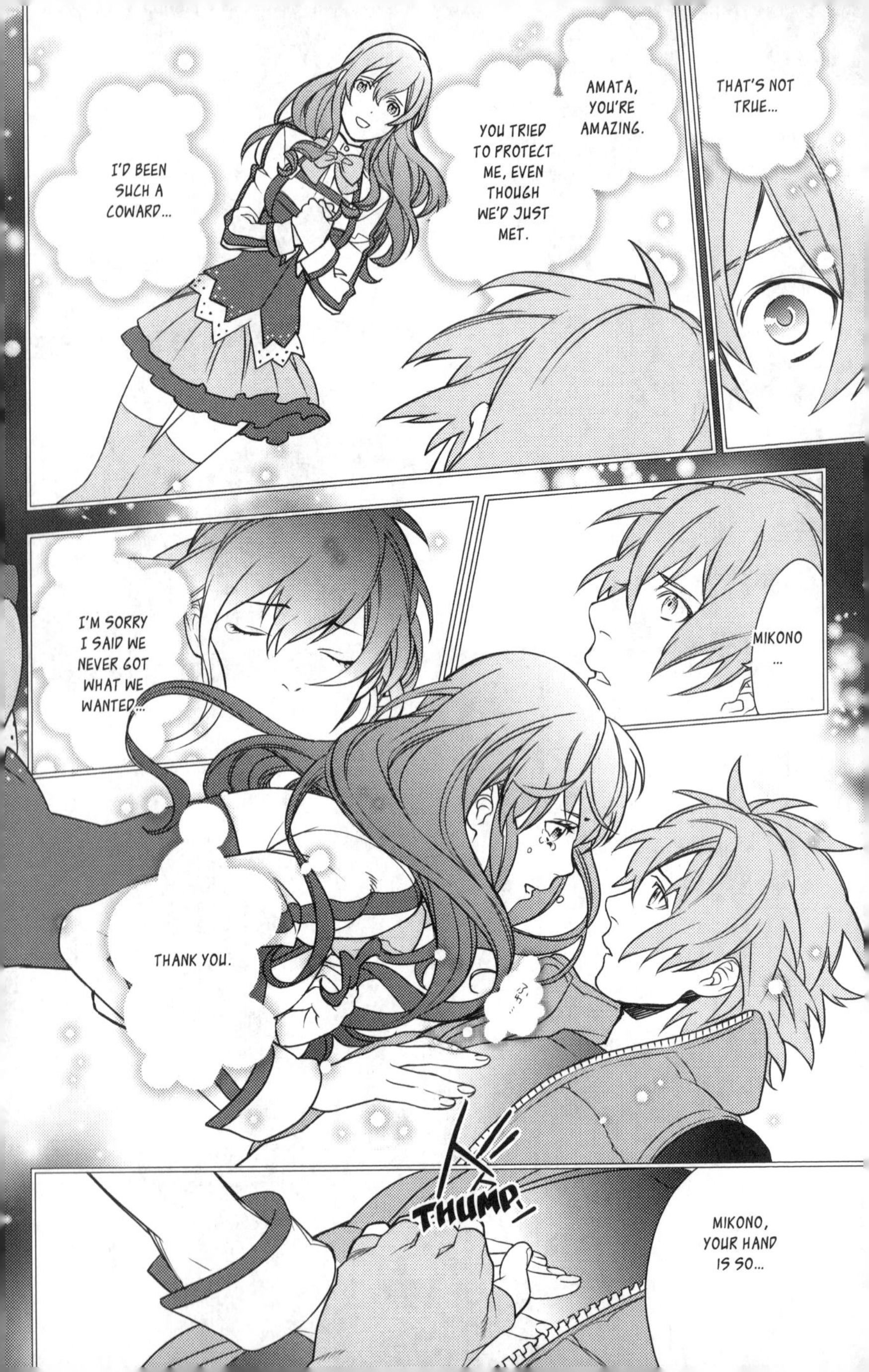
THAT'S NOT TRUE...
AMATA, YOU'RE AMAZING.
YOU TRIED TO PROTECT ME, EVEN THOUGH WE'D JUST MET.
I'D BEEN SUCH A COWARD...
MIKONO ...
I'M SORRY I SAID WE NEVER GOT WHAT WE WANTED...
THANK YOU.
MIKONO, YOUR HAND IS SO...
THUMP

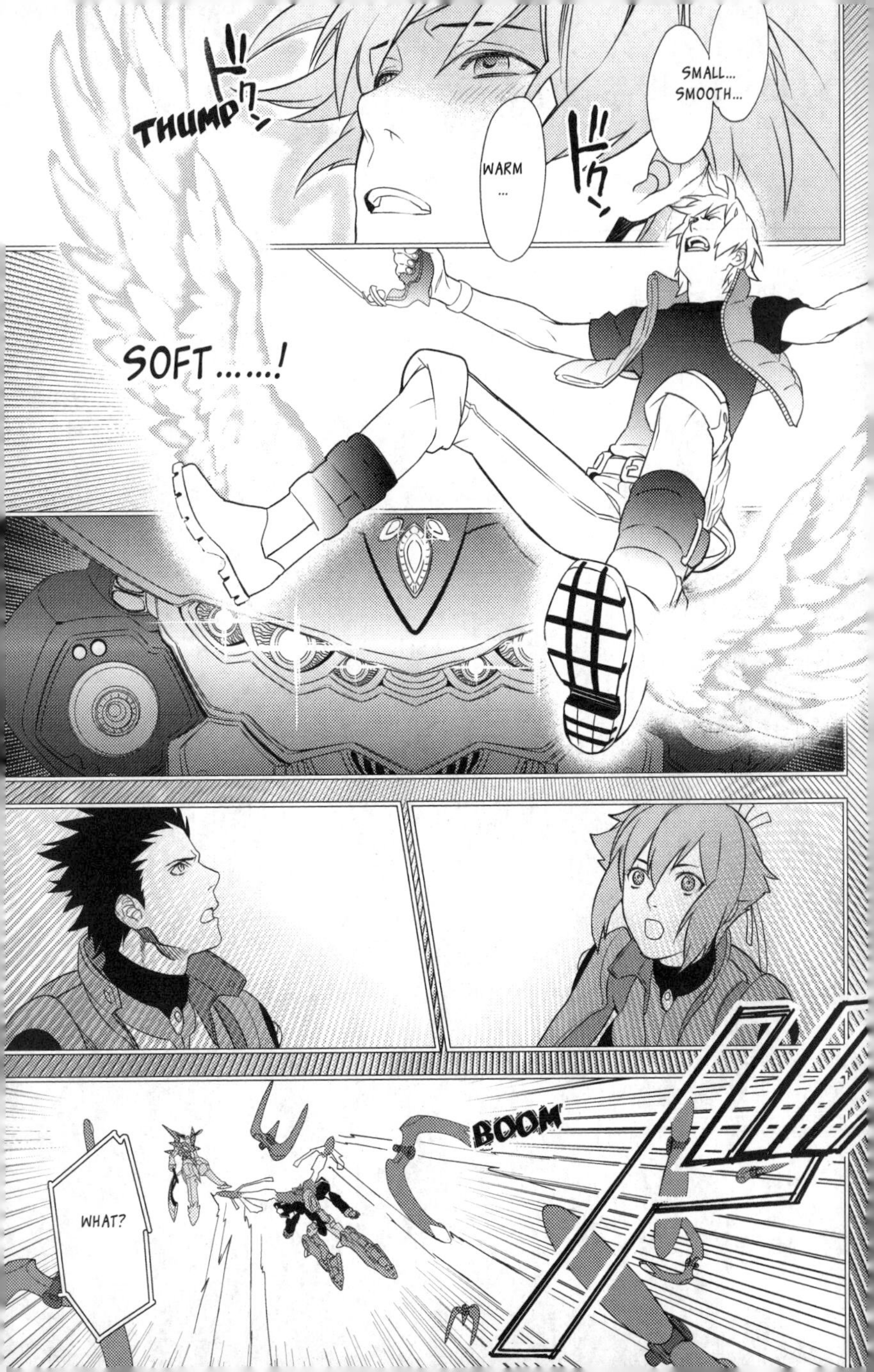
SMALL... SMOOTH...
WARM ...
THUMP
SOFT......!
BOOM
WHAT?

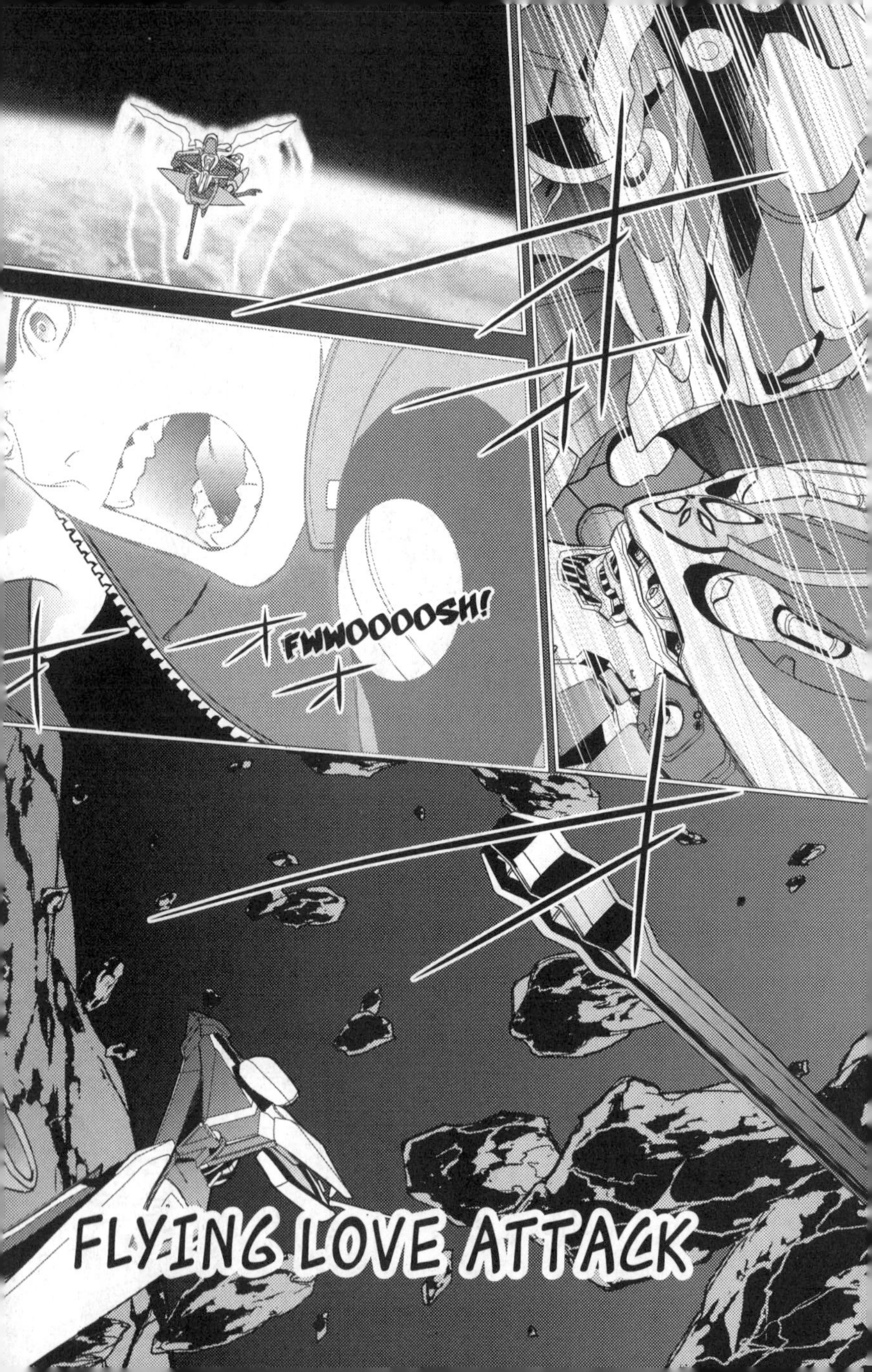
FWWOOOOOSH!
FLYING LOVE ATTACK

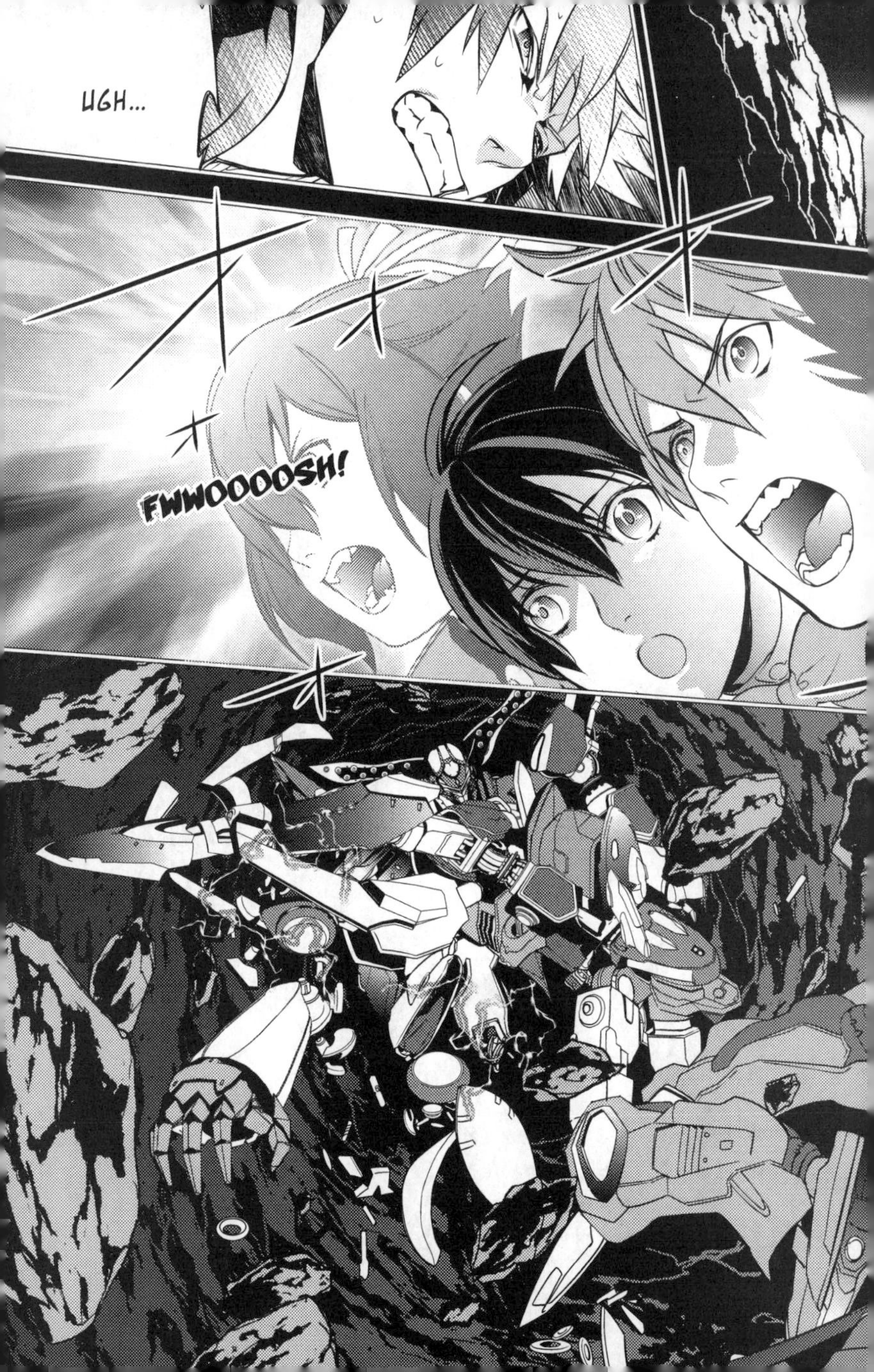
UGH...
FWWOOOOSH!

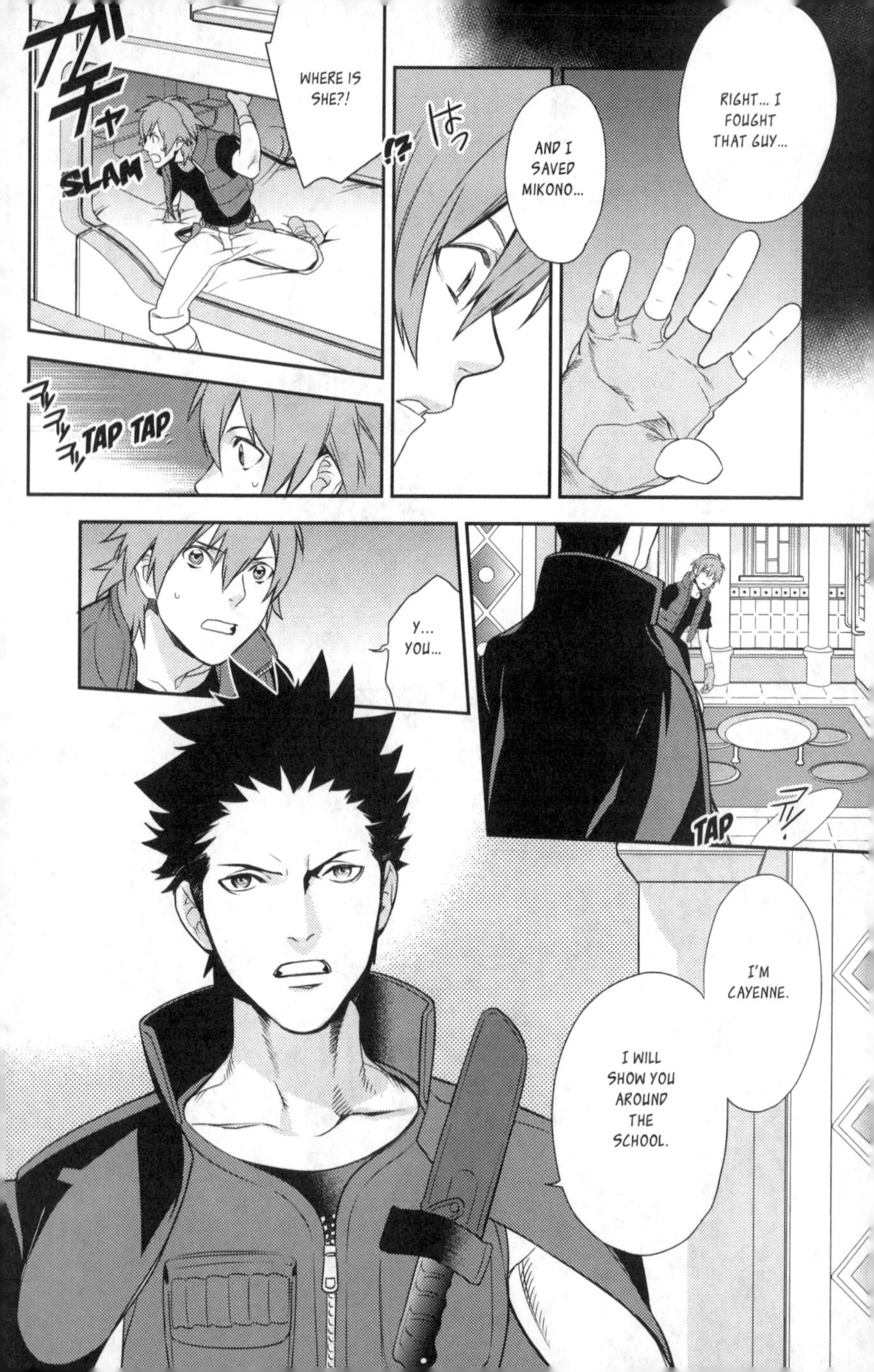
RIGHT... I FOUGHT THAT GUY...
はっ
!?
AND I SAVED MIKONO...
ガチャ
SLAM
WHERE IS SHE?!
TAP TAP
TAP
Y... YOU...
I'M CAYENNE.
I WILL SHOW YOU AROUND THE SCHOOL.

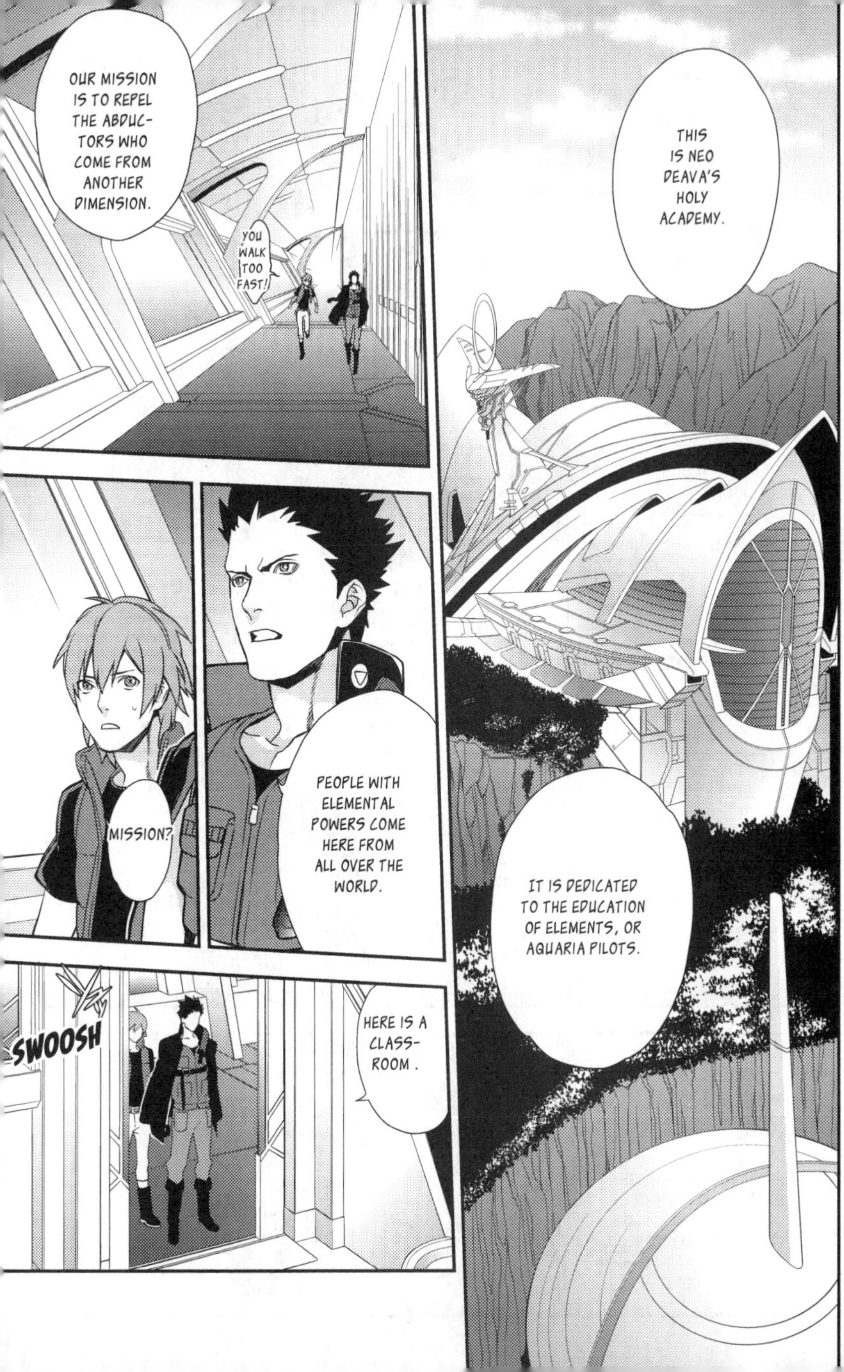
THIS IS NEO DEAVA'S HOLY ACADEMY.
IT IS DEDICATED TO THE EDUCATION OF ELEMENTS, OR AQUARIA PILOTS.
OUR MISSION IS TO REPEL THE ABDUC-TORS WHO COME FROM ANOTHER DIMENSION.
YOU WALK TOO FAST!
PEOPLE WITH ELEMENTAL POWERS COME HERE FROM ALL OVER THE WORLD.
MISSION?
HERE IS A CLASS-ROOM .
SWOOSH

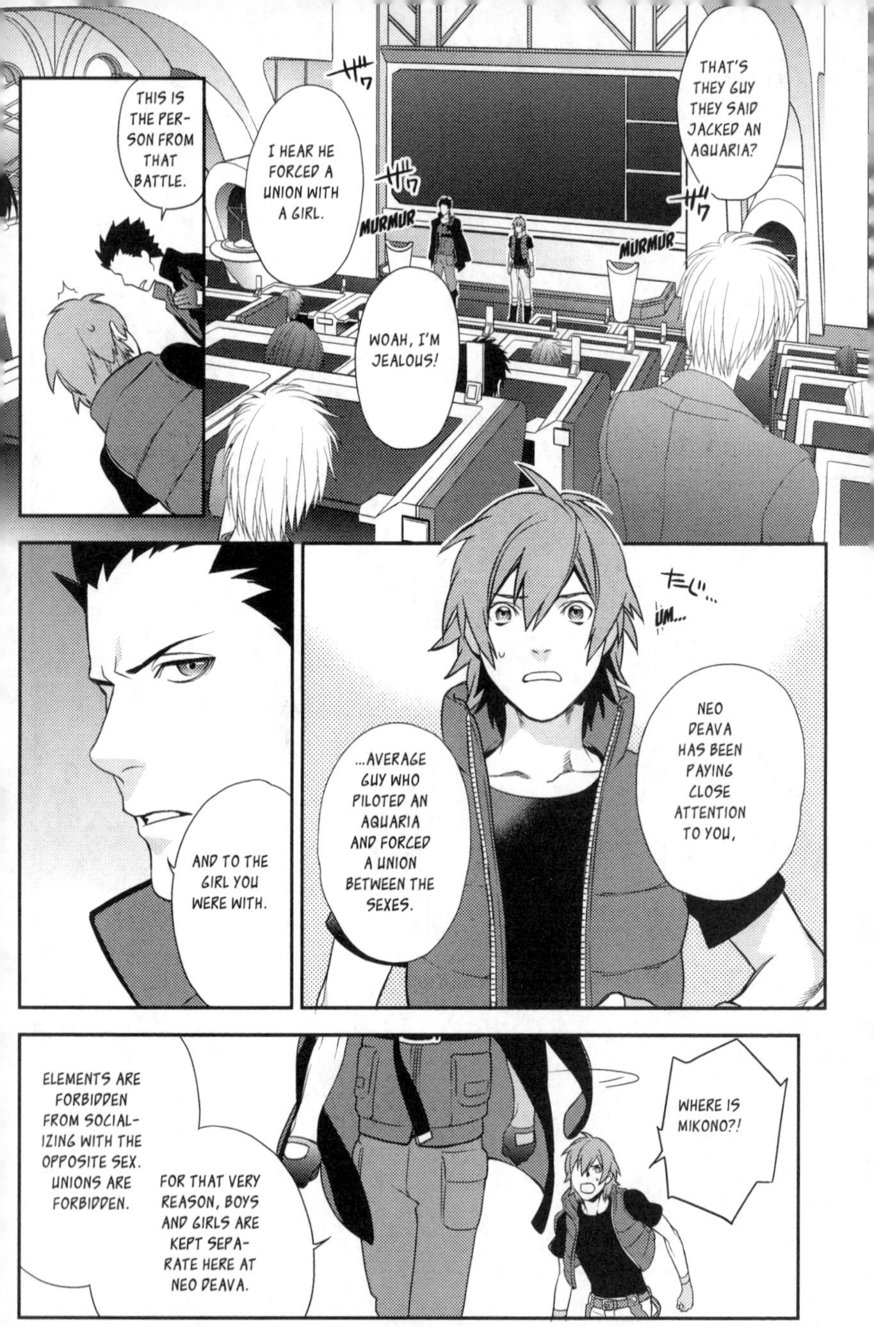
THAT'S THEY GUY THEY SAID JACKED AN AQUARIA?
ザワ
MURMUR
I HEAR HE FORCED A UNION WITH A GIRL.
MURMUR
WOAH, I'M JEALOUS!
THIS IS THE PERSON FROM THAT BATTLE.
UM...
NEO DEAVA HAS BEEN PAYING CLOSE ATTENTION TO YOU,
...AVERAGE GUY WHO PILOTED AN AQUARIA AND FORCED A UNION BETWEEN THE SEXES.
AND TO THE GIRL YOU WERE WITH.
WHERE IS MIKONO?!
ELEMENTS ARE FORBIDDEN FROM SOCIAL-IZING WITH THE OPPOSITE SEX. UNIONS ARE FORBIDDEN.
FOR THAT VERY REASON, BOYS AND GIRLS ARE KEPT SEPA-RATE HERE AT NEO DEAVA.

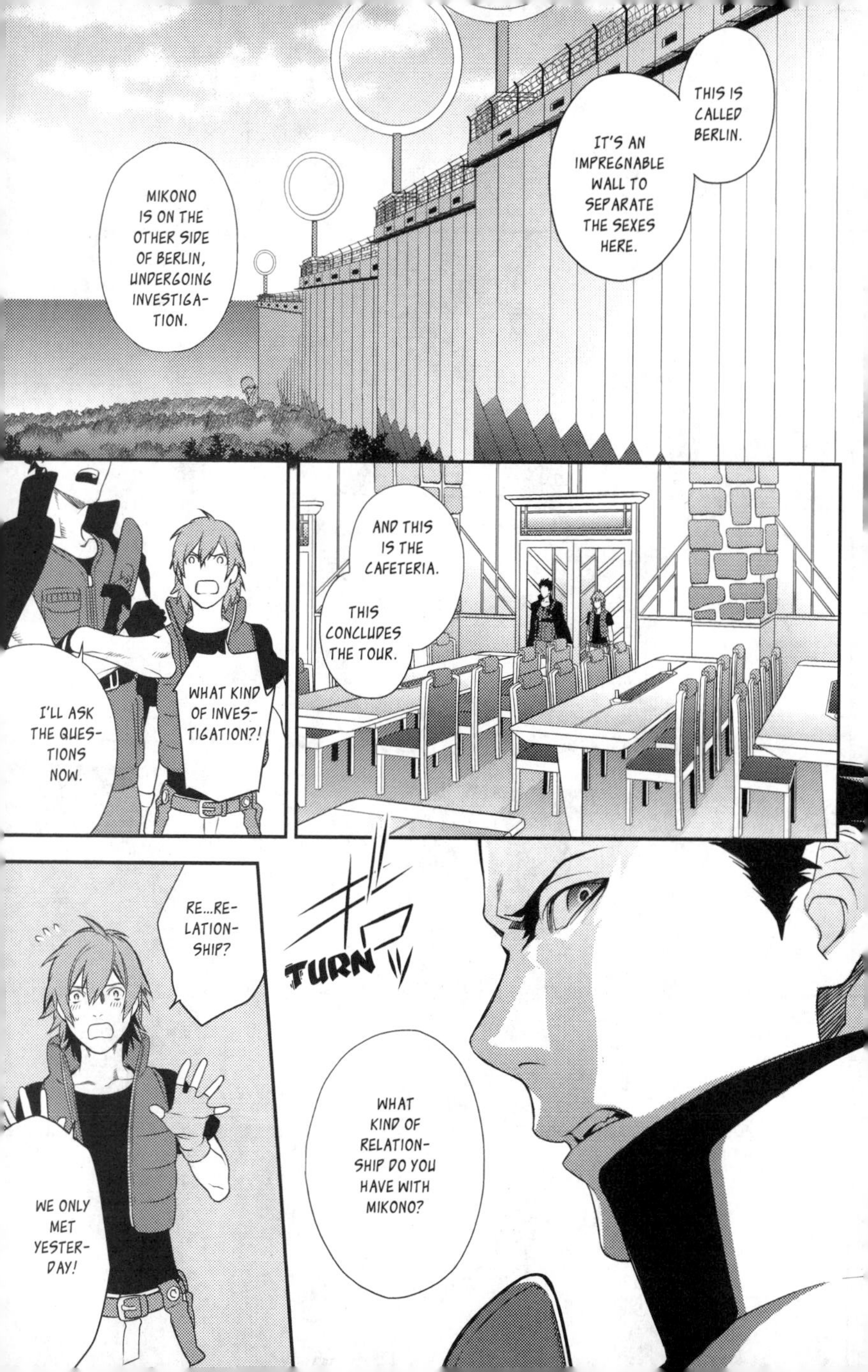
THIS IS CALLED BERLIN.
IT'S AN IMPREGNABLE WALL TO SEPARATE THE SEXES HERE.
MIKONO IS ON THE OTHER SIDE OF BERLIN, UNDERGOING INVESTIGA-TION.
AND THIS IS THE CAFETERIA.
THIS CONCLUDES THE TOUR.
WHAT KIND OF INVES-TIGATION?!
I'LL ASK THE QUES-TIONS NOW.
TURN
WHAT KIND OF RELATION-SHIP DO YOU HAVE WITH MIKONO?
RE...RE-LATION-SHIP?
WE ONLY MET YESTER-DAY!

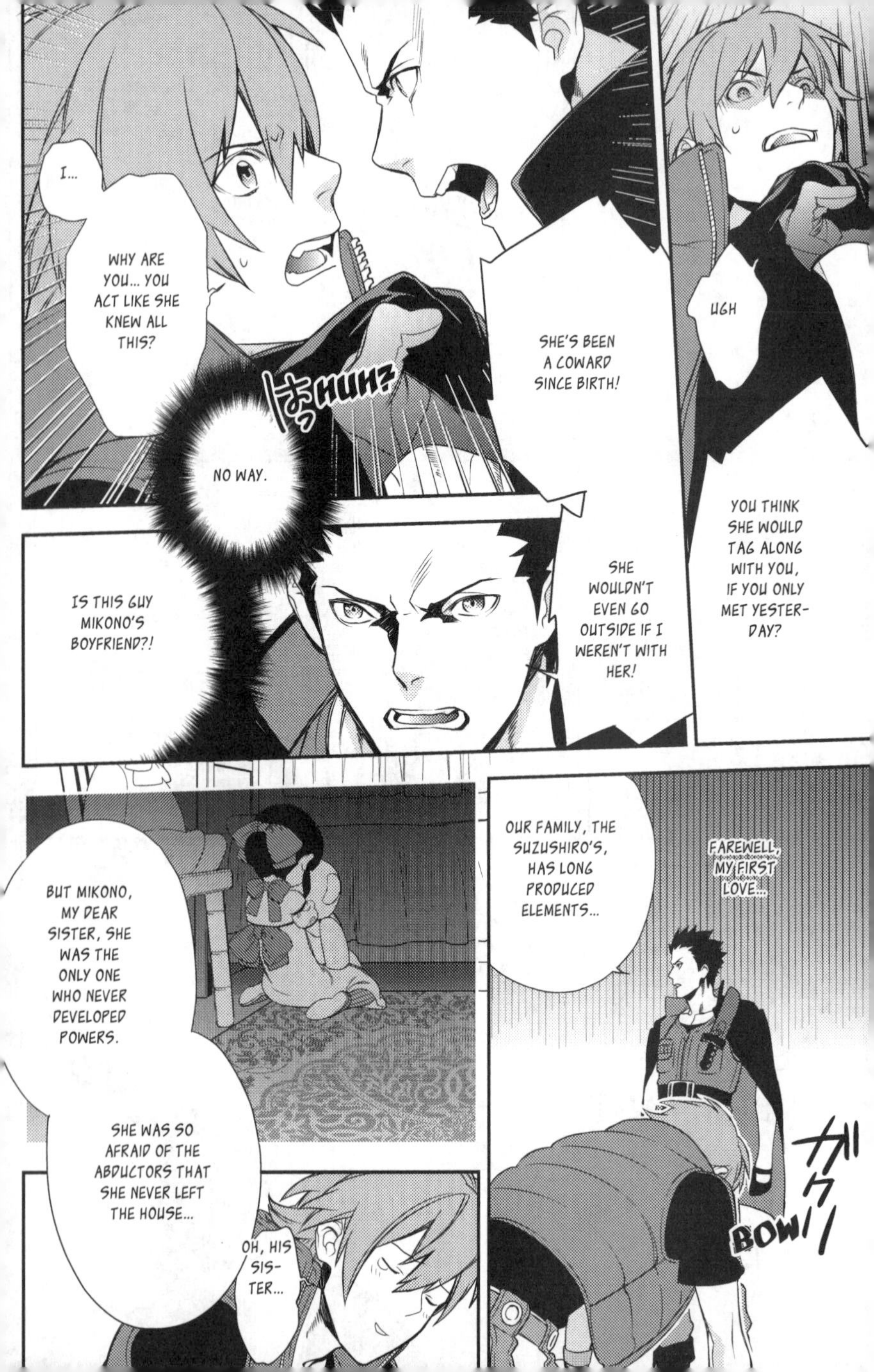
UGH
YOU THINK SHE WOULD TAG ALONG WITH YOU, IF YOU ONLY MET YESTER-DAY?
I...
WHY ARE YOU... YOU ACT LIKE SHE KNEW ALL THIS?
SHE'S BEEN A COWARD SINCE BIRTH!
SHE WOULDN'T EVEN GO OUTSIDE IF I WEREN'T WITH HER!
HUHZ
NO WAY.
IS THIS GUY MIKONO'S BOYFRIEND?!
OUR FAMILY, THE SUZUSHIRO'S, HAS LONG PRODUCED ELEMENTS...
FAREWELL, MY FIRST LOVE...
BOW
BUT MIKONO, MY DEAR SISTER, SHE WAS THE ONLY ONE WHO NEVER DEVELOPED POWERS.
SHE WAS SO AFRAID OF THE ABDUCTORS THAT SHE NEVER LEFT THE HOUSE...
OH, HIS SIS-TER...

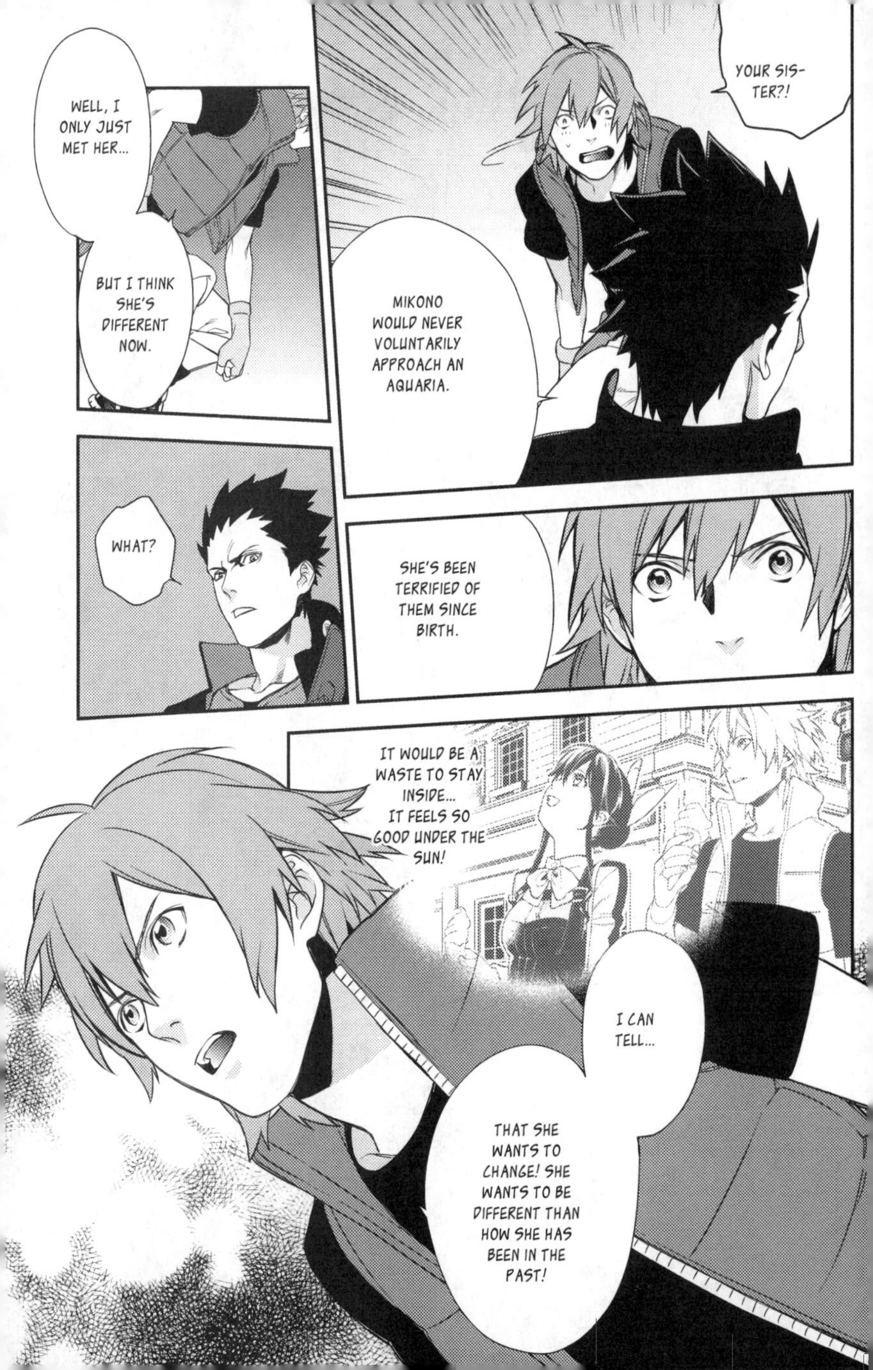
YOUR SISTER?!
MIKONO WOULD NEVER VOLUNTARILY APPROACH AN AQUARIA.
WELL, I ONLY JUST MET HER...
BUT I THINK SHE'S DIFFERENT NOW.
SHE'S BEEN TERRIFIED OF THEM SINCE BIRTH.
WHAT?
IT WOULD BE A WASTE TO STAY INSIDE... IT FEELS SO GOOD UNDER THE SUN!
I CAN TELL...
THAT SHE WANTS TO CHANGE! SHE WANTS TO BE DIFFERENT THAN HOW SHE HAS BEEN IN THE PAST!

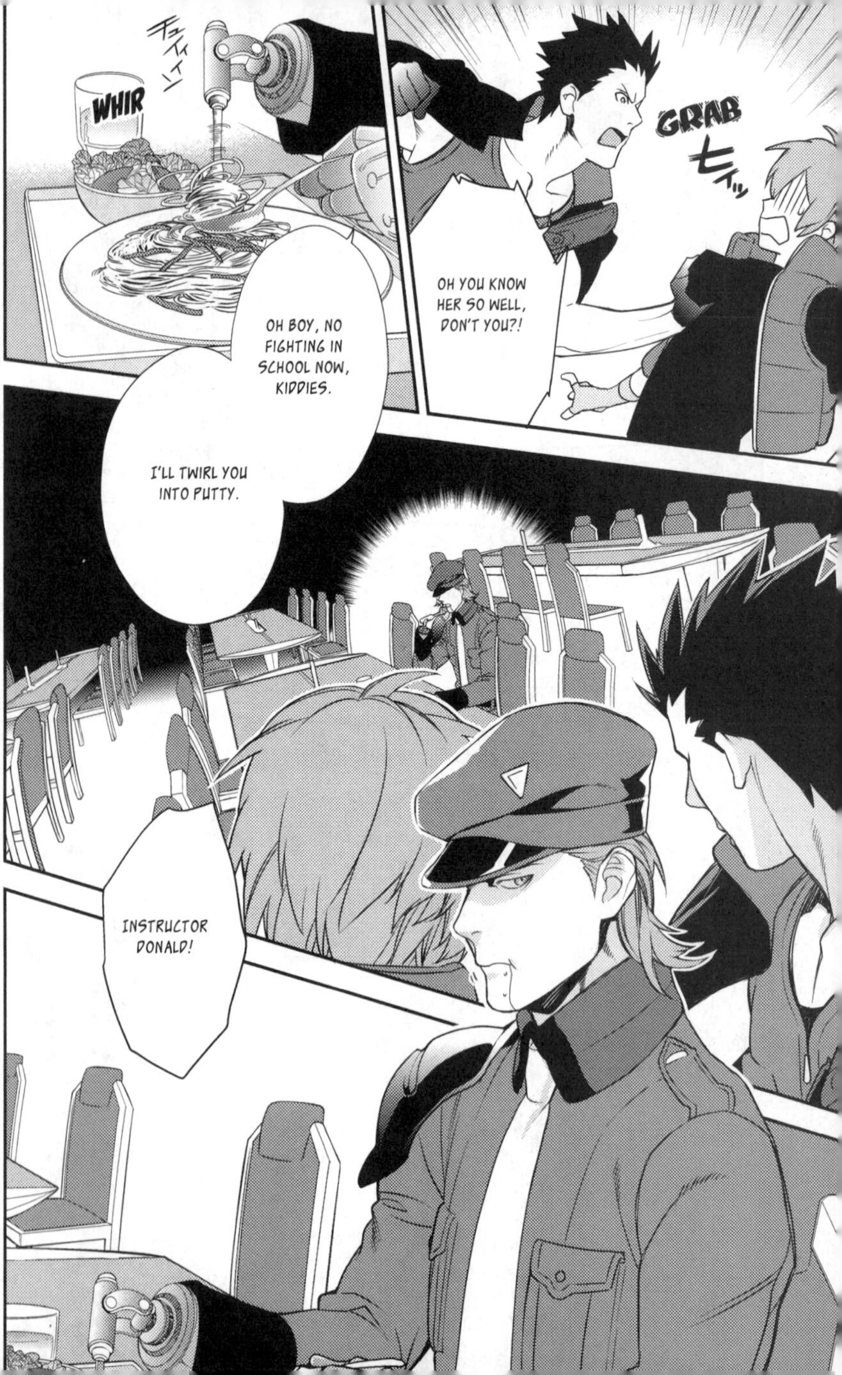
GRAB
OH YOU KNOW HER SO WELL, DON'T YOU?!
WHIR
OH BOY, NO FIGHTING IN SCHOOL NOW, KIDDIES.
I'LL TWIRL YOU INTO PUTTY.
INSTRUCTOR DONALD!

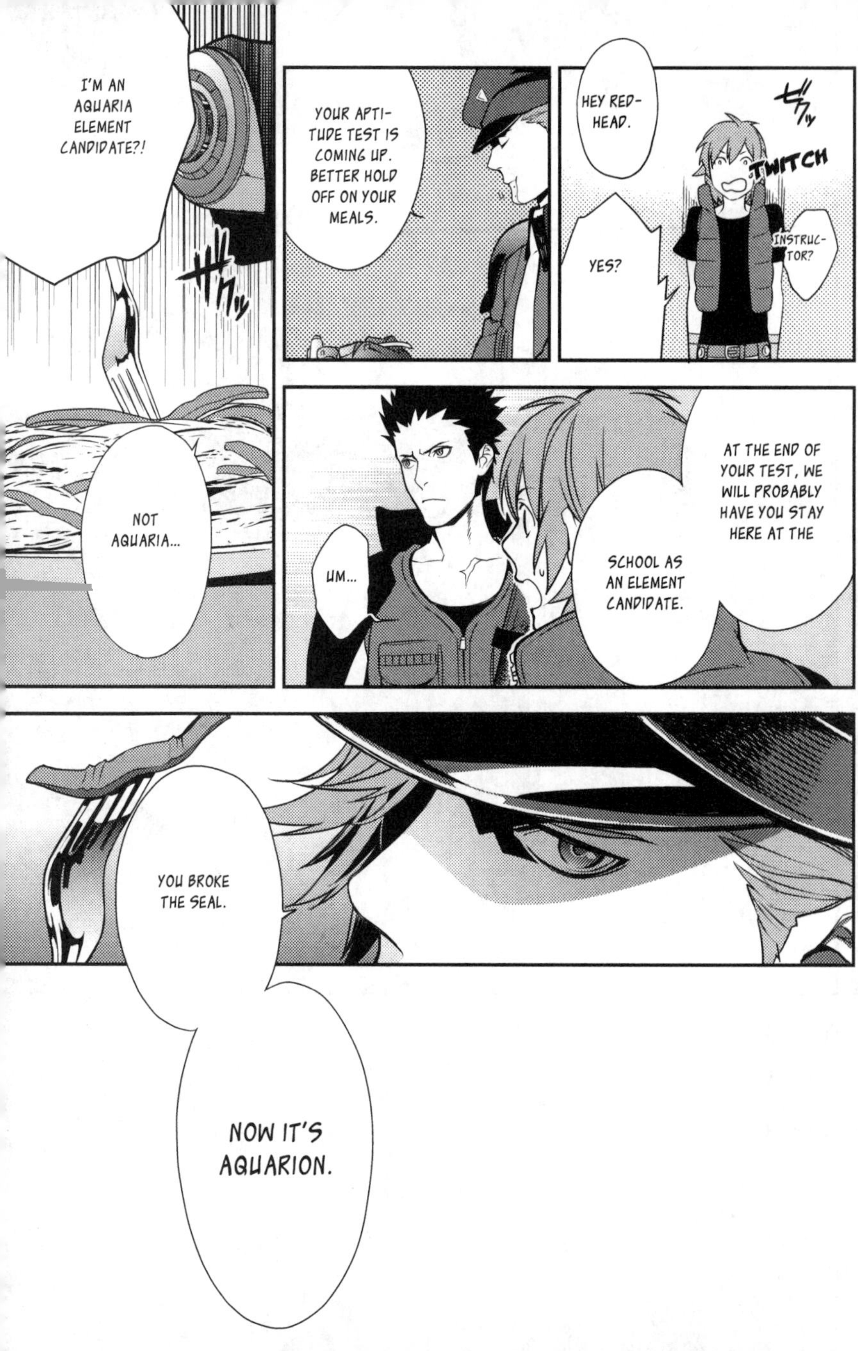
HEY RED-HEAD.
TWITCH
INSTRUCTOR?
YES?
YOUR APTITUDE TEST IS COMING UP. BETTER HOLD OFF ON YOUR MEALS.
AT THE END OF YOUR TEST, WE WILL PROBABLY HAVE YOU STAY HERE AT THE
SCHOOL AS AN ELEMENT CANDIDATE.
UM...
I'M AN AQUARIA ELEMENT CANDIDATE?!
NOT AQUARIA...
YOU BROKE THE SEAL.
NOW IT'S AQUARION.

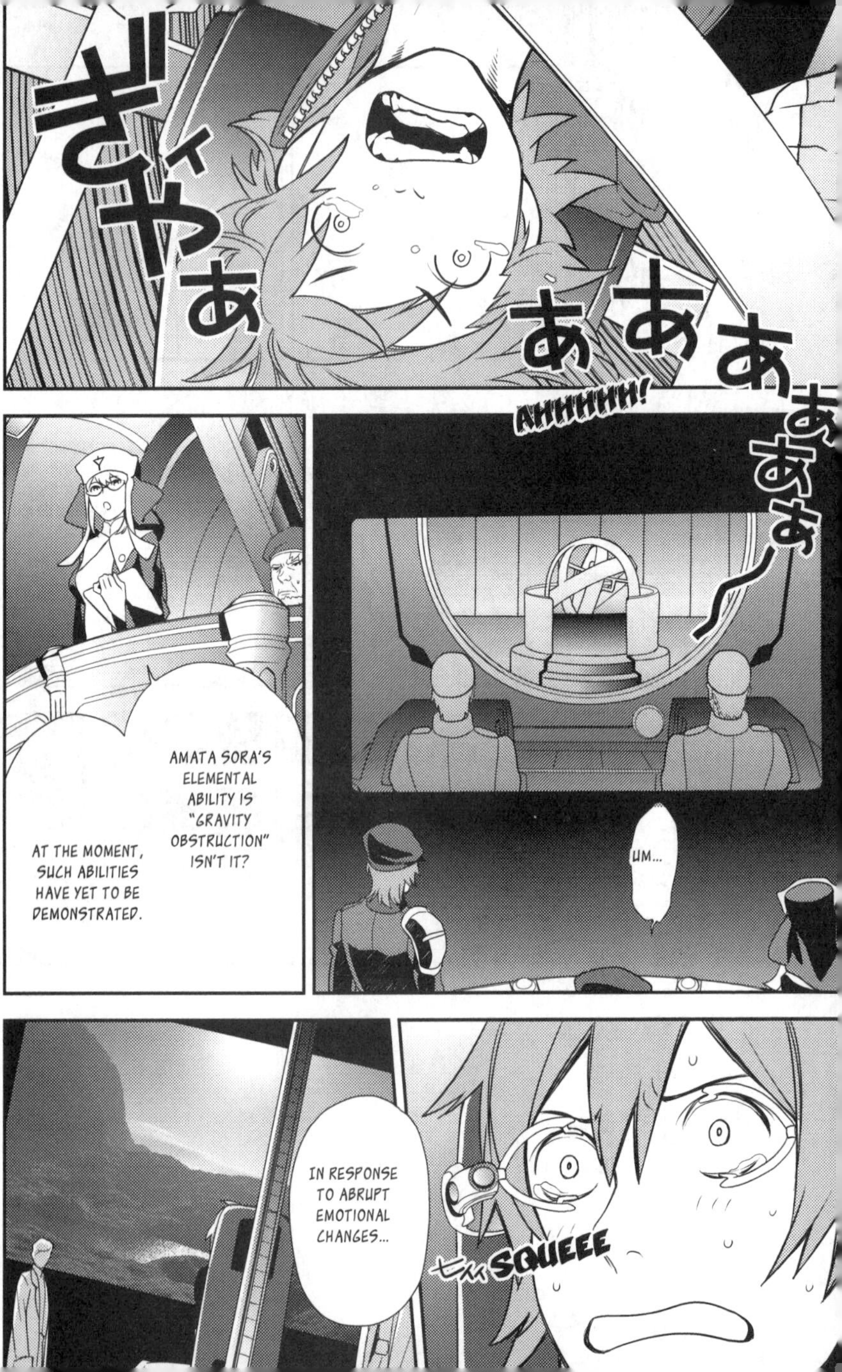
ぎィやぁあああぁあぁ～
AHHHHHH!
UM...
AMATA SORA'S ELEMENTAL ABILITY IS "GRAVITY OBSTRUCTION" ISN'T IT?
AT THE MOMENT, SUCH ABILITIES HAVE YET TO BE DEMONSTRATED.
IN RESPONSE TO ABRUPT EMOTIONAL CHANGES...
ヒィ SQUEEE

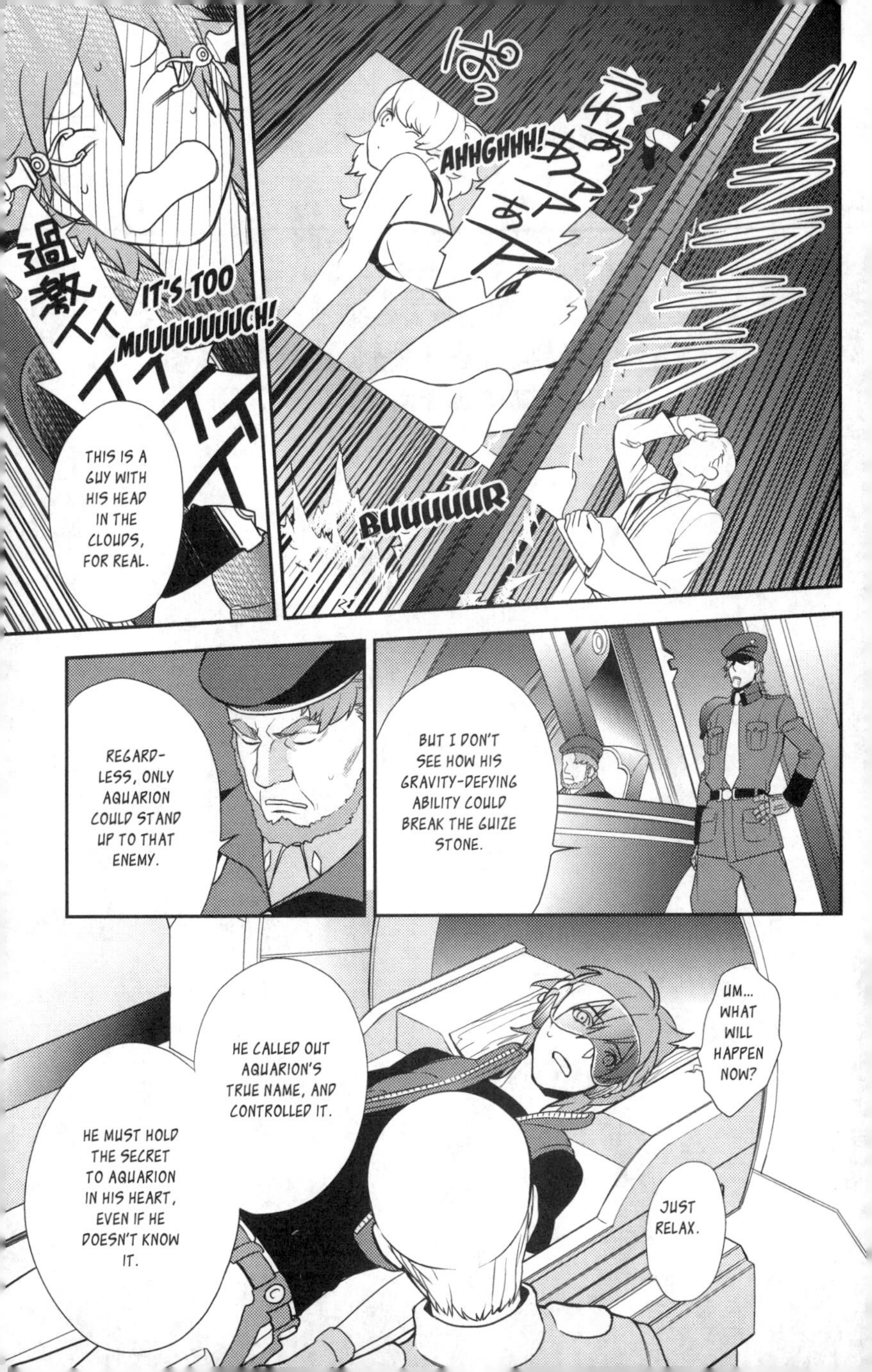
ぱっ
AHHGHHH!
BUUUUUR
過激イィィィ
IT'S TOO MUUUUUUUUCH!
THIS IS A GUY WITH HIS HEAD IN THE CLOUDS, FOR REAL.
BUT I DON'T SEE HOW HIS GRAVITY-DEFYING ABILITY COULD BREAK THE GUIZE STONE.
REGARD-LESS, ONLY AQUARION COULD STAND UP TO THAT ENEMY.
UM... WHAT WILL HAPPEN NOW?
HE CALLED OUT AQUARION'S TRUE NAME, AND CONTROLLED IT.
JUST RELAX.
HE MUST HOLD THE SECRET TO AQUARION IN HIS HEART, EVEN IF HE DOESN'T KNOW IT.

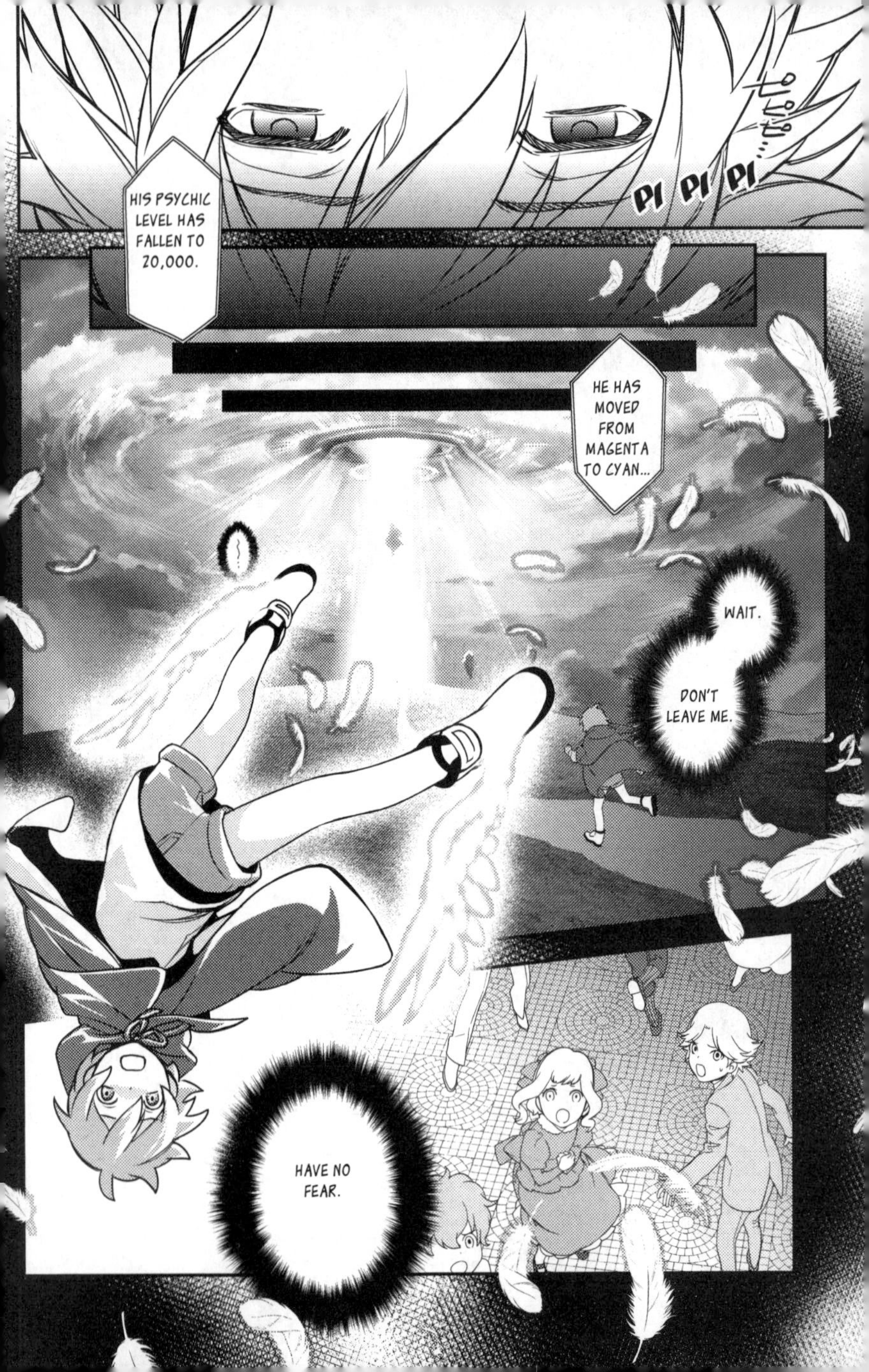
PI PI PI
HIS PSYCHIC LEVEL HAS FALLEN TO 20,000.
HE HAS MOVED FROM MAGENTA TO CYAN...
WAIT.
DON'T LEAVE ME.
HAVE NO FEAR.

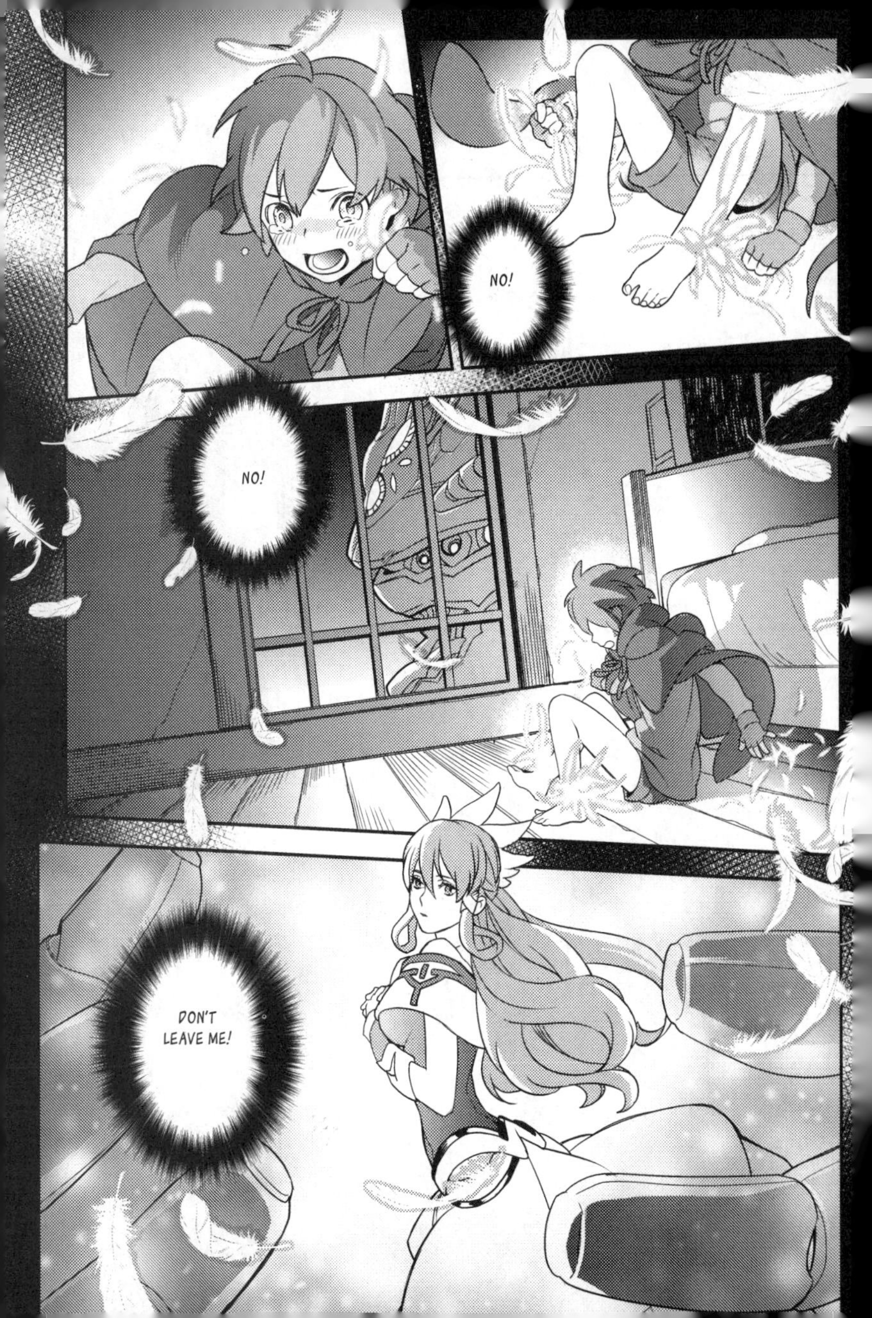
NO!
NO!
DON'T LEAVE ME!

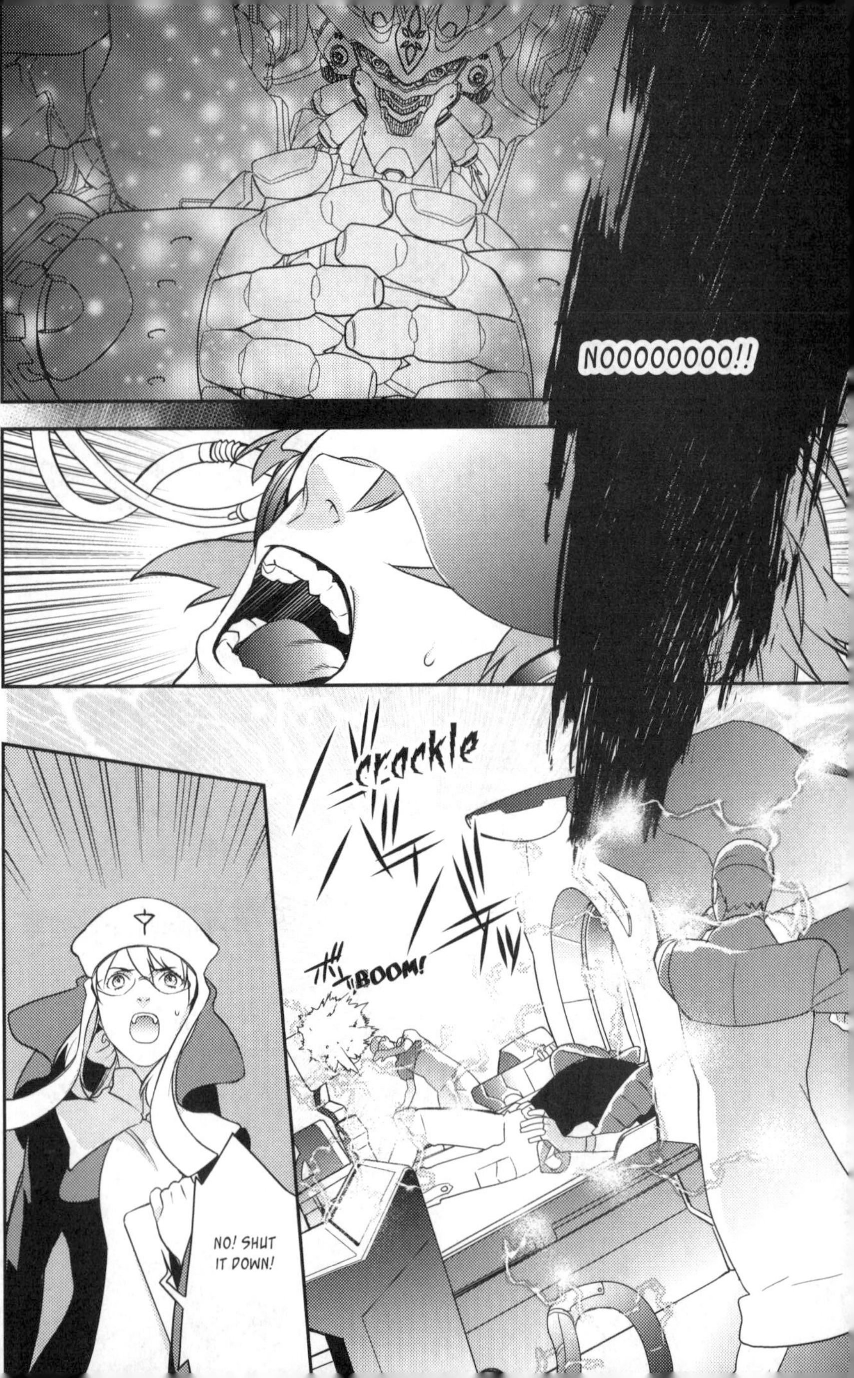
NOOOOOOOO!!
crackle
BOOM!
NO! SHUT IT DOWN!

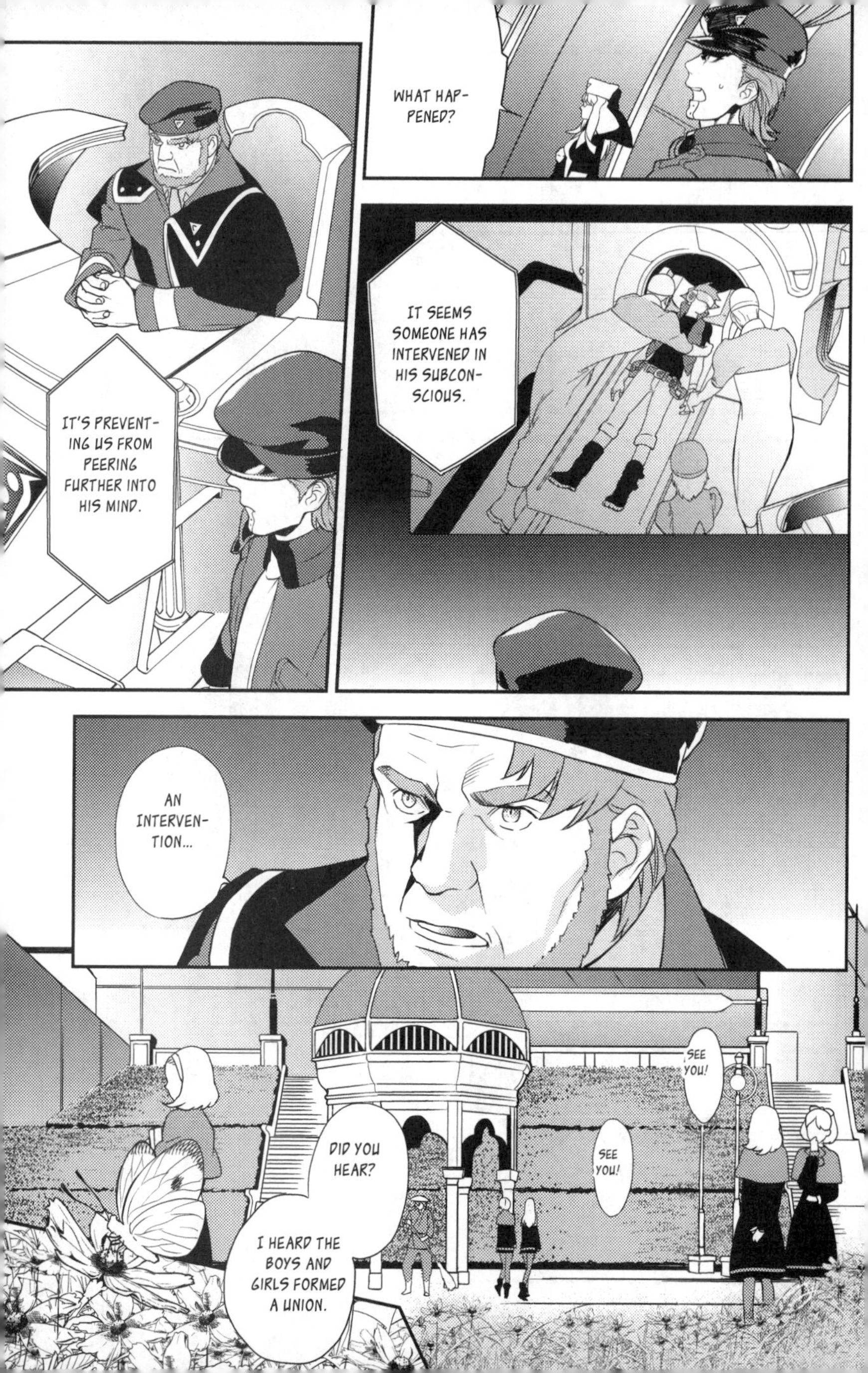
WHAT HAP-PENED?
IT SEEMS SOMEONE HAS INTERVENED IN HIS SUBCON-SCIOUS.
IT'S PREVENT-ING US FROM PEERING FURTHER INTO HIS MIND.
AN INTERVEN-TION...
SEE YOU!
SEE YOU!
DID YOU HEAR?
I HEARD THE BOYS AND GIRLS FORMED A UNION.

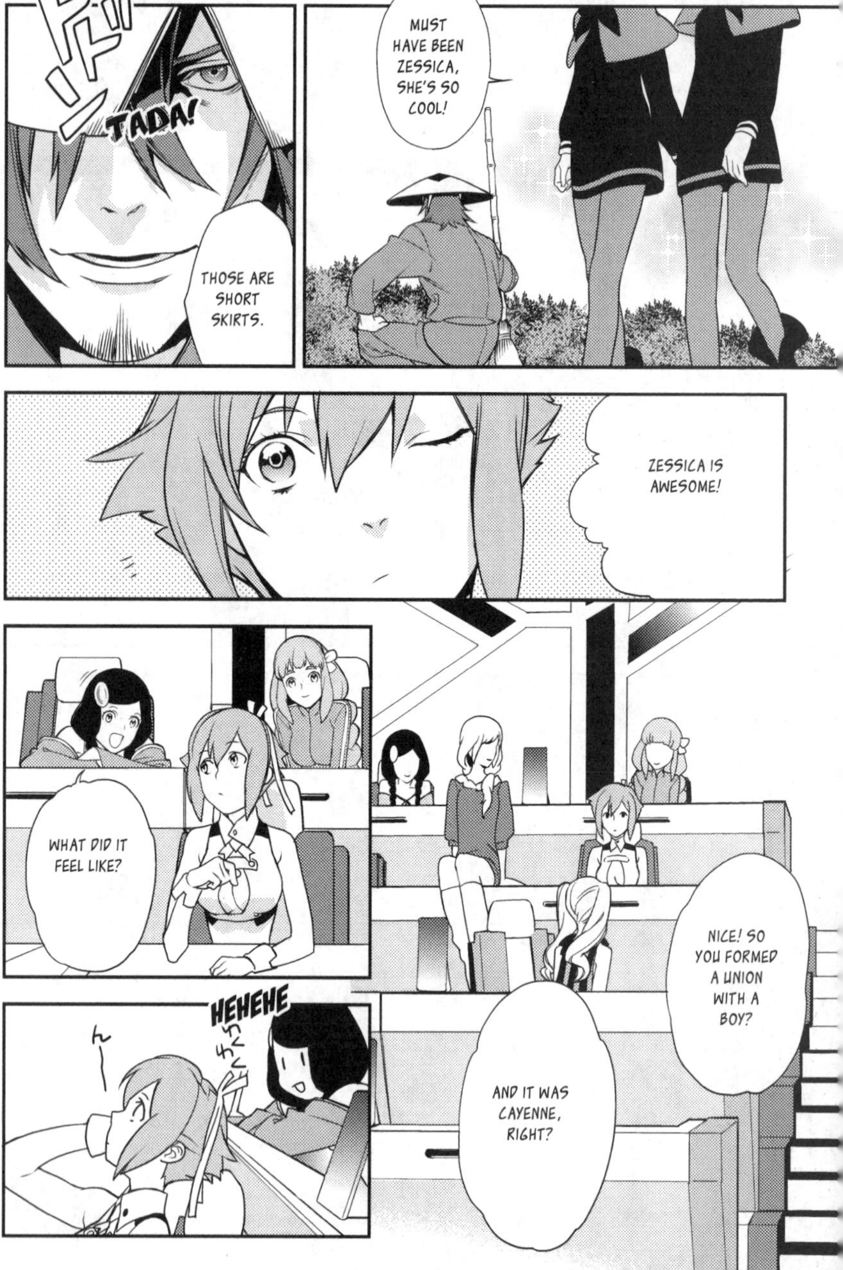
MUST HAVE BEEN ZESSICA, SHE'S SO COOL!
TADA!
THOSE ARE SHORT SKIRTS.
ZESSICA IS AWESOME!
NICE! SO YOU FORMED A UNION WITH A BOY?
AND IT WAS CAYENNE, RIGHT?
WHAT DID IT FEEL LIKE?
HEHEHE

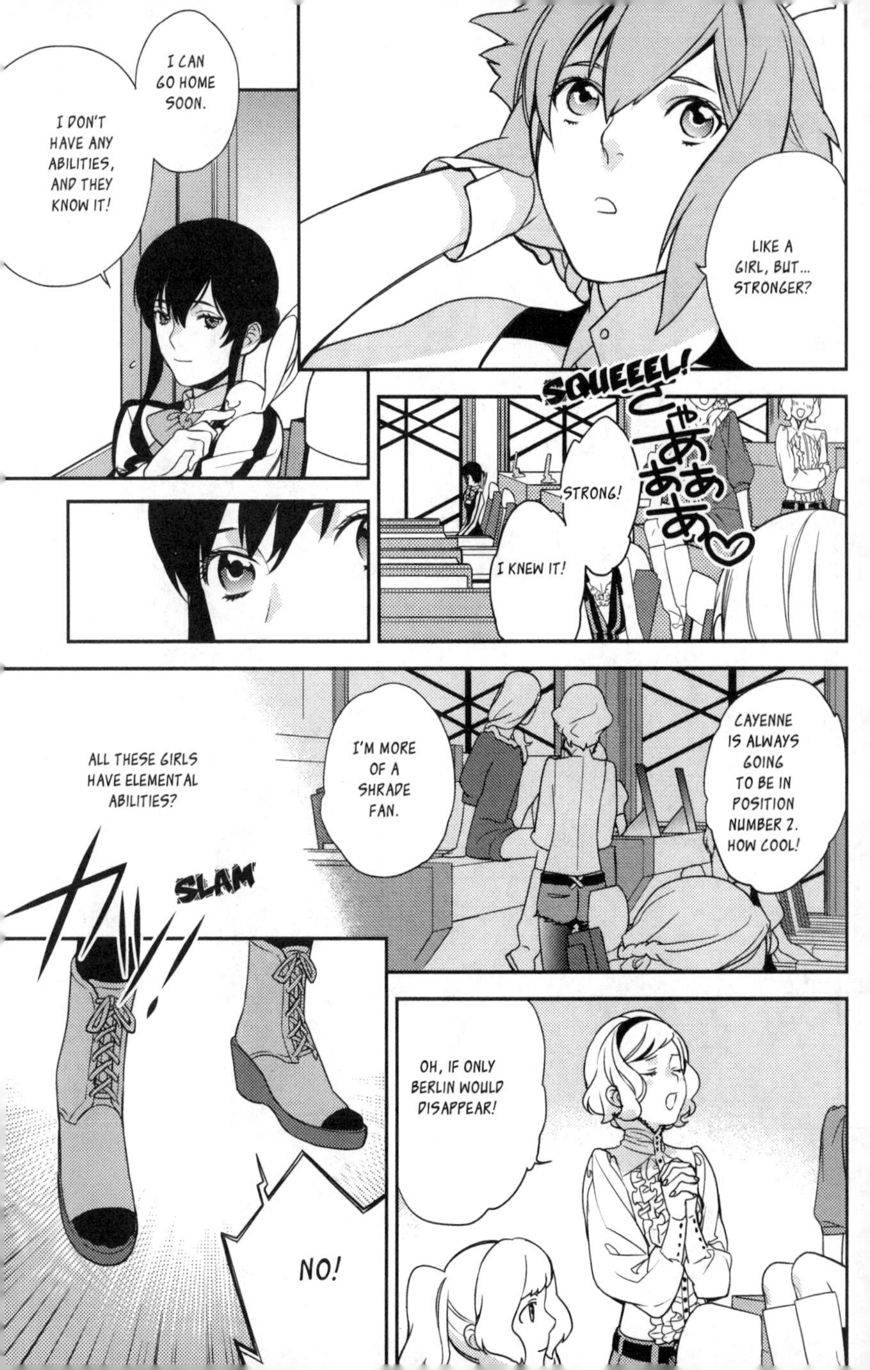
LIKE A GIRL, BUT... STRONGER?
I CAN GO HOME SOON.
I DON'T HAVE ANY ABILITIES, AND THEY KNOW IT!
SQUEEEL!
きゃああああ
STRONG!
I KNEW IT!
CAYENNE IS ALWAYS GOING TO BE IN POSITION NUMBER 2. HOW COOL!
I'M MORE OF A SHRADE FAN.
ALL THESE GIRLS HAVE ELEMENTAL ABILITIES?
OH, IF ONLY BERLIN WOULD DISAPPEAR!
SLAM
NO!

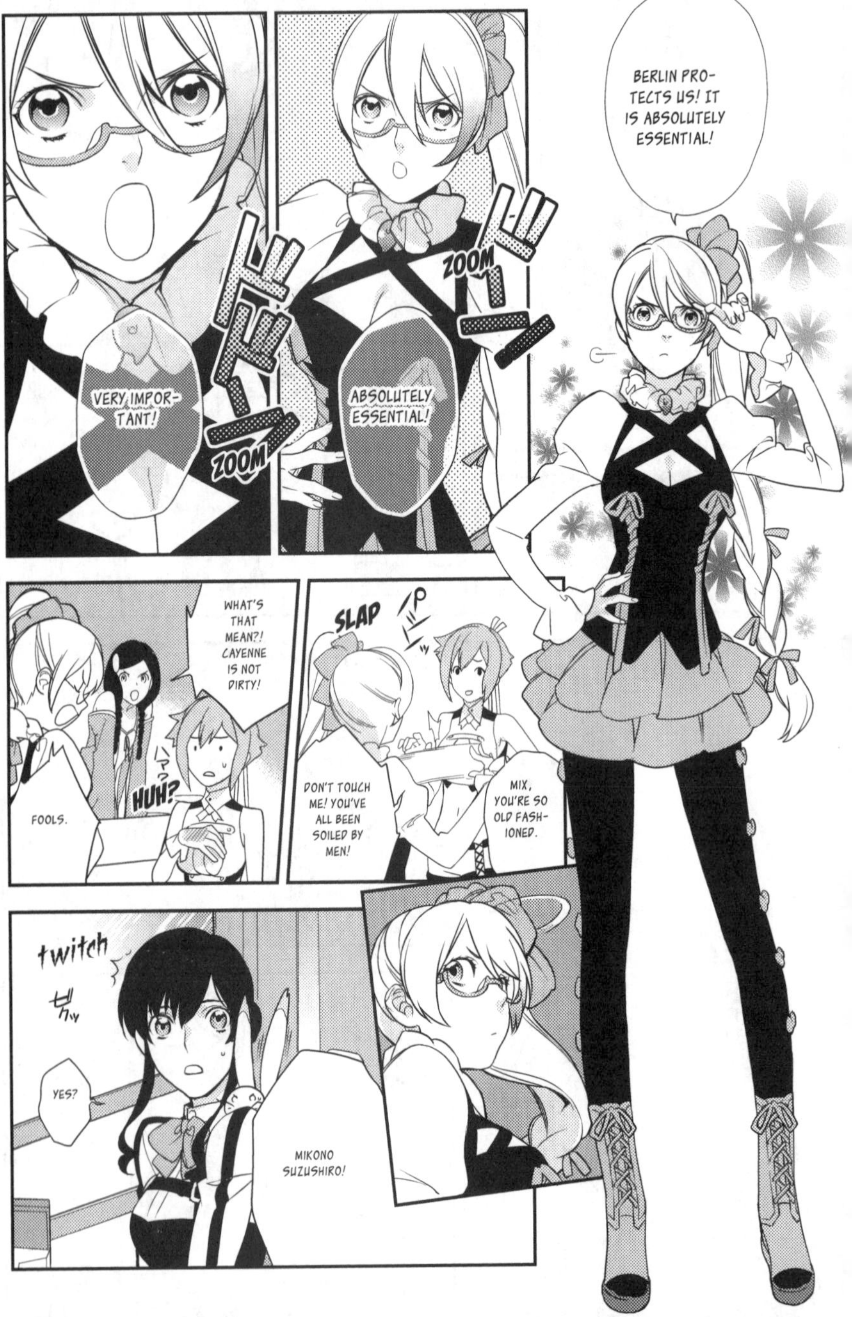
BERLIN PROTECTS US! IT IS ABSOLUTELY ESSENTIAL!
ZOOM
ABSOLUTELY ESSENTIAL!
ZOOM
VERY IMPORTANT!
SLAP
MIX, YOU'RE SO OLD FASHIONED.
DON'T TOUCH ME! YOU'VE ALL BEEN SOILED BY MEN!
WHAT'S THAT MEAN?! CAYENNE IS NOT DIRTY!
HUH?
FOOLS.
MIKONO SUZUSHIRO!
twitch
YES?

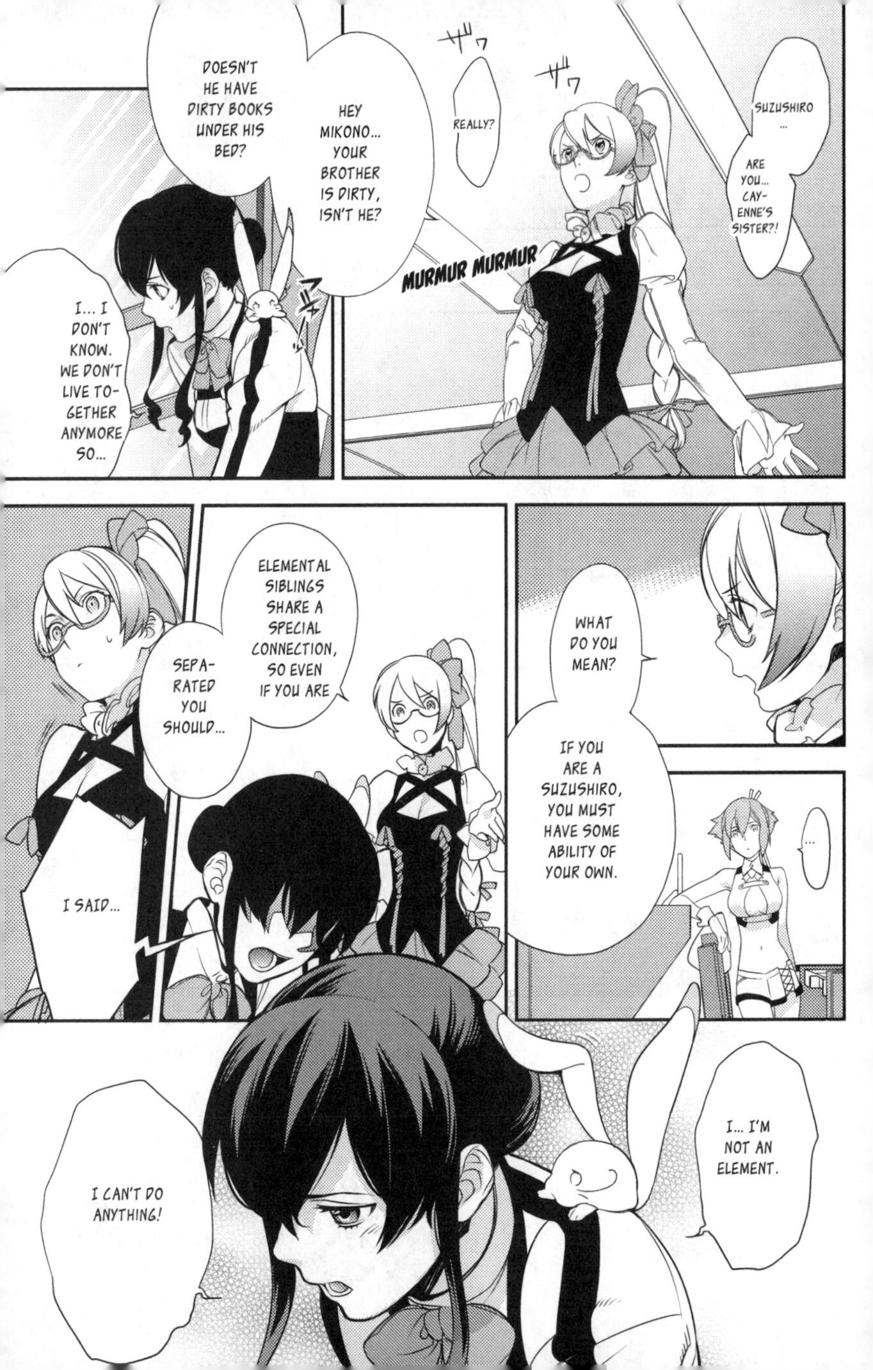
SUZUSHIRO ...
ARE YOU... CAY-ENNE'S SISTER?!
ザワ
ザワ
REALLY?
MURMUR MURMUR
HEY MIKONO... YOUR BROTHER IS DIRTY, ISN'T HE?
DOESN'T HE HAVE DIRTY BOOKS UNDER HIS BED?
I... I DON'T KNOW. WE DON'T LIVE TO-GETHER ANYMORE SO...
WHAT DO YOU MEAN?
IF YOU ARE A SUZUSHIRO, YOU MUST HAVE SOME ABILITY OF YOUR OWN.
...
ELEMENTAL SIBLINGS SHARE A SPECIAL CONNECTION, SO EVEN IF YOU ARE
SEPA-RATED YOU SHOULD...
I SAID...
I... I'M NOT AN ELEMENT.
I CAN'T DO ANYTHING!

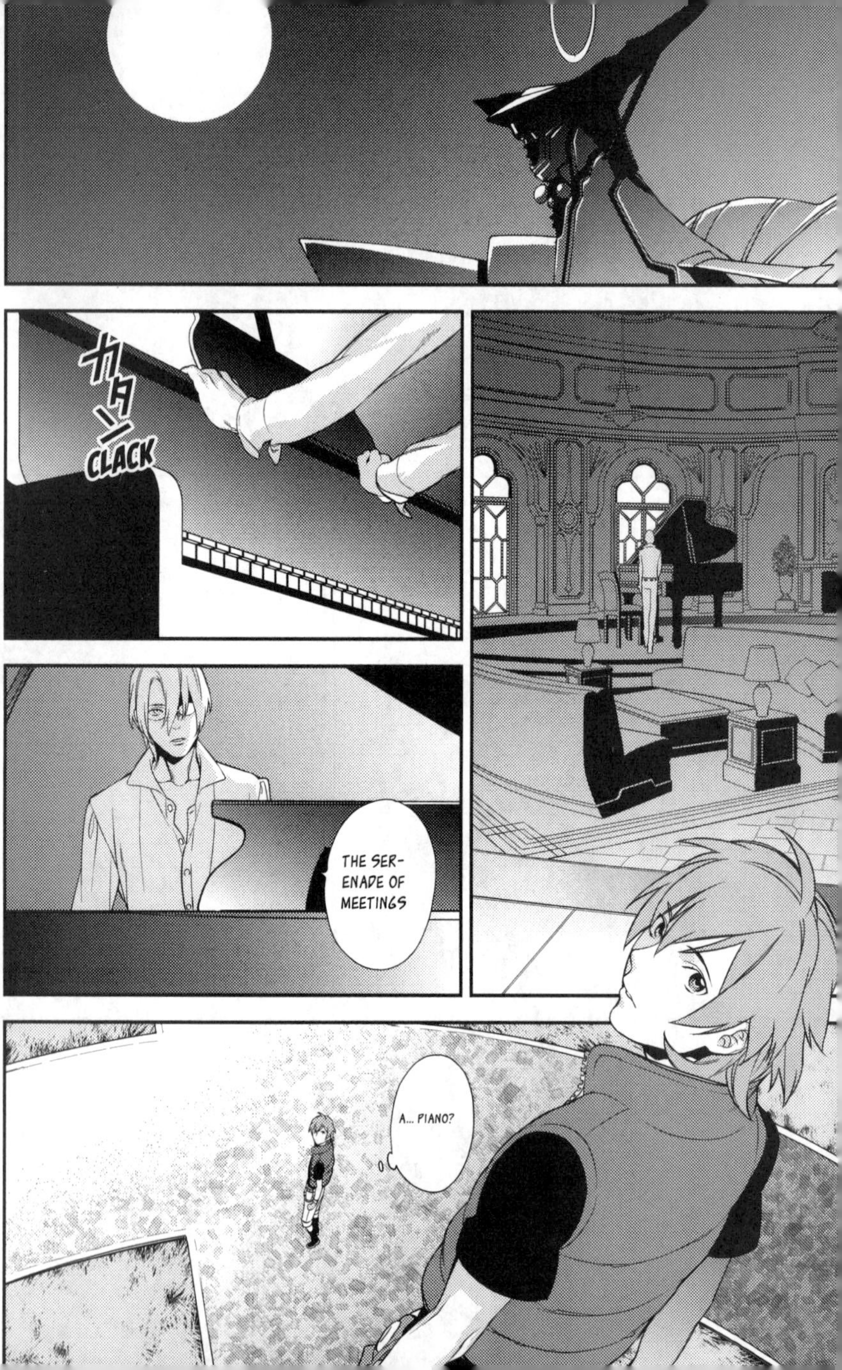
カタン
CLACK
THE SER-
ENADE OF
MEETINGS
A... PIANO?

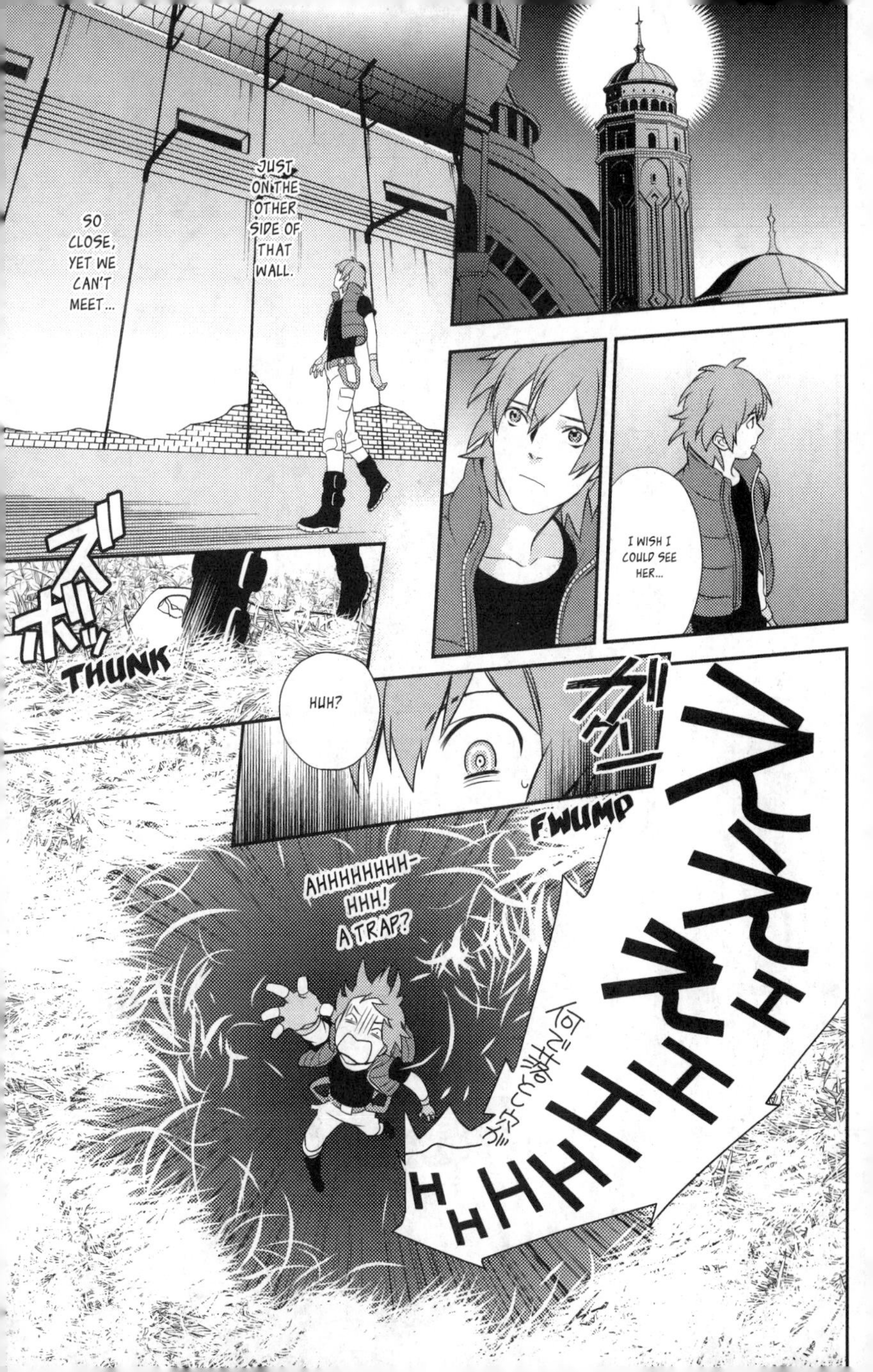
I WISH I COULD SEE HER...
JUST ON THE OTHER SIDE OF THAT WALL.
SO CLOSE, YET WE CAN'T MEET...
ズボッ
THUNK
HUH?
FWUMP
AHHHHHHHH-HHH! A TRAP?
HHHHHHH
何で落とし穴が

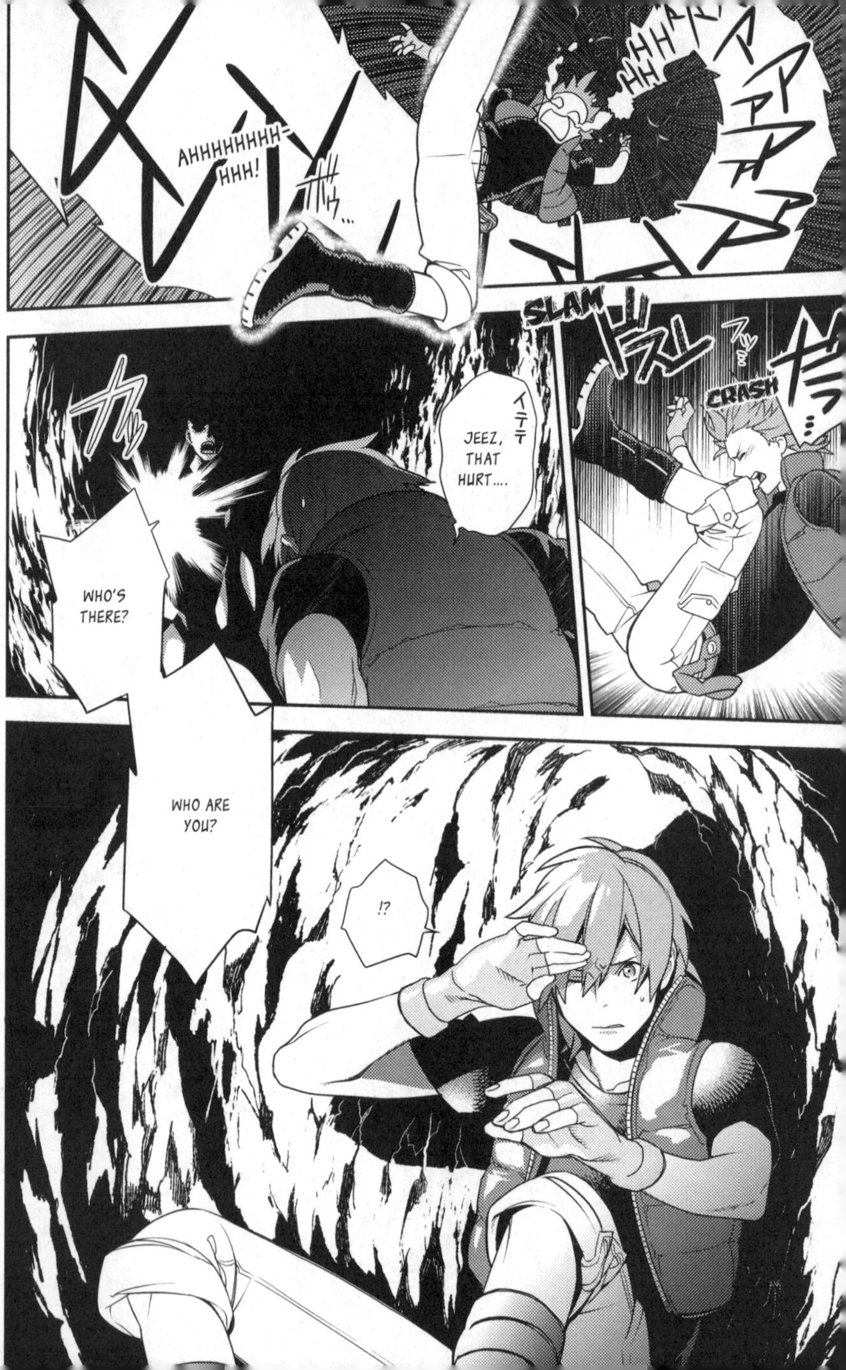
AHHHHHHHH-HHH!
SLAM
CRASH
JEEZ, THAT HURT....
WHO'S THERE?
WHO ARE YOU?
!?

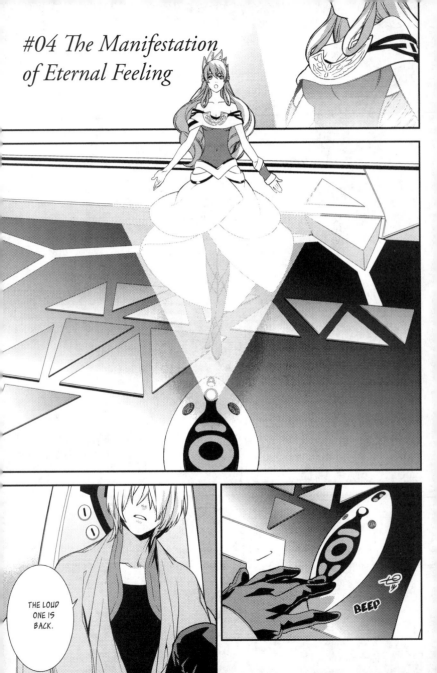

#04 The Manifestation
of Eternal Feeling

THE LOUD
ONE IS
BACK.

BEEP

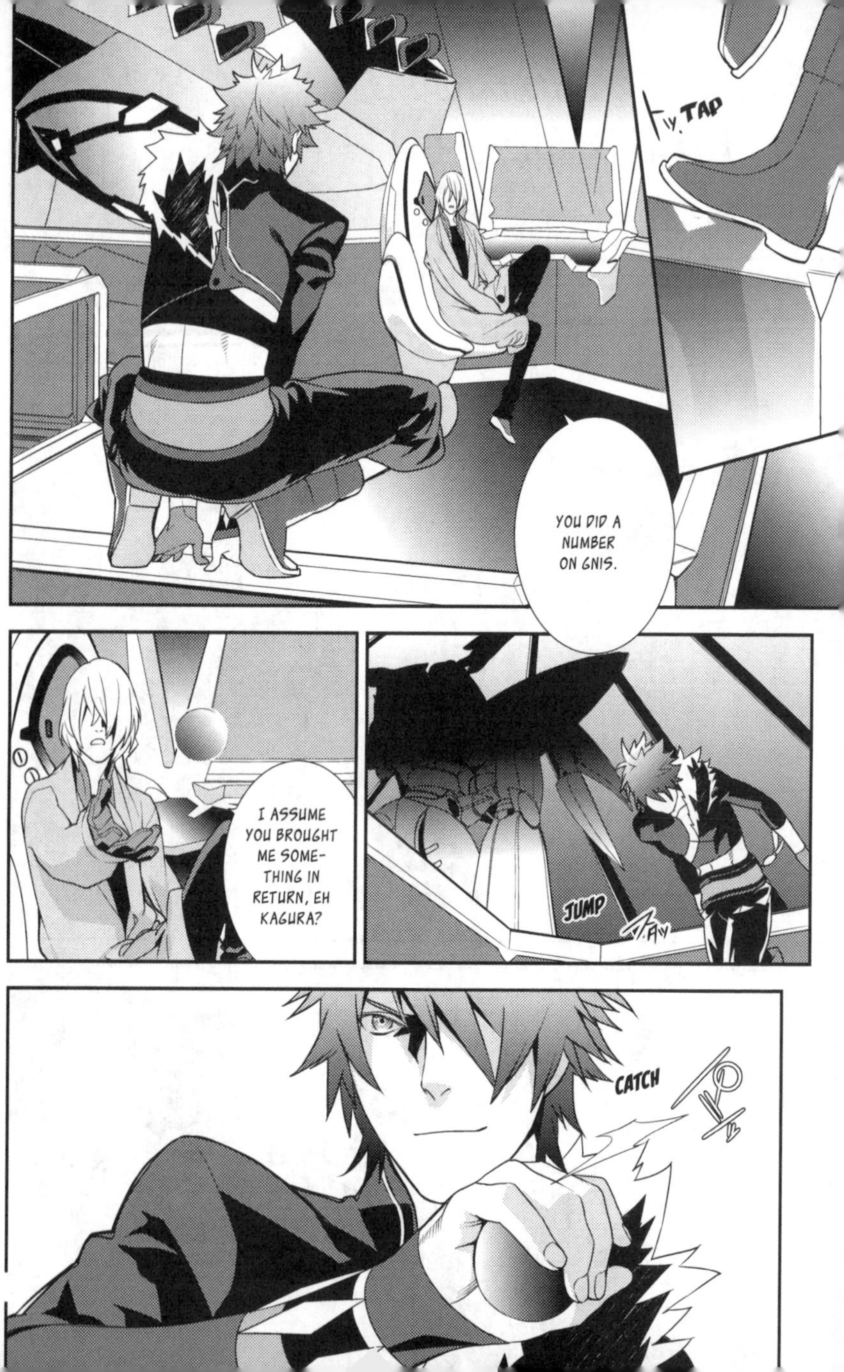
TAP
YOU DID A NUMBER ON GNIS.
JUMP
I ASSUME YOU BROUGHT ME SOME-THING IN RETURN, EH KAGURA?
CATCH

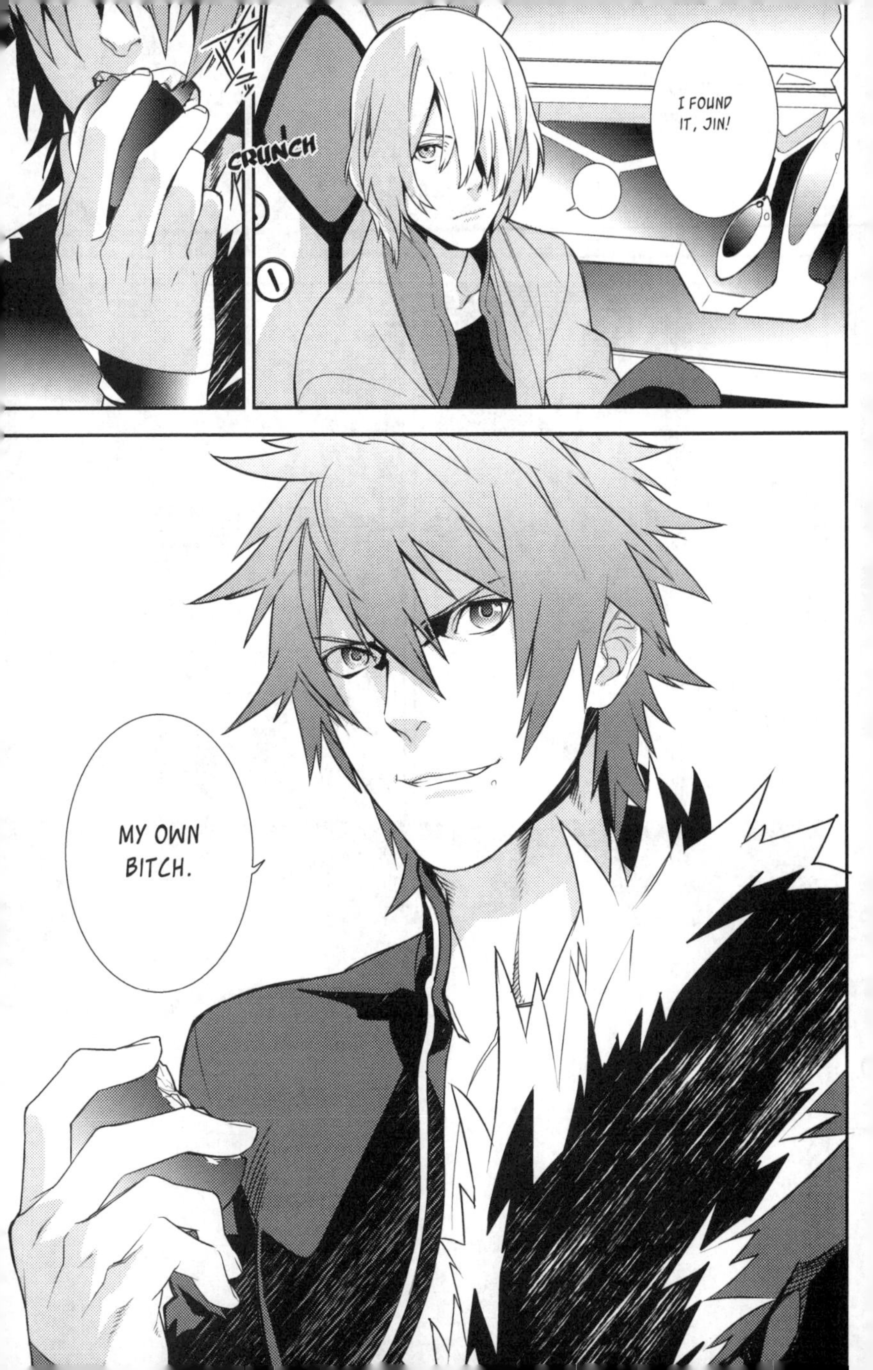
I FOUND IT, JIN!
CRUNCH
MY OWN BITCH.

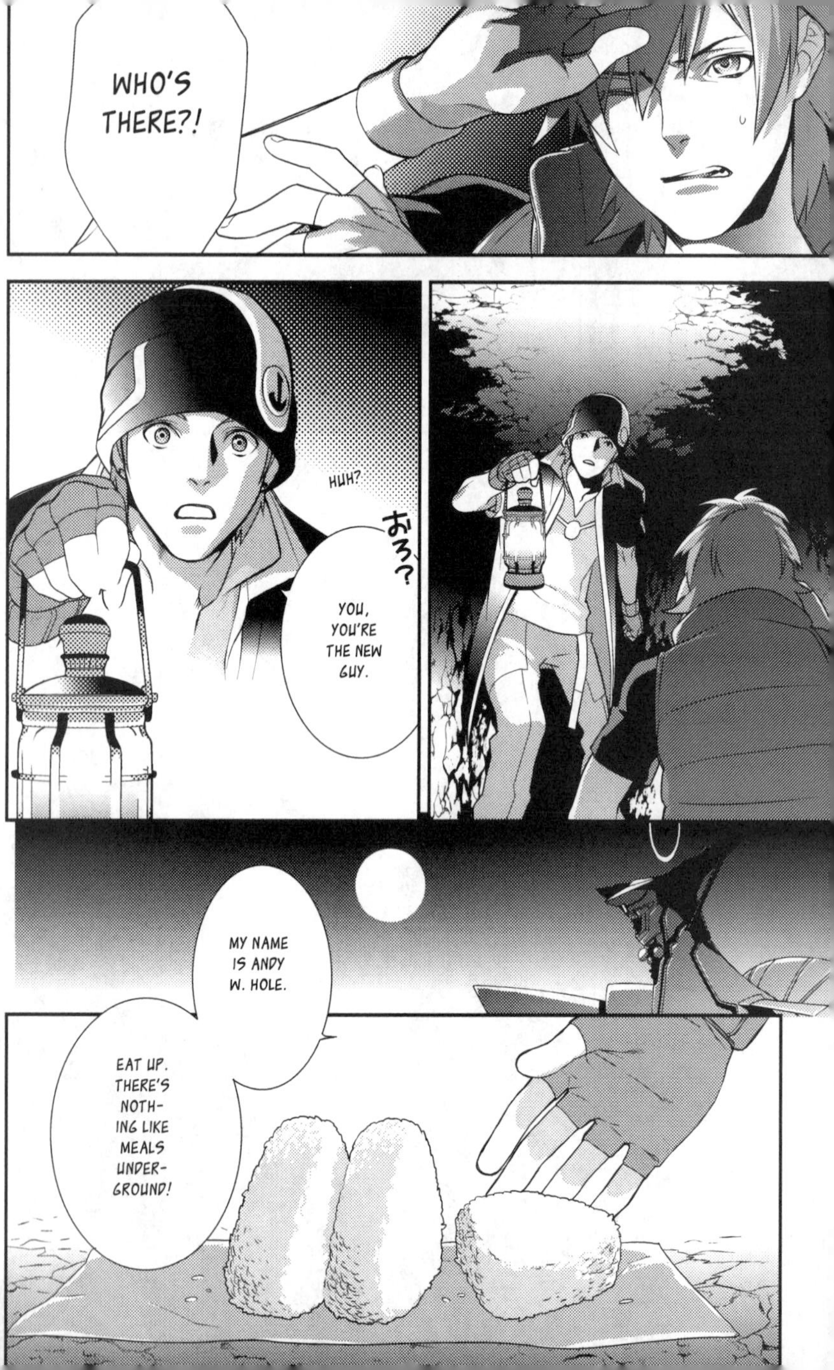
WHO'S THERE?!
HUH?
おろ?
YOU, YOU'RE THE NEW GUY.
MY NAME IS ANDY W. HOLE.
EAT UP. THERE'S NOTHING LIKE MEALS UNDERGROUND!

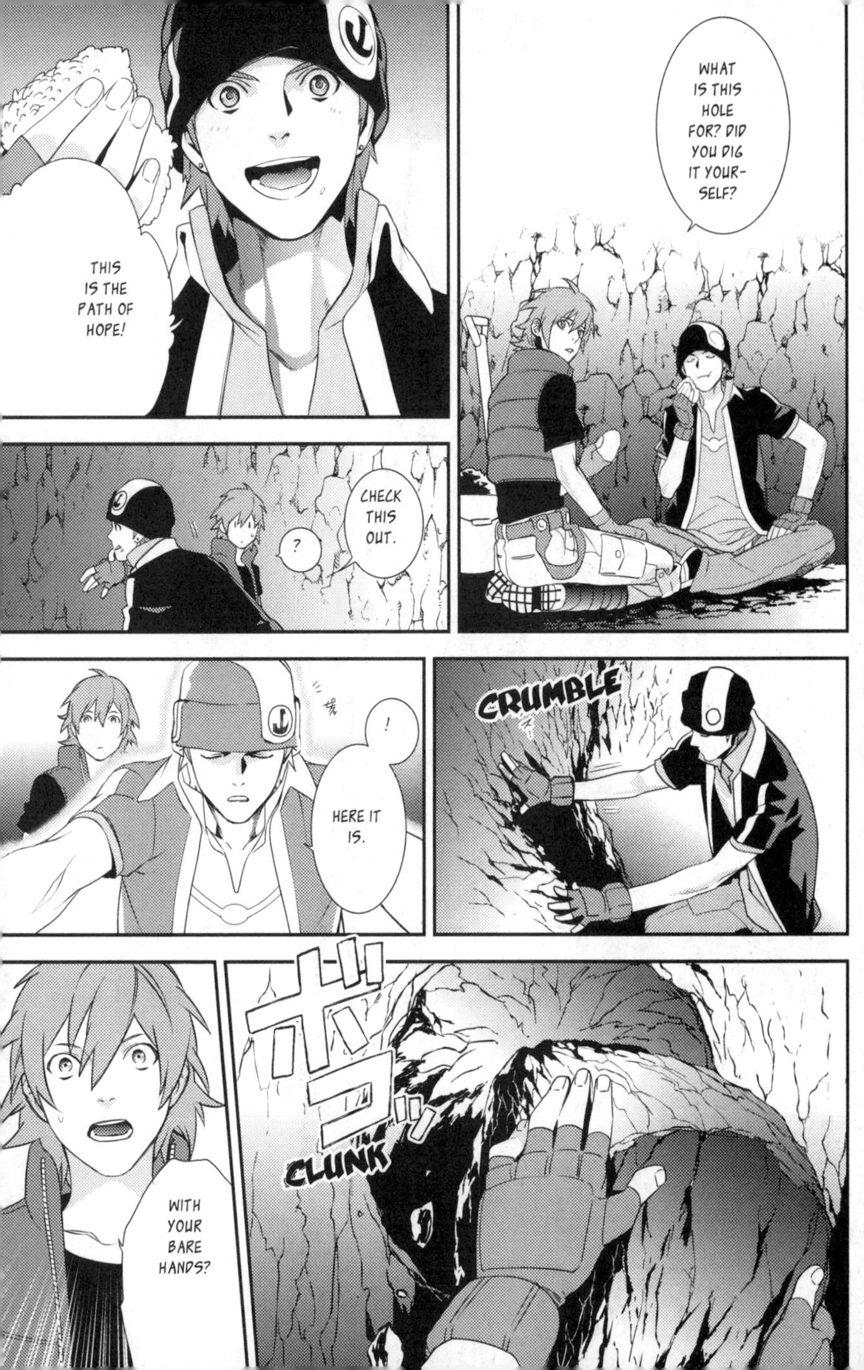
WHAT IS THIS HOLE FOR? DID YOU DIG IT YOURSELF?
THIS IS THE PATH OF HOPE!
CHECK THIS OUT.
?
CRUMBLE
!
HERE IT IS.
CLUNK
WITH YOUR BARE HANDS?

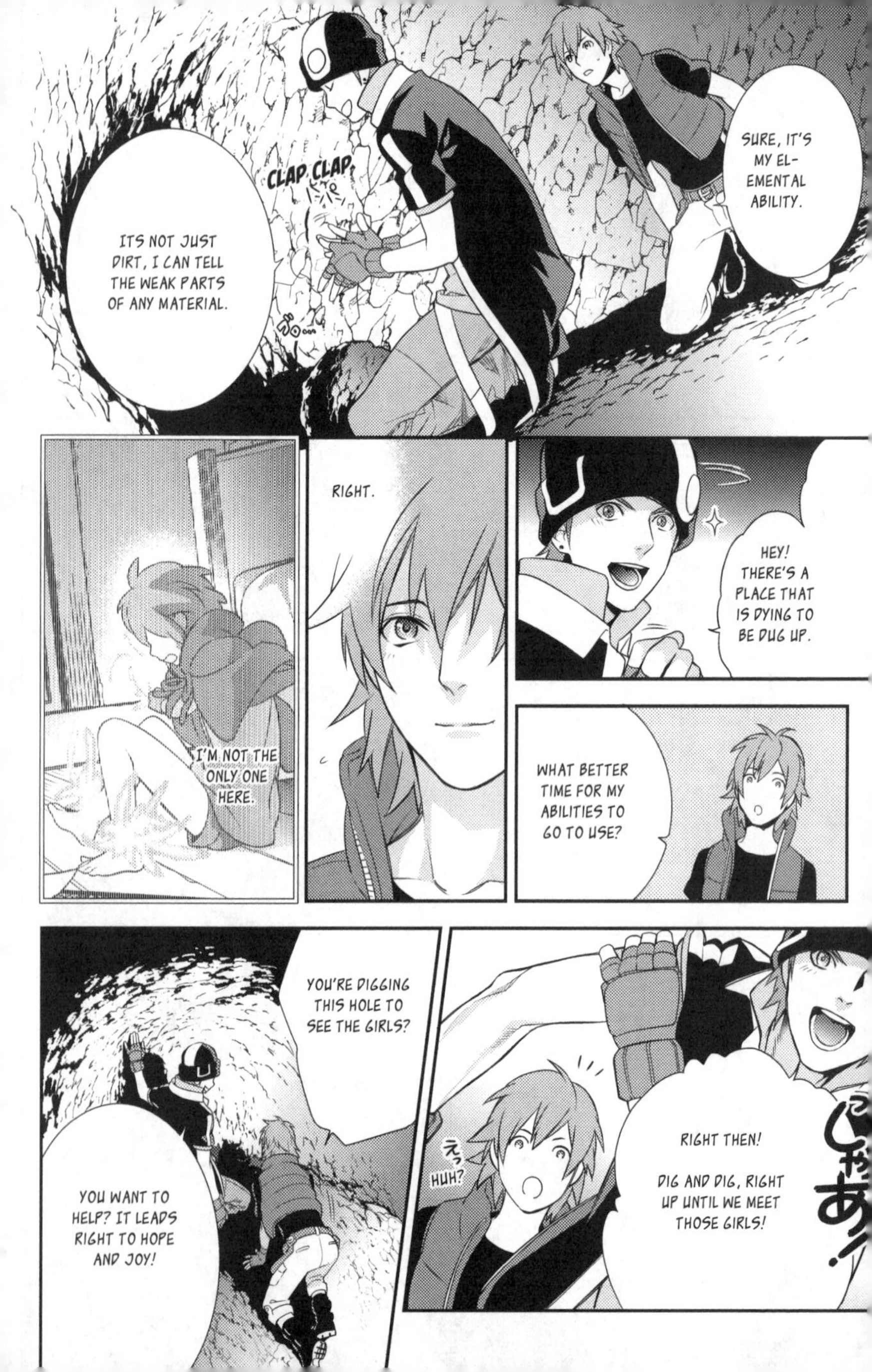

SURE, IT'S MY EL-EMENTAL ABILITY.
CLAP CLAP
ITS NOT JUST DIRT, I CAN TELL THE WEAK PARTS OF ANY MATERIAL.
HEY! THERE'S A PLACE THAT IS DYING TO BE DUG UP.
WHAT BETTER TIME FOR MY ABILITIES TO GO TO USE?
RIGHT.
I'M NOT THE ONLY ONE HERE.
RIGHT THEN!
DIG AND DIG, RIGHT UP UNTIL WE MEET THOSE GIRLS!
えっ
HUH?
YOU'RE DIGGING THIS HOLE TO SEE THE GIRLS?
YOU WANT TO HELP? IT LEADS RIGHT TO HOPE AND JOY!

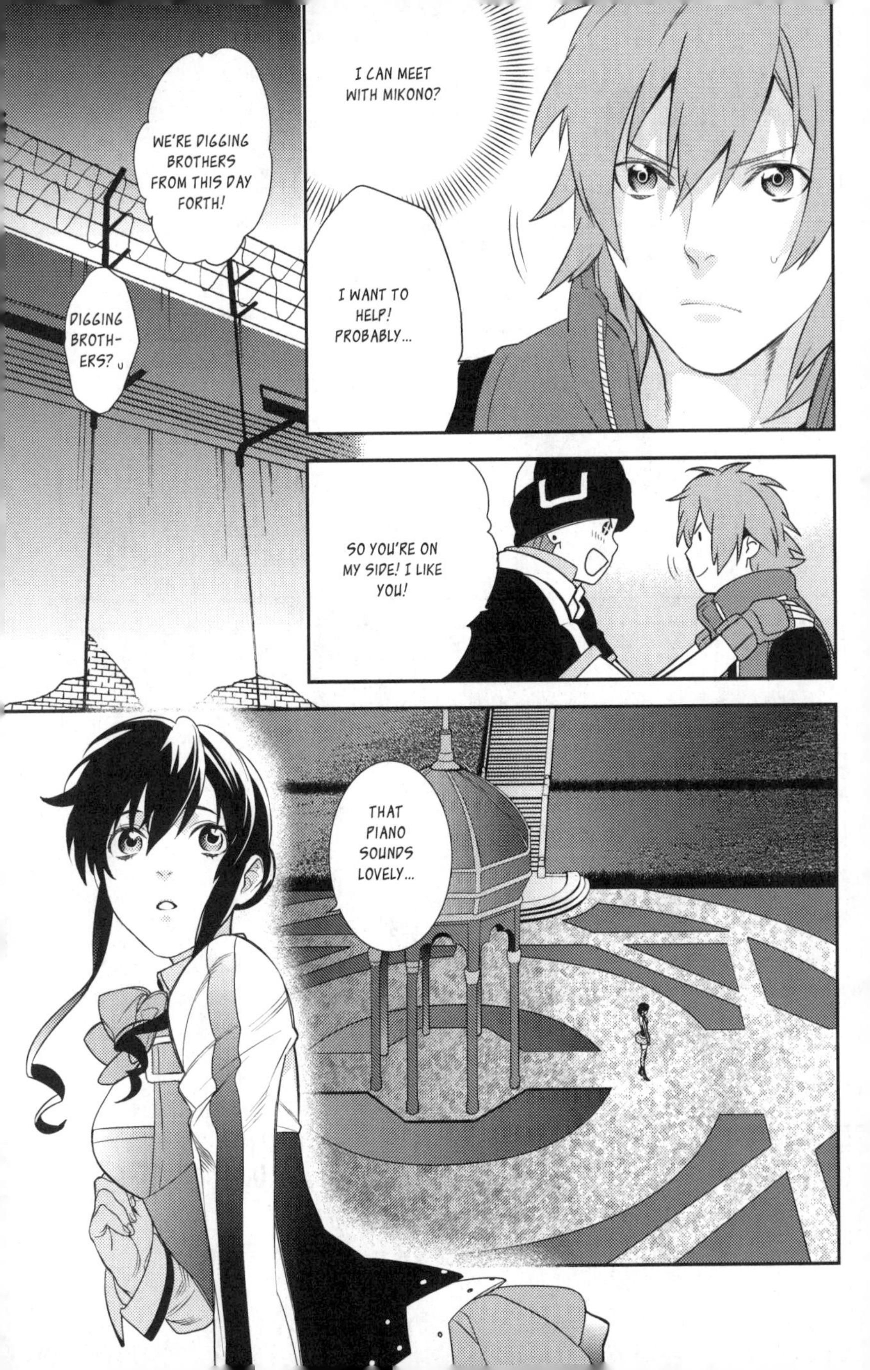
I CAN MEET WITH MIKONO?
I WANT TO HELP! PROBABLY...
WE'RE DIGGING BROTHERS FROM THIS DAY FORTH!
DIGGING BROTH-ERS?
SO YOU'RE ON MY SIDE! I LIKE YOU!
THAT PIANO SOUNDS LOVELY...

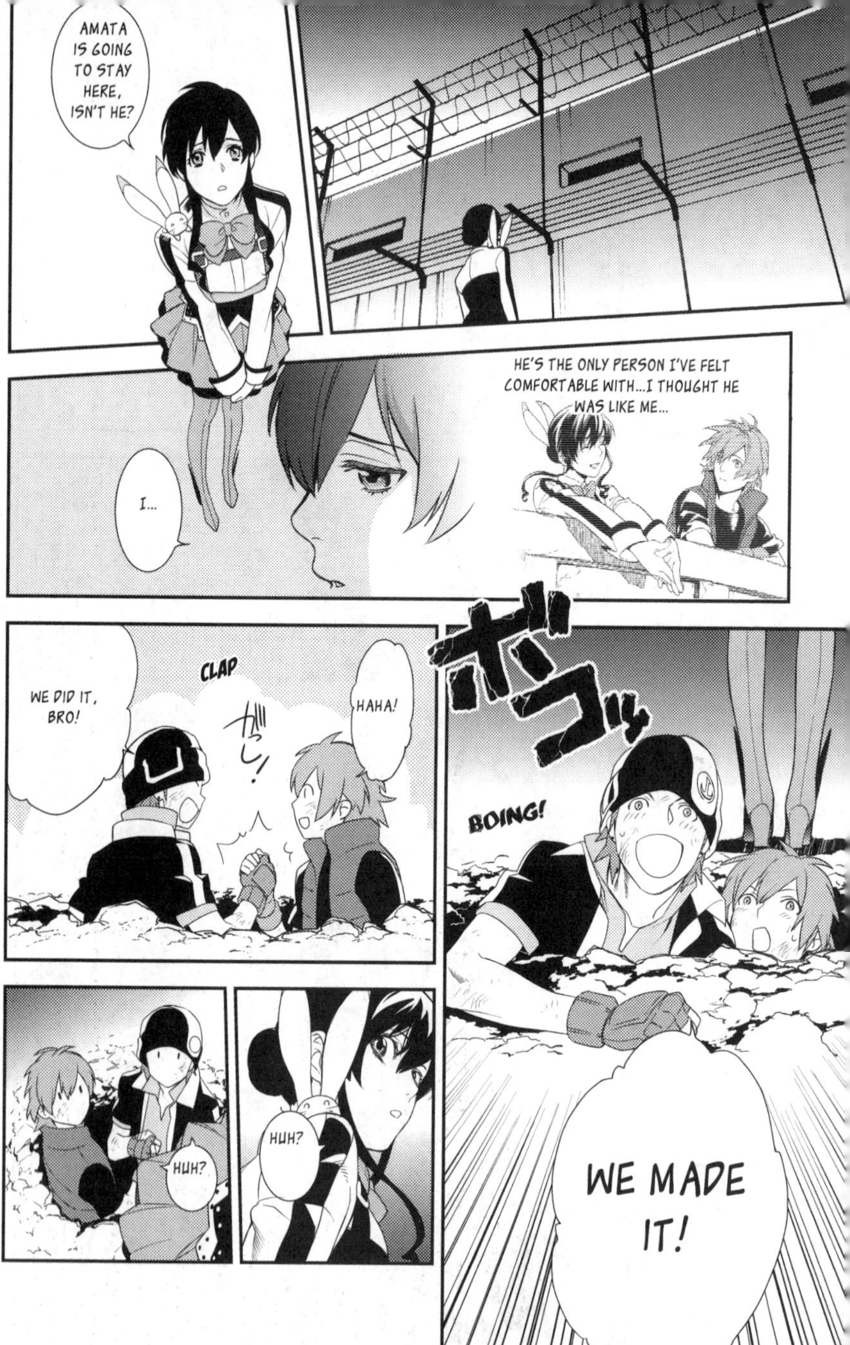
AMATA IS GOING TO STAY HERE, ISN'T HE?
HE'S THE ONLY PERSON I'VE FELT COMFORTABLE WITH...I THOUGHT HE WAS LIKE ME...
I...
ボゴッ
BOING!
WE MADE IT!
HAHA!
CLAP
がしっ!
WE DID IT, BRO!
HUH?
HUH?

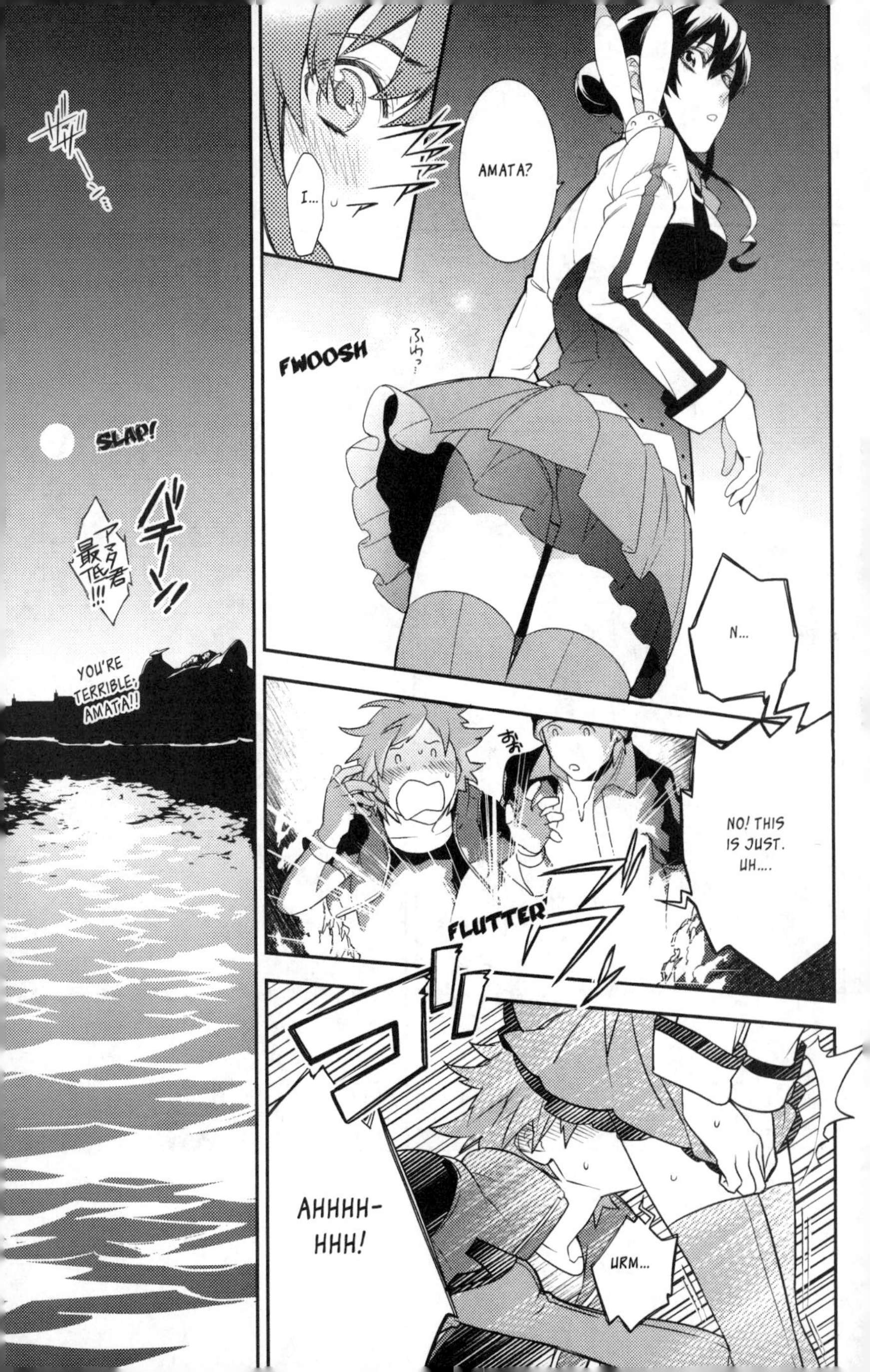
AMATA?
I...
FWOOSH
ふわっ…
N...
おお
NO! THIS IS JUST. UH....
FLUTTER
AHHHH-HHH!
URM...
SLAP!
アマタ君最低!!!
YOU'RE TERRIBLE, AMATA!!

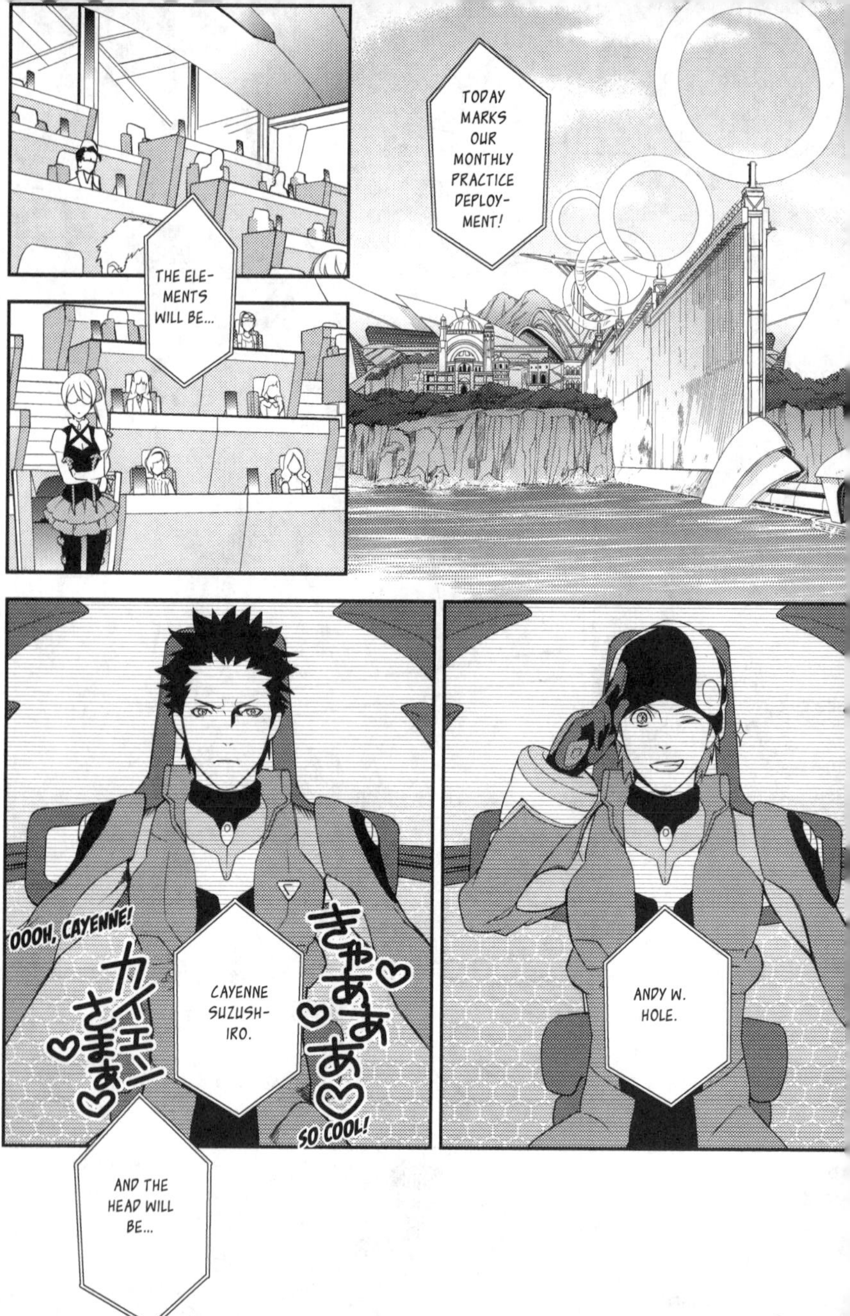
TODAY MARKS OUR MONTHLY PRACTICE DEPLOYMENT!
THE ELEMENTS WILL BE...
ANDY W. HOLE.
きゃあああ♡
CAYENNE SUZUSHIRO.
OOOH, CAYENNE!
カイエンさまぁ♡
SO COOL!
AND THE HEAD WILL BE...

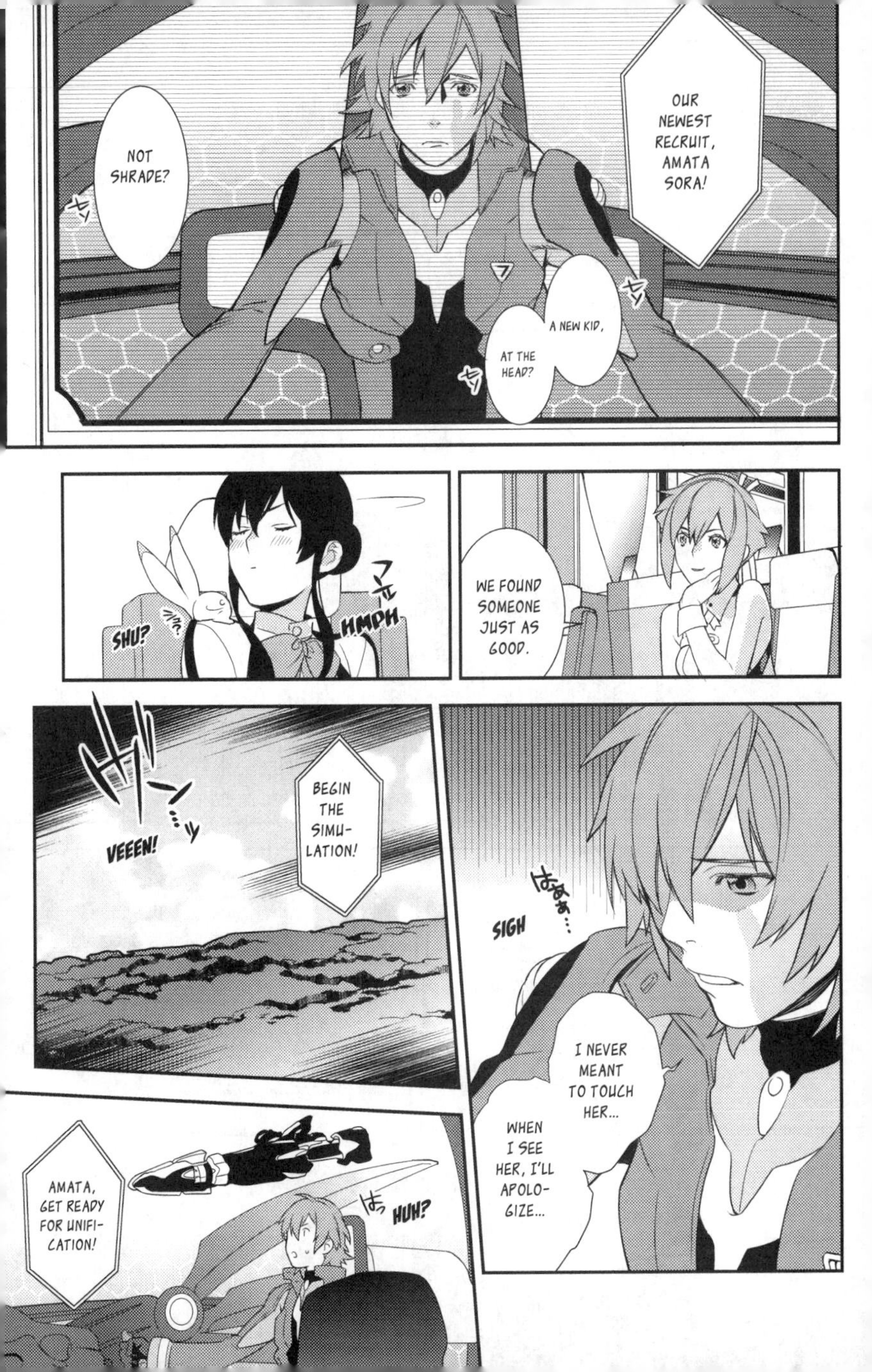
OUR NEWEST RECRUIT, AMATA SORA!
A NEW KID,
AT THE HEAD?
NOT SHRADE?
WE FOUND SOMEONE JUST AS GOOD.
SHU?
HMPH
SIGH
I NEVER MEANT TO TOUCH HER...
WHEN I SEE HER, I'LL APOLOGIZE...
BEGIN THE SIMULATION!
VEEEN!
HUH?
AMATA, GET READY FOR UNIFICATION!

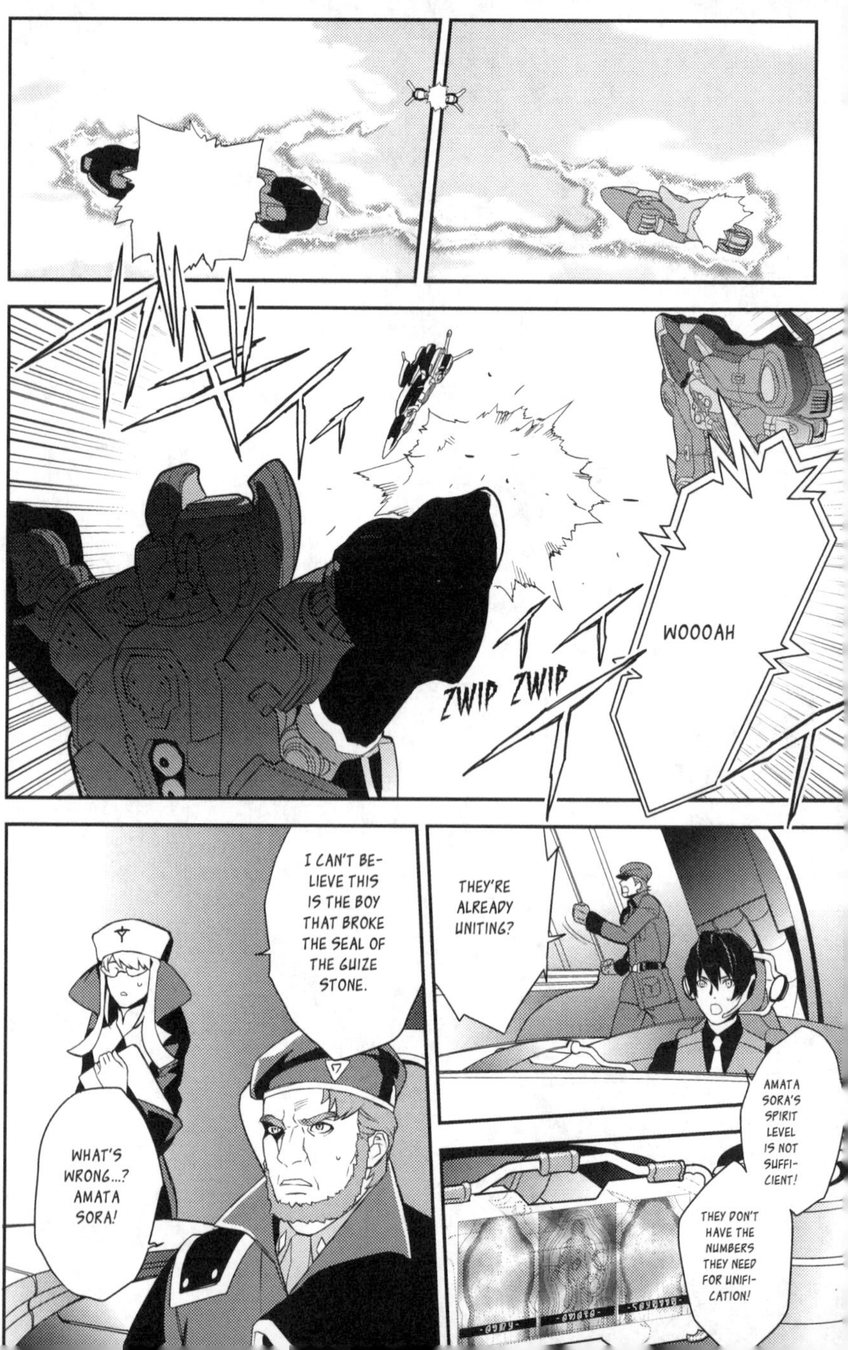
WOOOAH
ZWIP ZWIP
THEY'RE ALREADY UNITING?
AMATA SORA'S SPIRIT LEVEL IS NOT SUFFI- CIENT!
THEY DON'T HAVE THE NUMBERS THEY NEED FOR UNIFI- CATION!
I CAN'T BE- LIEVE THIS IS THE BOY THAT BROKE THE SEAL OF THE GUIZE STONE.
WHAT'S WRONG...? AMATA SORA!

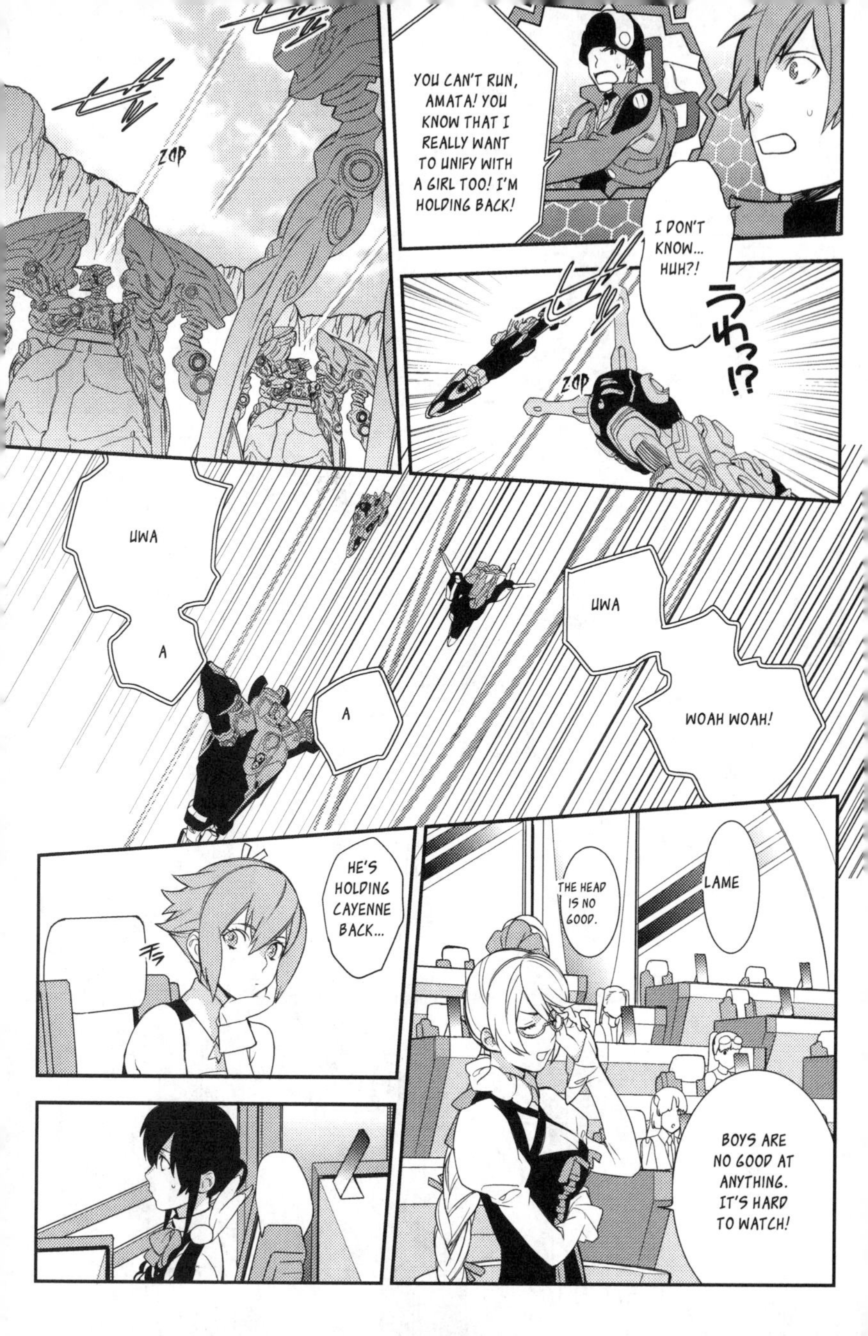
YOU CAN'T RUN, AMATA! YOU KNOW THAT I REALLY WANT TO UNIFY WITH A GIRL TOO! I'M HOLDING BACK!
I DON'T KNOW... HUH?!
うわっ!?
ZAP
ZAP
UWA
WOAH WOAH!
UWA
A
A
LAME
THE HEAD IS NO GOOD.
BOYS ARE NO GOOD AT ANYTHING. IT'S HARD TO WATCH!
HE'S HOLDING CAYENNE BACK...

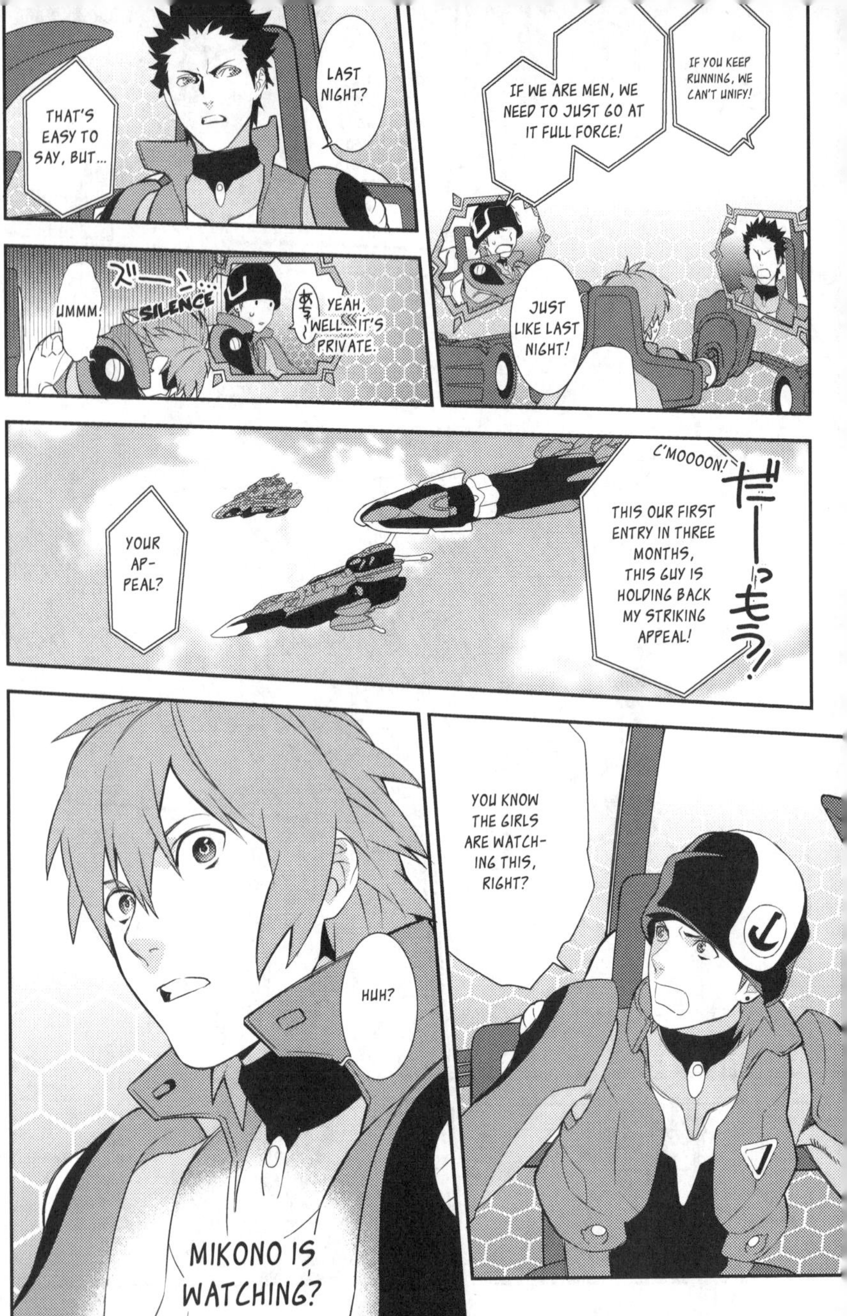
IF YOU KEEP RUNNING, WE CAN'T UNIFY!
IF WE ARE MEN, WE NEED TO JUST GO AT IT FULL FORCE!
JUST LIKE LAST NIGHT!
LAST NIGHT?
THAT'S EASY TO SAY, BUT...
ズーン…
SILENCE
YEAH, WELL... IT'S PRIVATE.
UMMM.
C'MOOOON!
だーっもう?!
THIS OUR FIRST ENTRY IN THREE MONTHS, THIS GUY IS HOLDING BACK MY STRIKING APPEAL!
YOUR AP-PEAL?
YOU KNOW THE GIRLS ARE WATCHING THIS, RIGHT?
HUH?
MIKONO IS WATCHING?

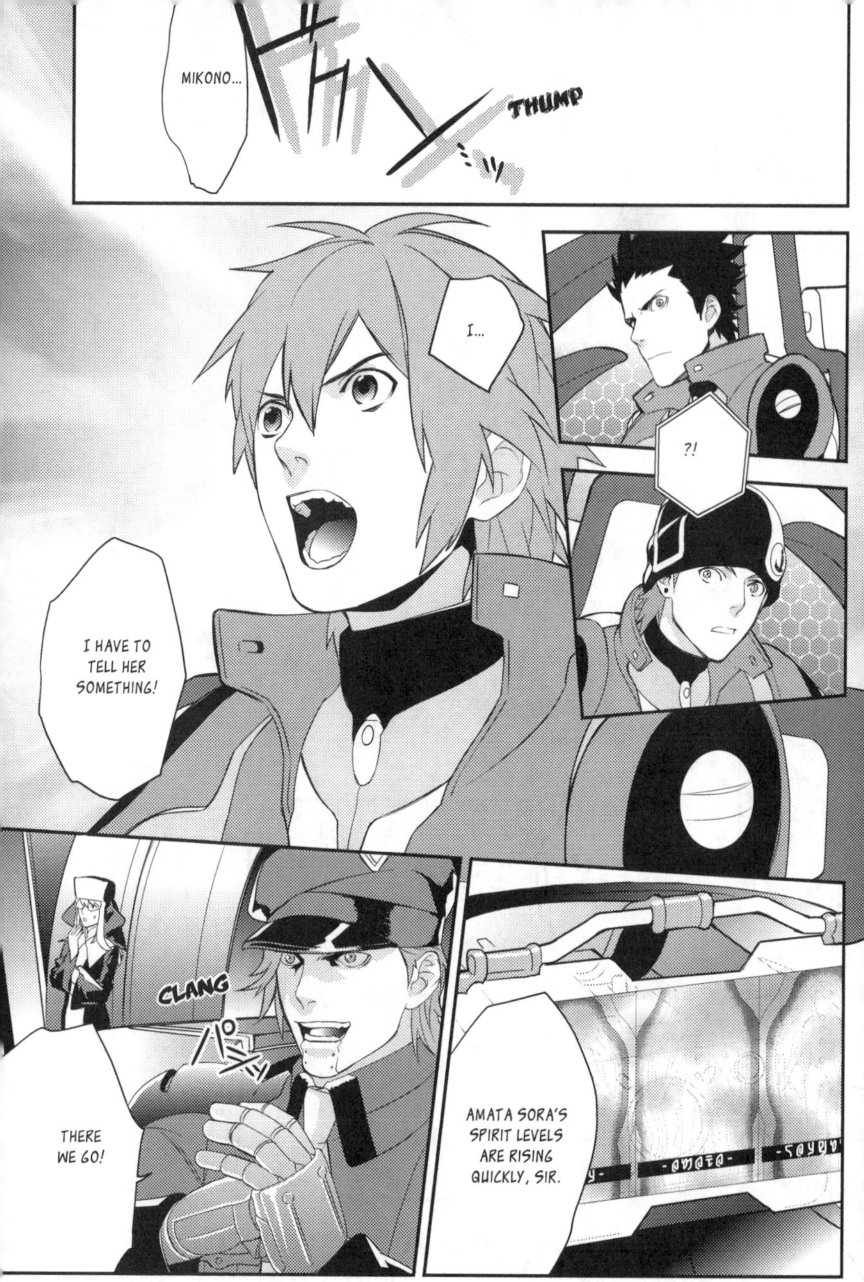
MIKONO...
THUMP
?!
I...
I HAVE TO TELL HER SOMETHING!
AMATA SORA'S SPIRIT LEVELS ARE RISING QUICKLY, SIR.
CLANG
THERE WE GO!

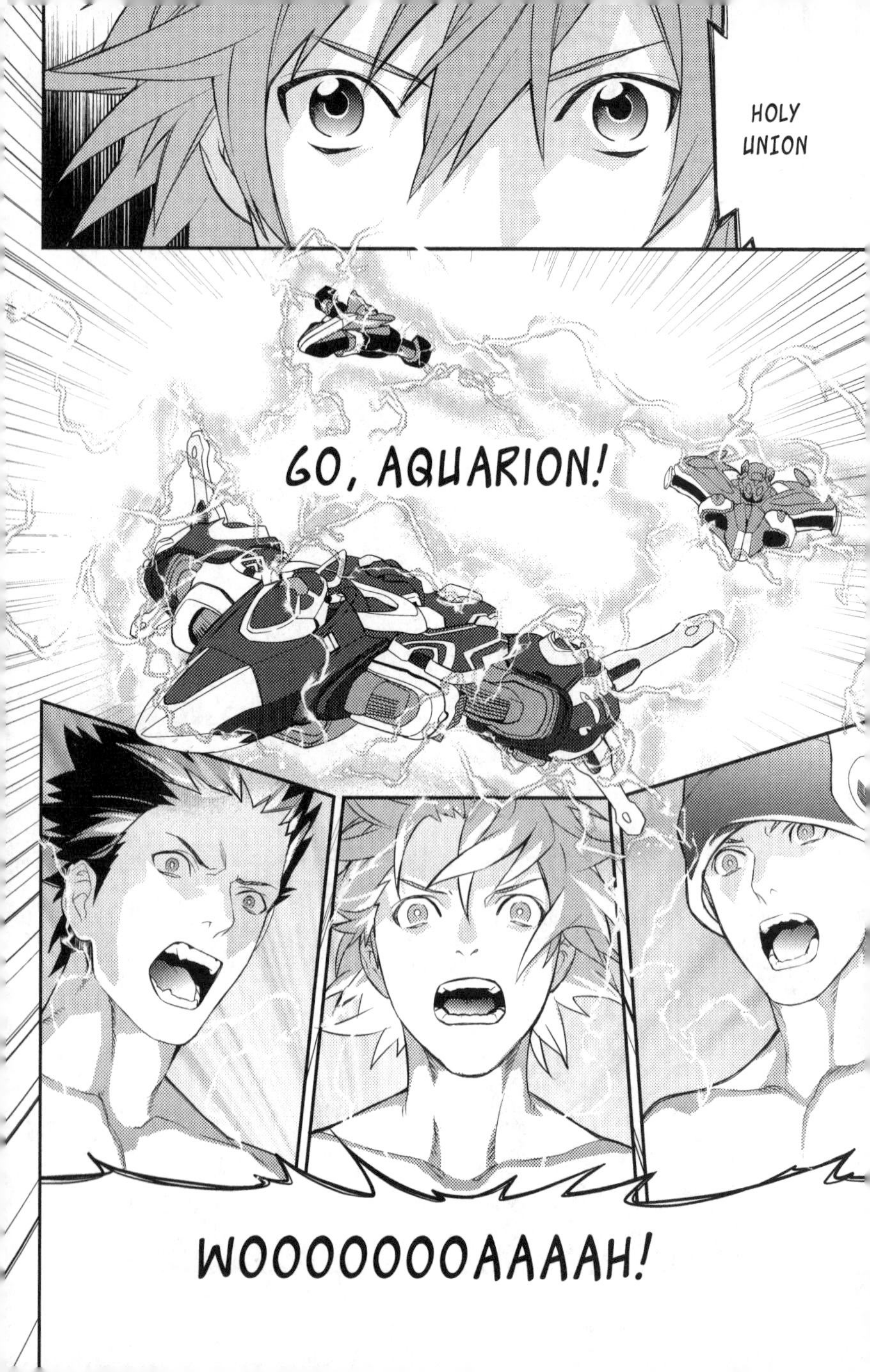
HOLY UNION
GO, AQUARION!
WOOOOOOOAAAAH!

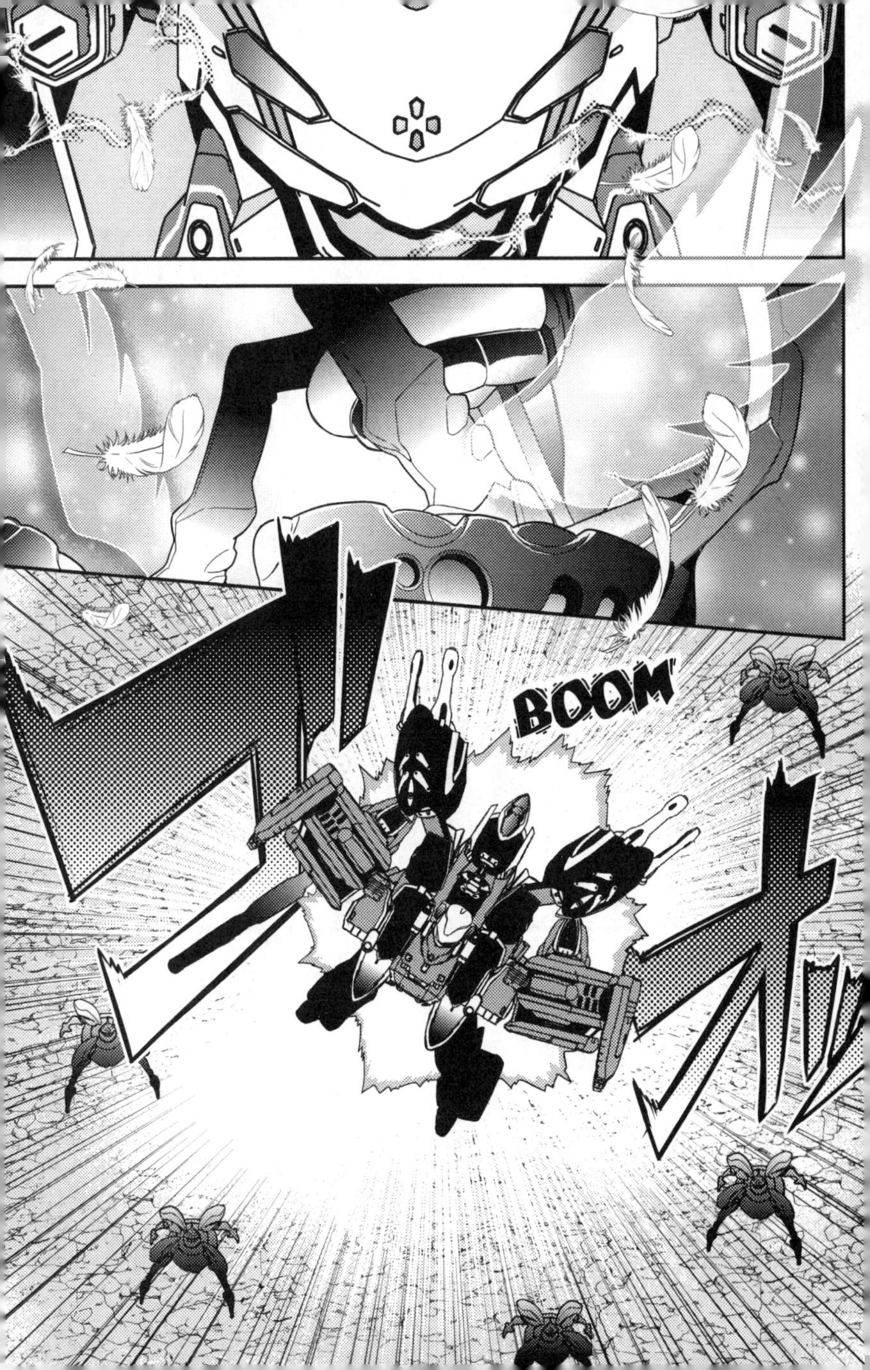
BOOM

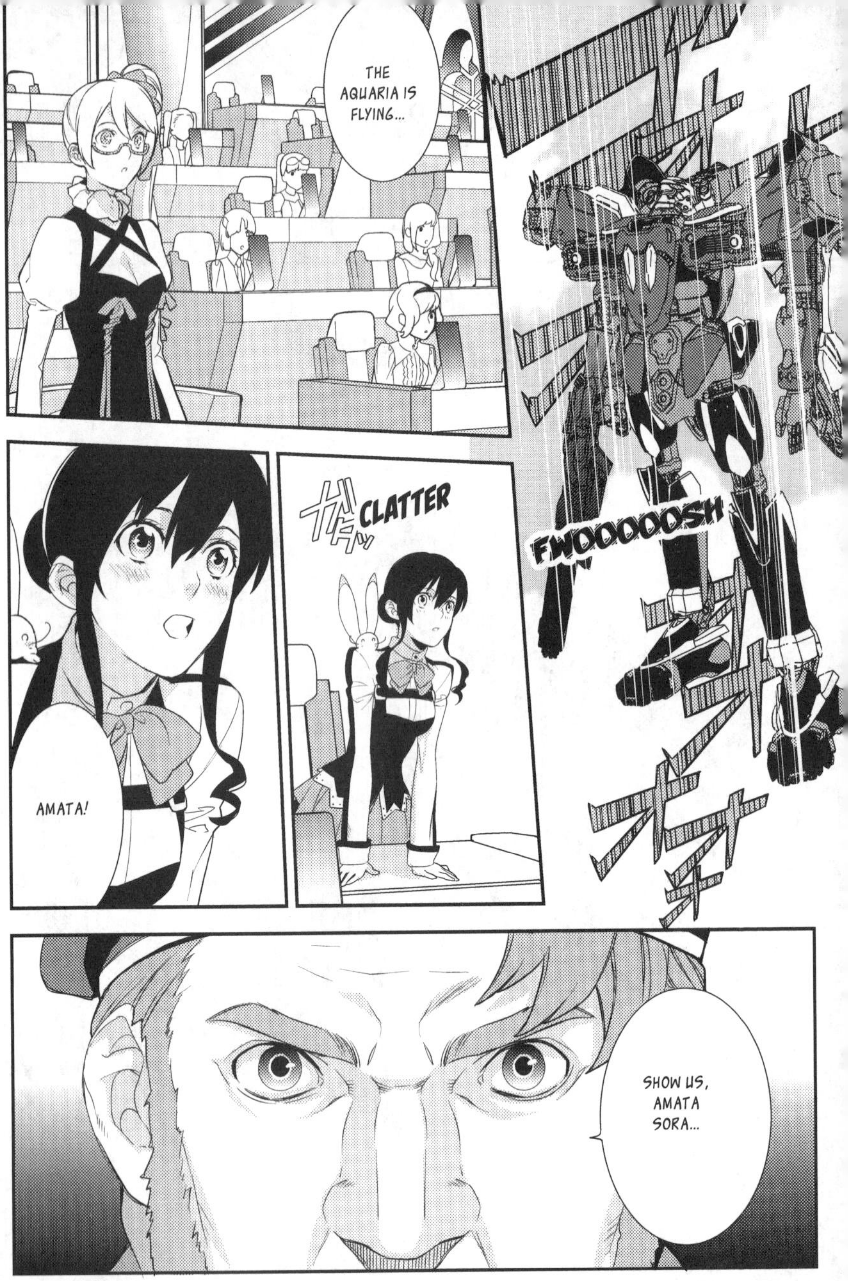
FWOOOOOOSH
THE AQUARIA IS FLYING...
CLATTER
AMATA!
SHOW US, AMATA SORA...

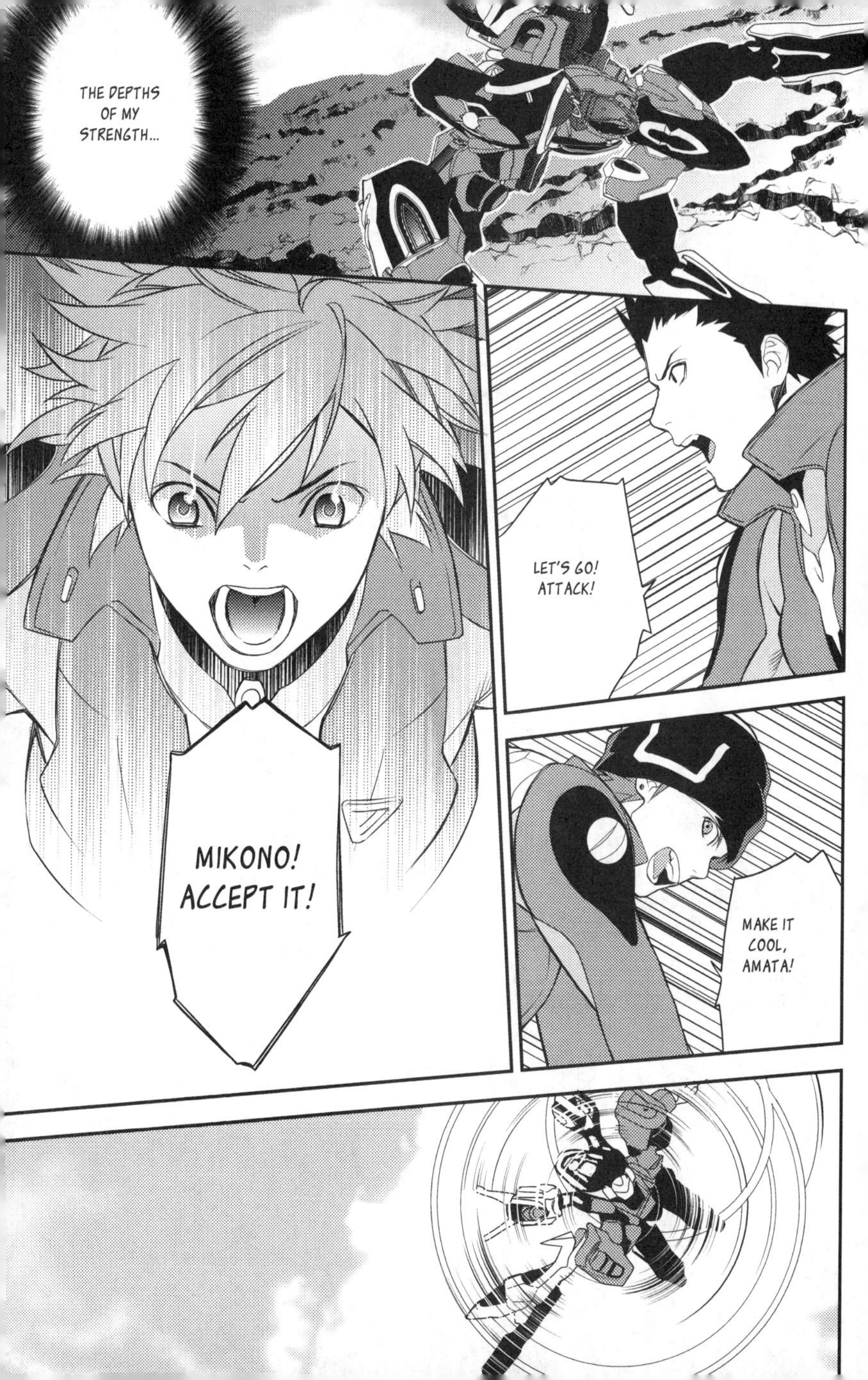
THE DEPTHS OF MY STRENGTH...
LET'S GO! ATTACK!
MAKE IT COOL, AMATA!
MIKONO! ACCEPT IT!

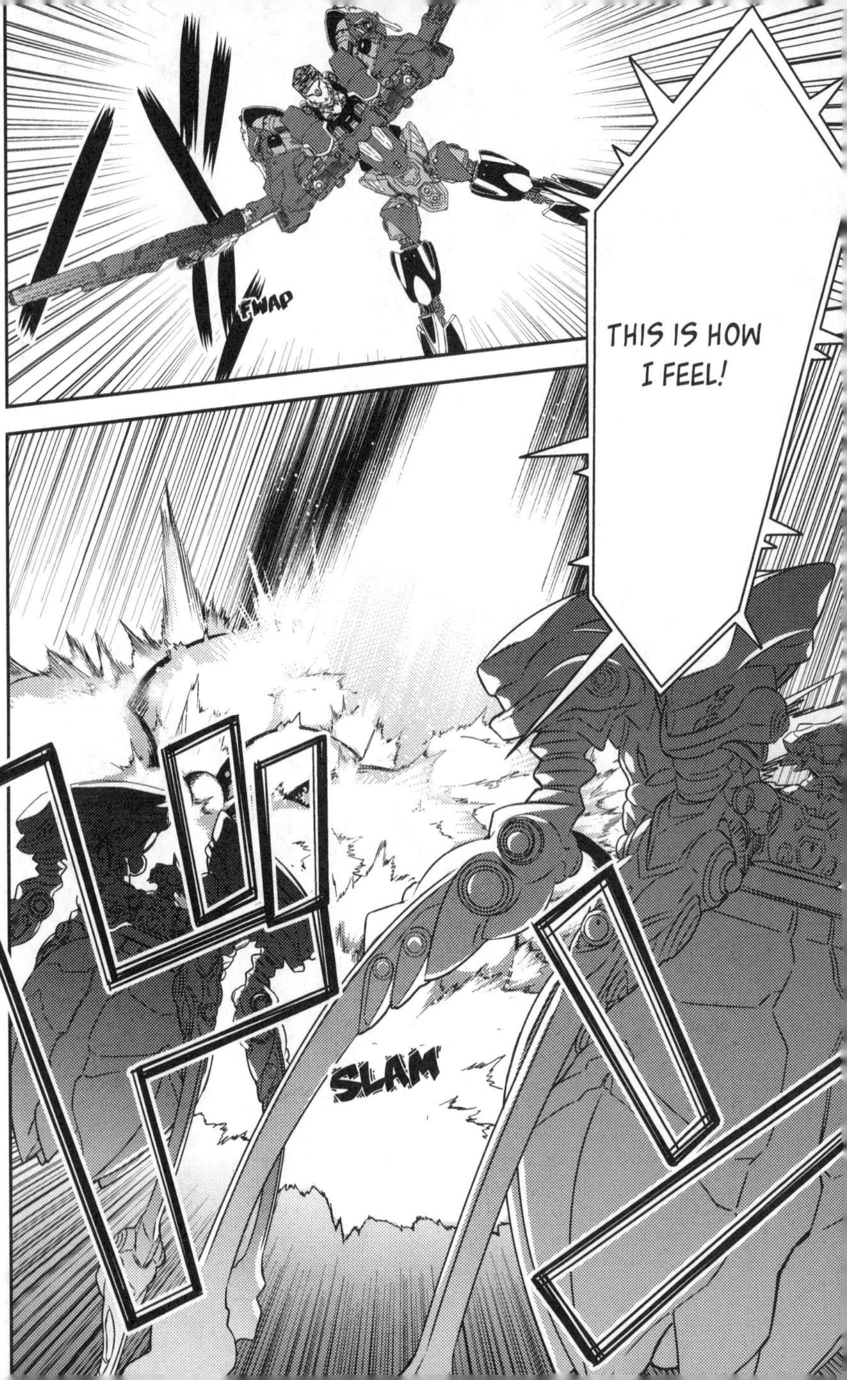
THIS IS HOW I FEEL!
FWAP
SLAM

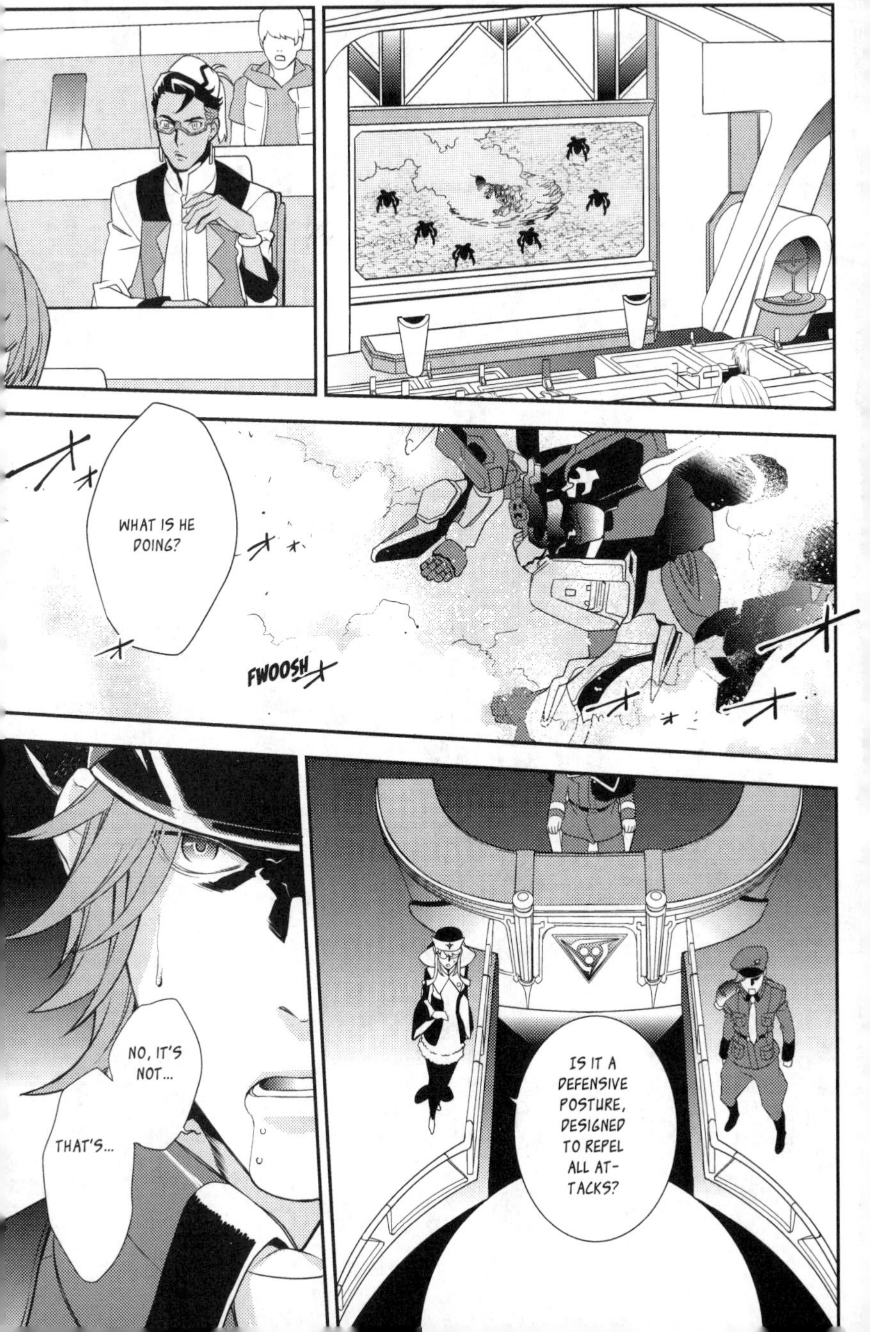
WHAT IS HE DOING?
FWOOSH
IS IT A DEFENSIVE POSTURE, DESIGNED TO REPEL ALL AT-TACKS?
NO, IT'S NOT...
THAT'S...

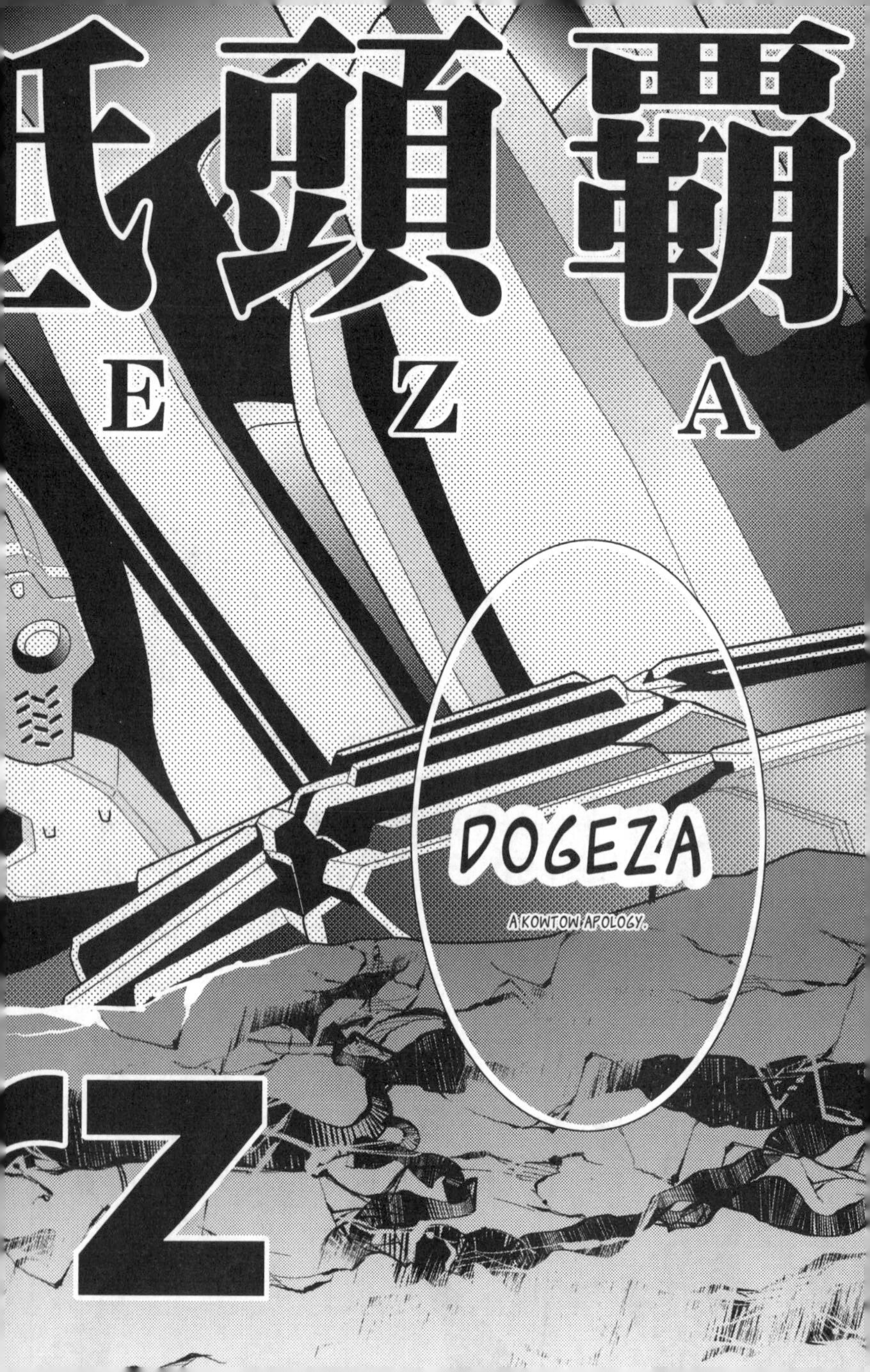
DOGEZA
A KOWTOW APOLOGY.

平身低

D O G

0

FATAL ERROR

SIZZLE

?

??

AMATA SORA HAS PERFORMED AN UNKNOWN ACTION, RESULTING IN A PROGRAM ERROR!

THE SIMULATION HAS BEEN CANCELED!

...

WHY....

WHAT A FOOL...

SIGH

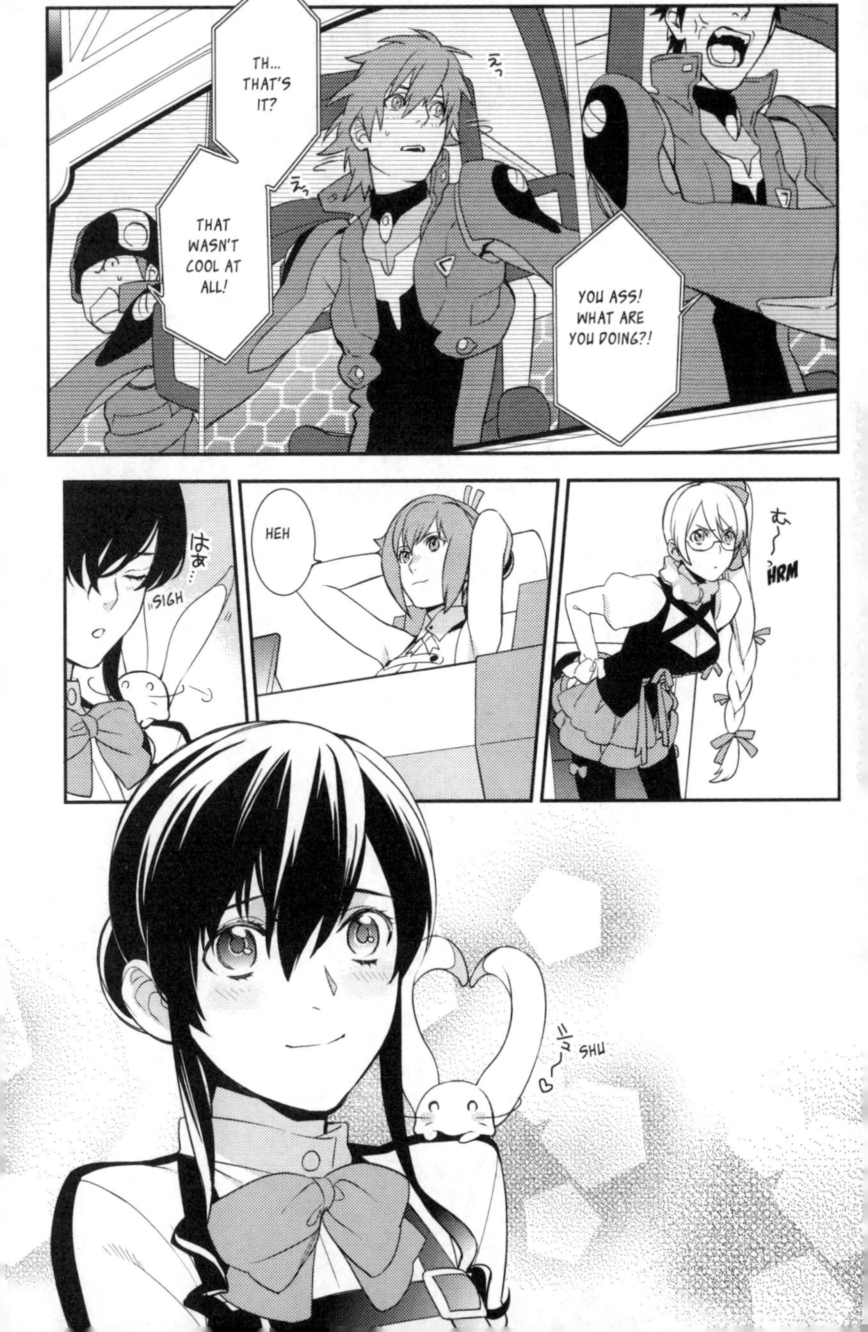
えっ
YOU ASS! WHAT ARE YOU DOING?!
TH... THAT'S IT?
えっ
THAT WASN'T COOL AT ALL!
む~
HRM
HEH
はぁ…
SIGH
SHU

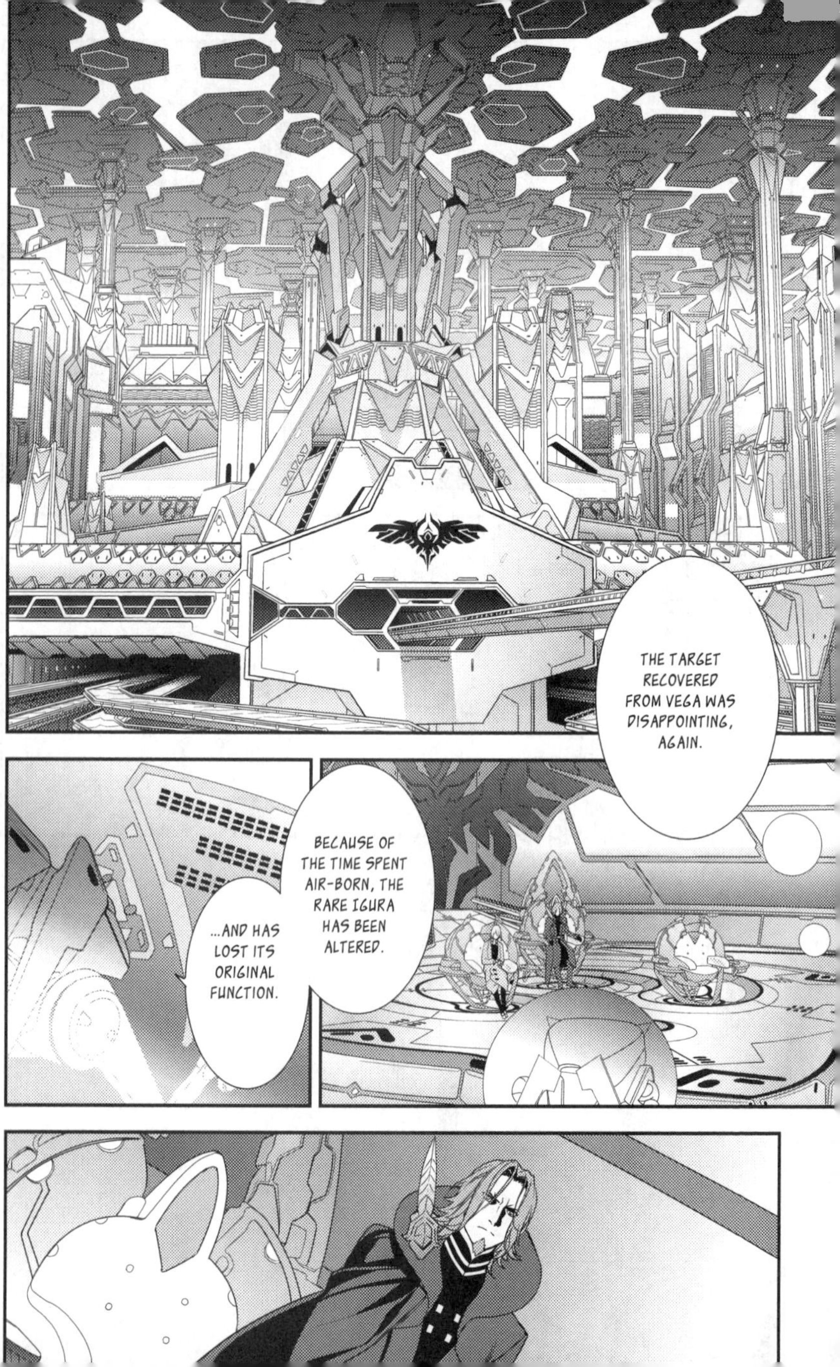
THE TARGET RECOVERED FROM VEGA WAS DISAPPOINTING, AGAIN.
BECAUSE OF THE TIME SPENT AIR-BORN, THE RARE IGURA HAS BEEN ALTERED.
...AND HAS LOST ITS ORIGINAL FUNCTION.

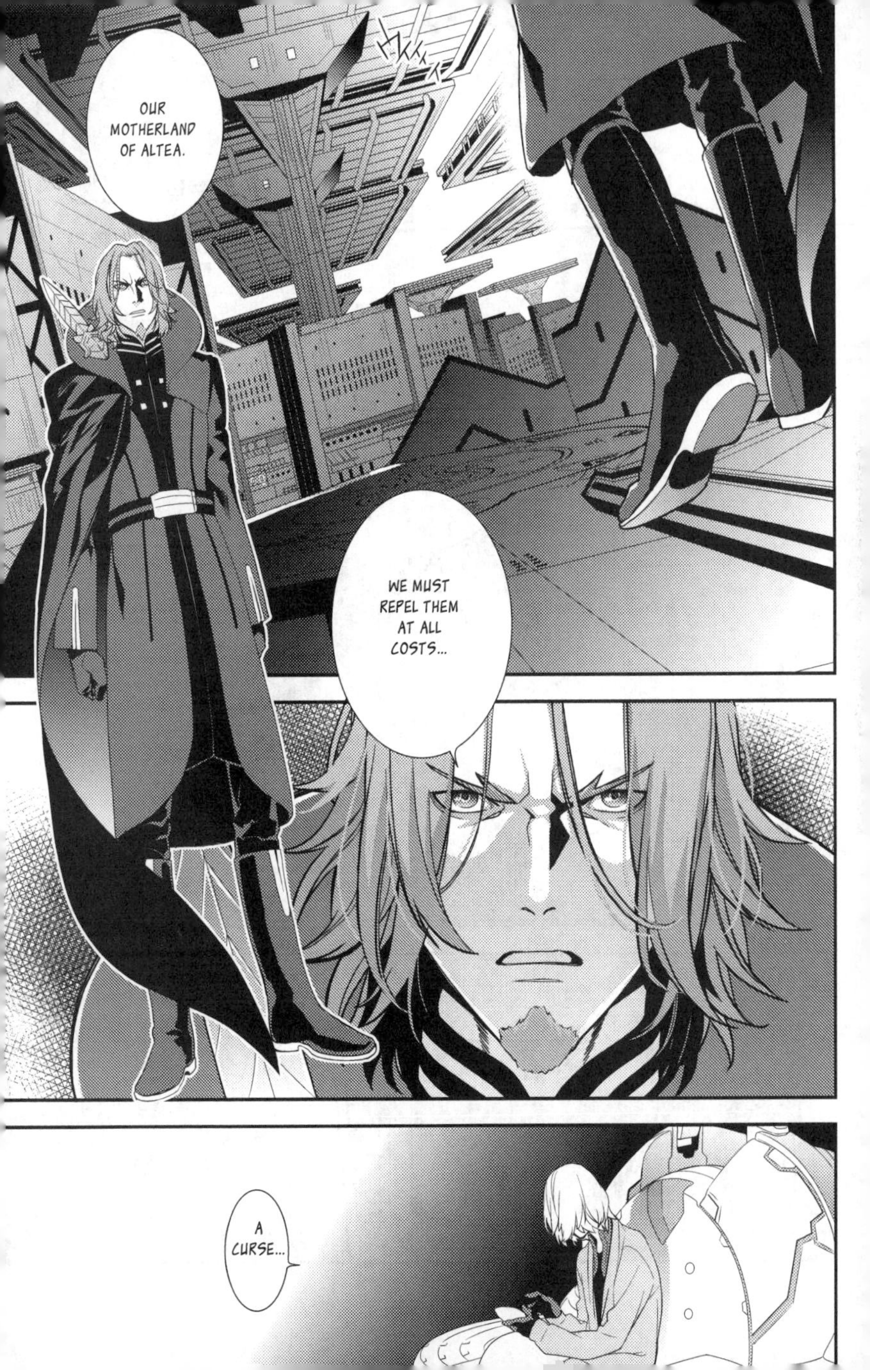
OUR MOTHERLAND OF ALTEA.
WE MUST REPEL THEM AT ALL COSTS...
A CURSE...

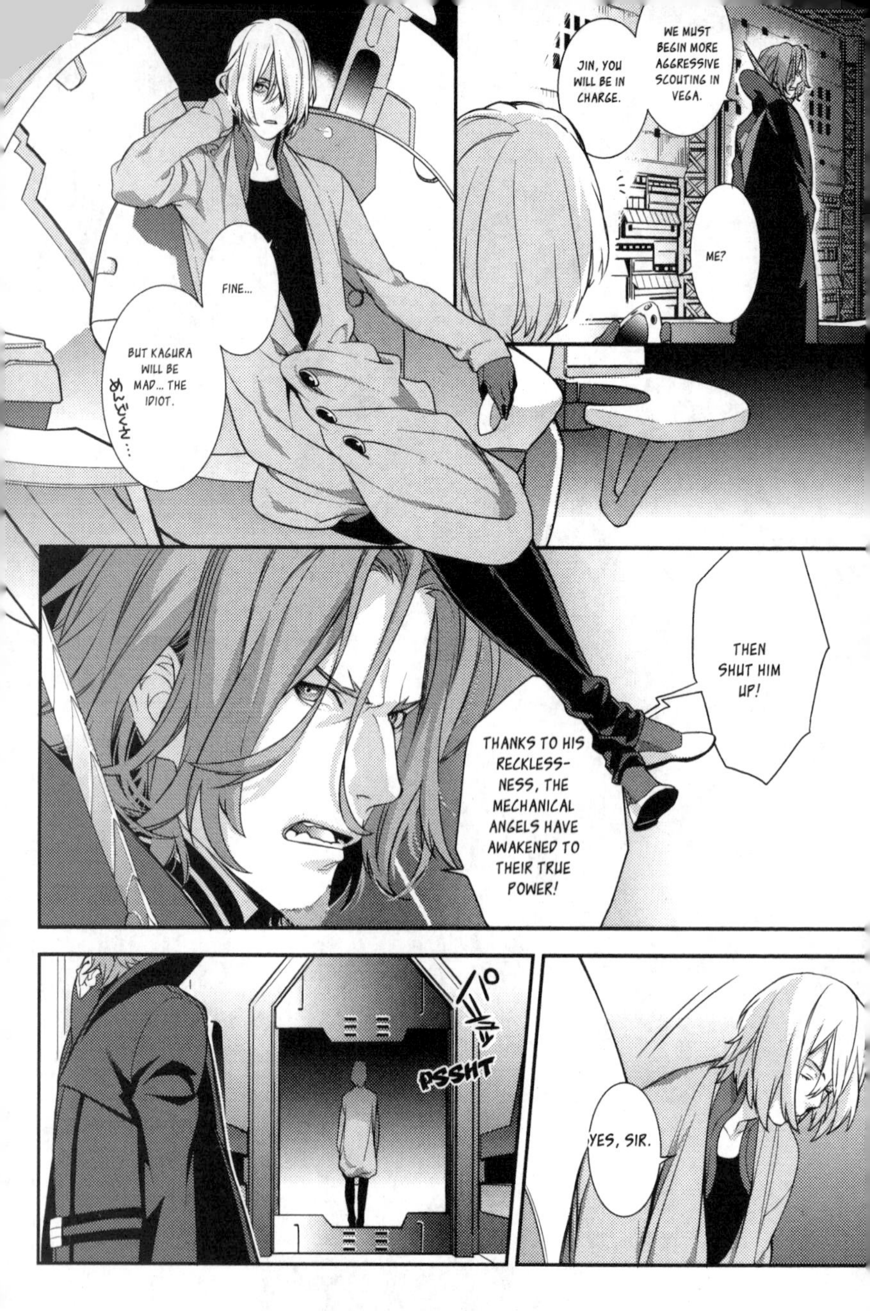
WE MUST BEGIN MORE AGGRESSIVE SCOUTING IN VEGA.
JIN, YOU WILL BE IN CHARGE.
ME?
FINE...
BUT KAGURA WILL BE MAD... THE IDIOT.
THEN SHUT HIM UP!
THANKS TO HIS RECKLESS-NESS, THE MECHANICAL ANGELS HAVE AWAKENED TO THEIR TRUE POWER!
YES, SIR.
PSSHT

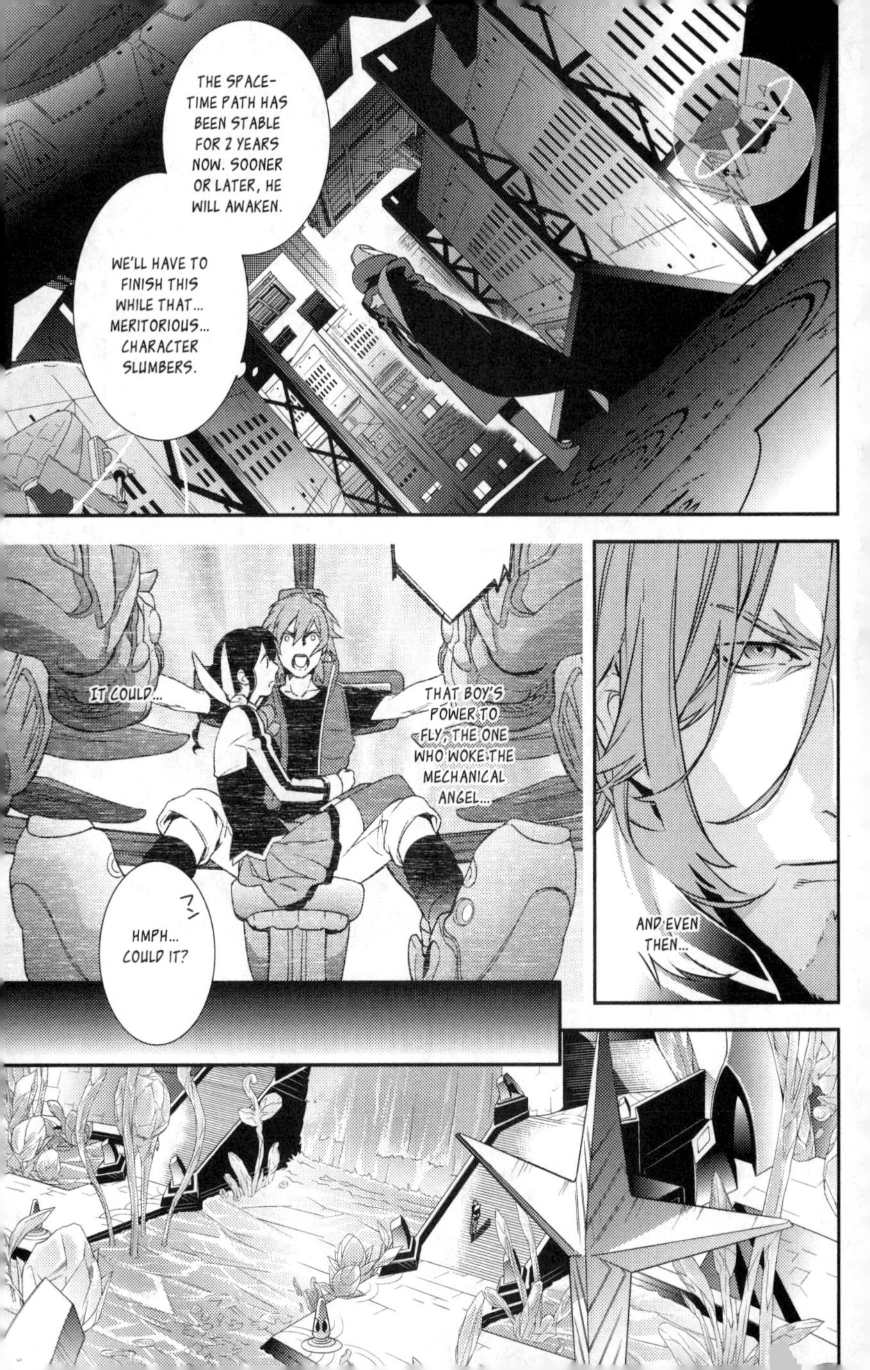
THE SPACE-TIME PATH HAS BEEN STABLE FOR 2 YEARS NOW. SOONER OR LATER, HE WILL AWAKEN.
WE'LL HAVE TO FINISH THIS WHILE THAT... MERITORIOUS... CHARACTER SLUMBERS.
AND EVEN THEN...
THAT BOY'S POWER TO FLY, THE ONE WHO WOKE THE MECHANICAL ANGEL...
IT COULD...
HMPH... COULD IT?

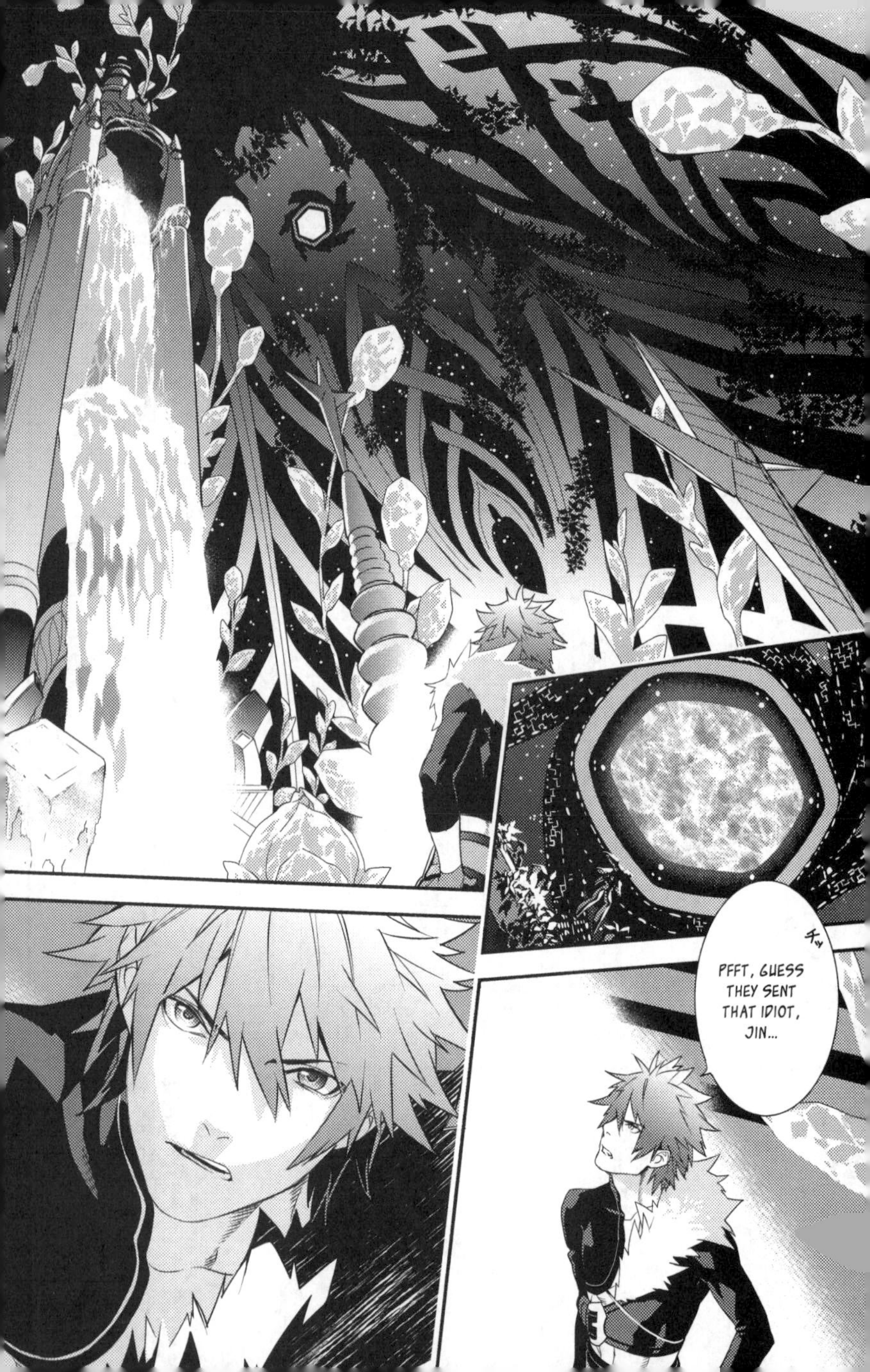
チッ
PFFT, GUESS THEY SENT THAT IDIOT, JIN...

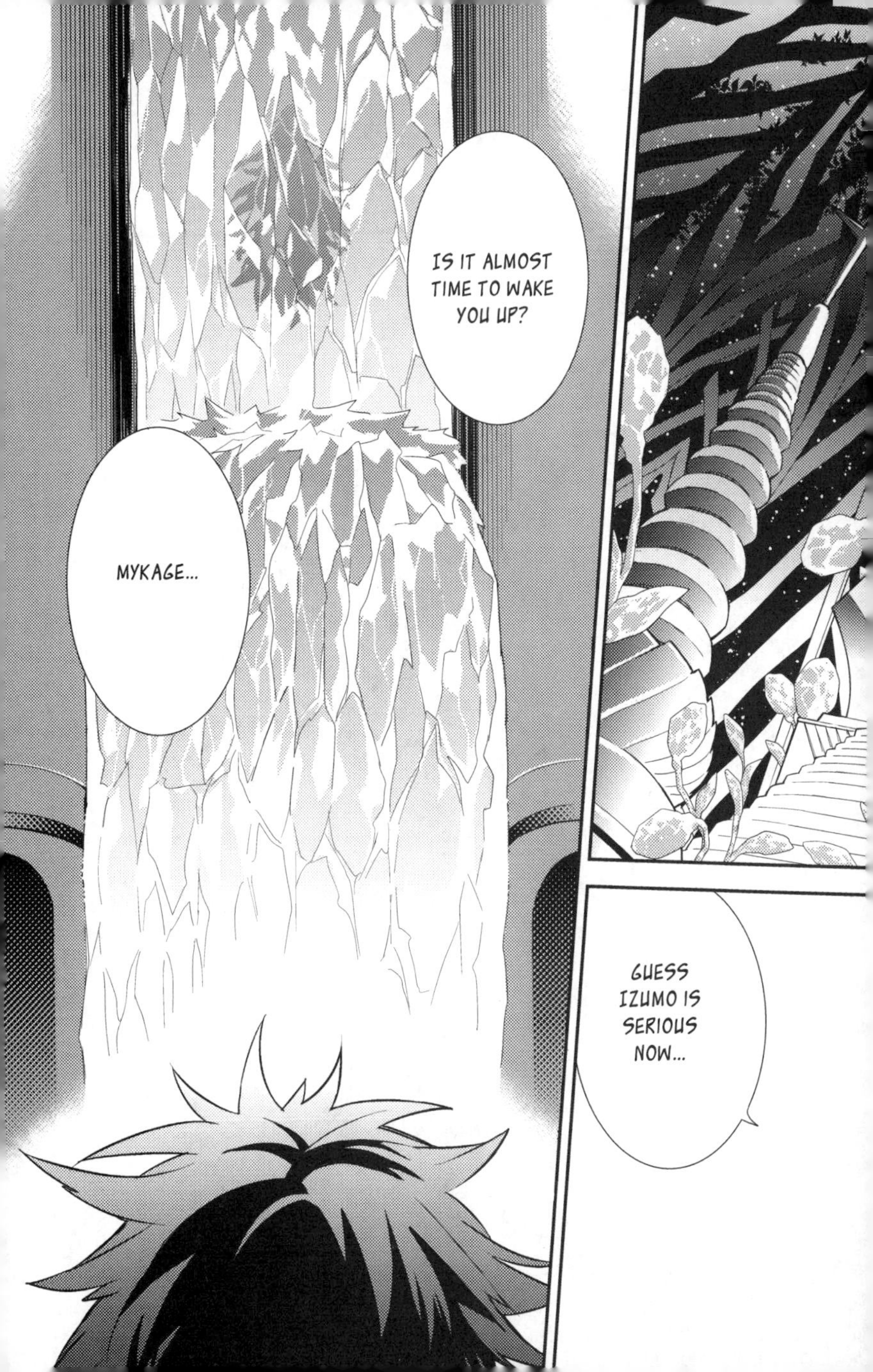
GUESS IZUMO IS SERIOUS NOW...
IS IT ALMOST TIME TO WAKE YOU UP?
MYKAGE...

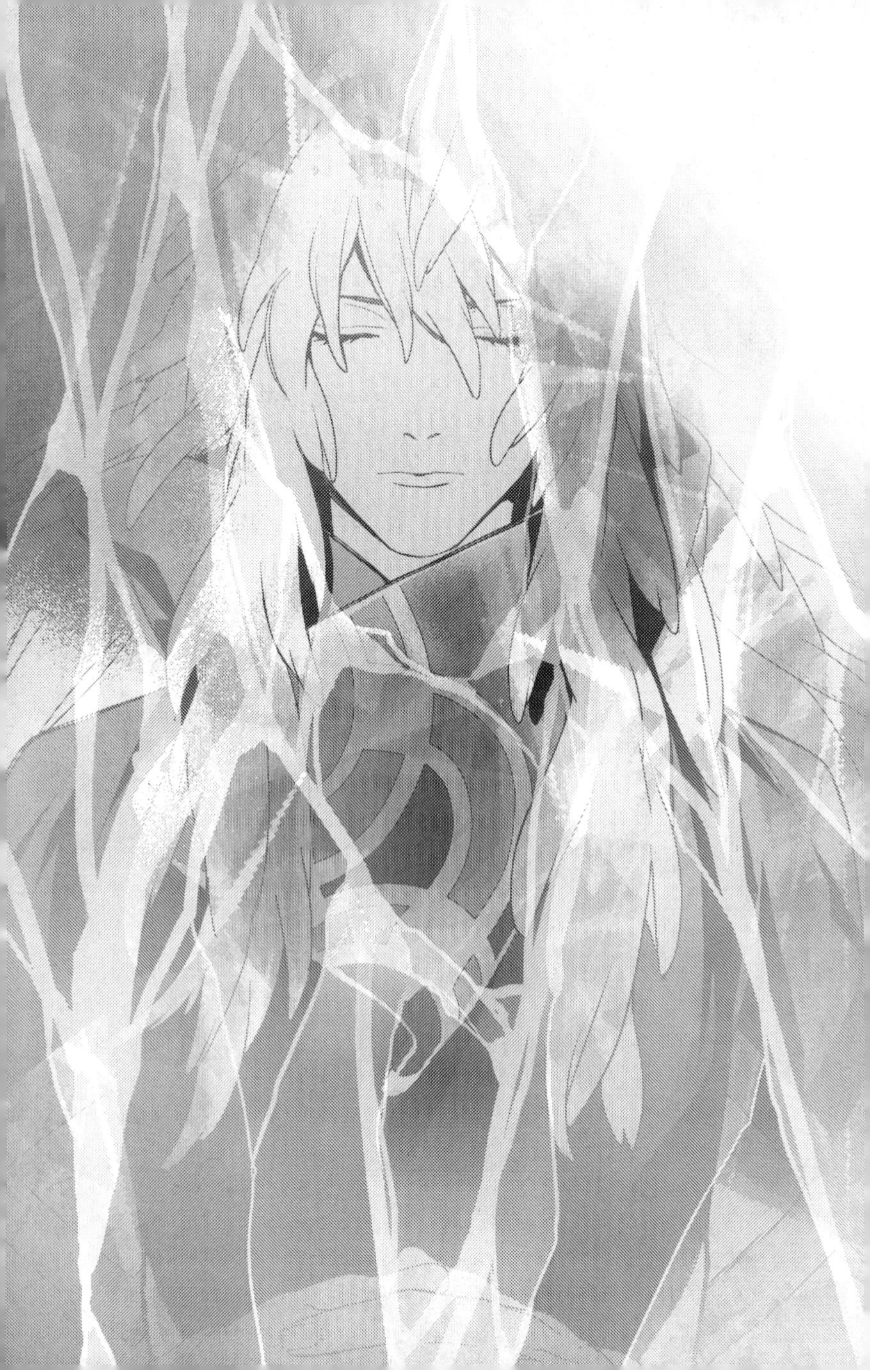

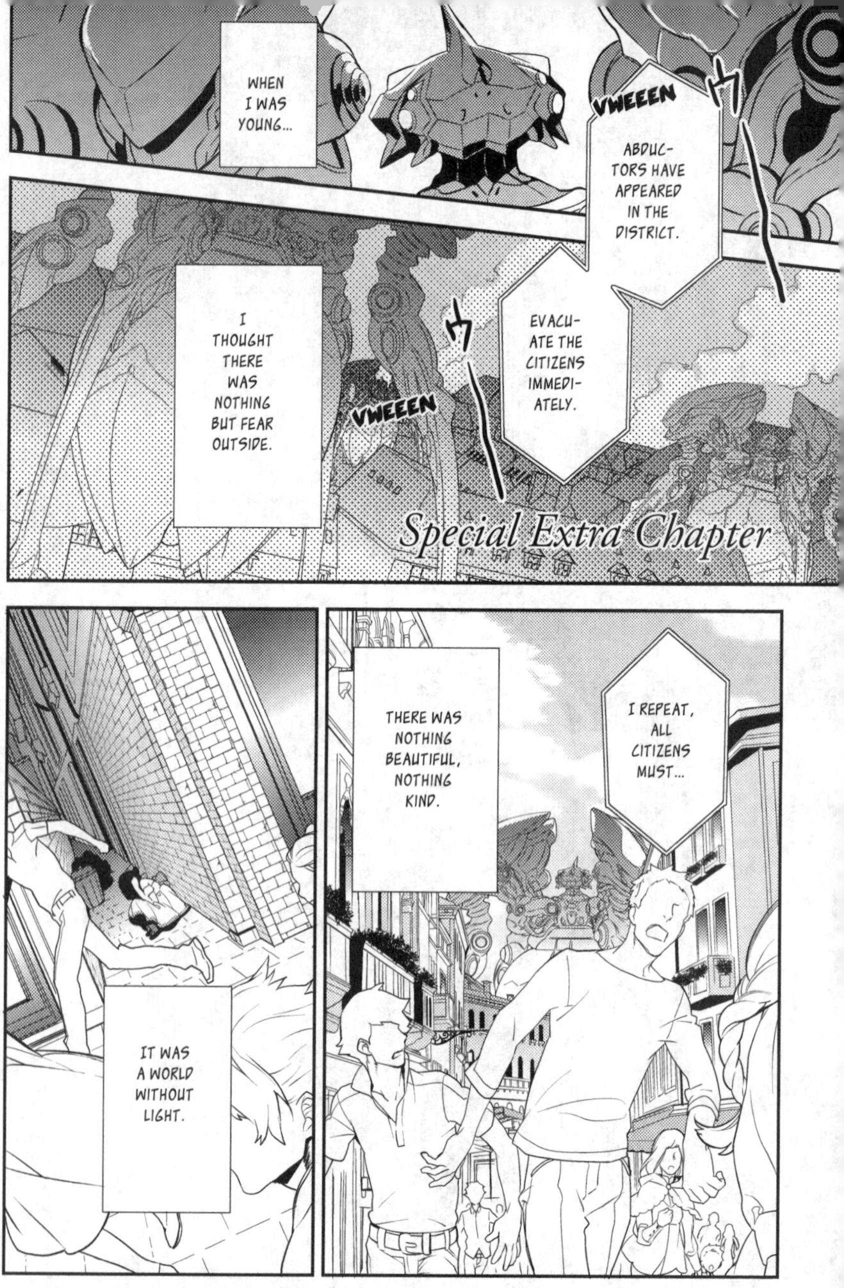
ウ
VWEEEN
ABDUCTORS HAVE APPEARED IN THE DISTRICT.
WHEN I WAS YOUNG...
EVACUATE THE CITIZENS IMMEDIATELY.
ウ
VWEEEN
I THOUGHT THERE WAS NOTHING BUT FEAR OUTSIDE.
Special Extra Chapter
I REPEAT, ALL CITIZENS MUST...
THERE WAS NOTHING BEAUTIFUL, NOTHING KIND.
IT WAS A WORLD WITHOUT LIGHT.

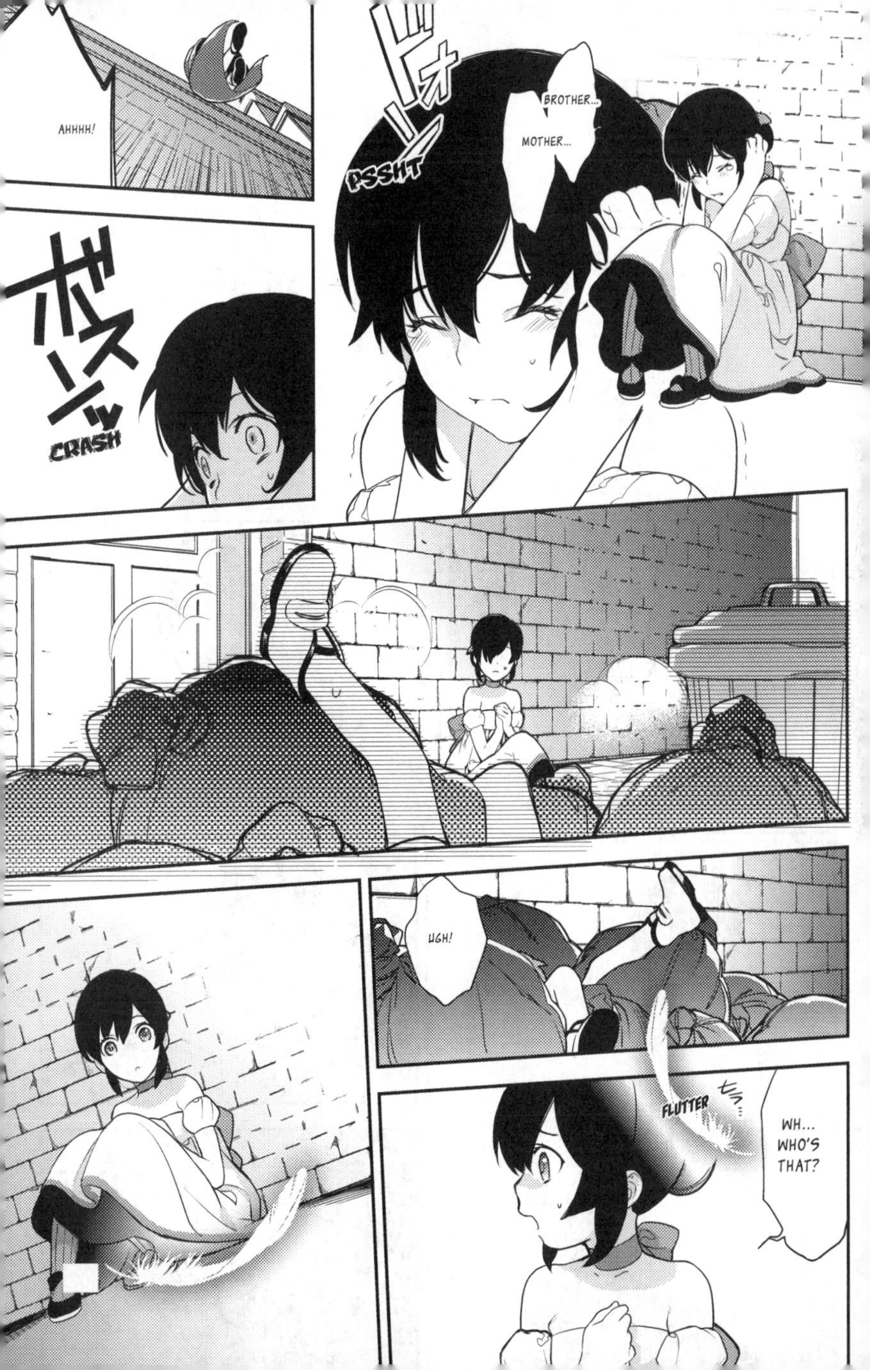
BROTHER...
MOTHER...
ドォン
PSSHT
AHHHH!
ボスンッ
CRASH
UGH!
ヒラ…
FLUTTER
WH... WHO'S THAT?

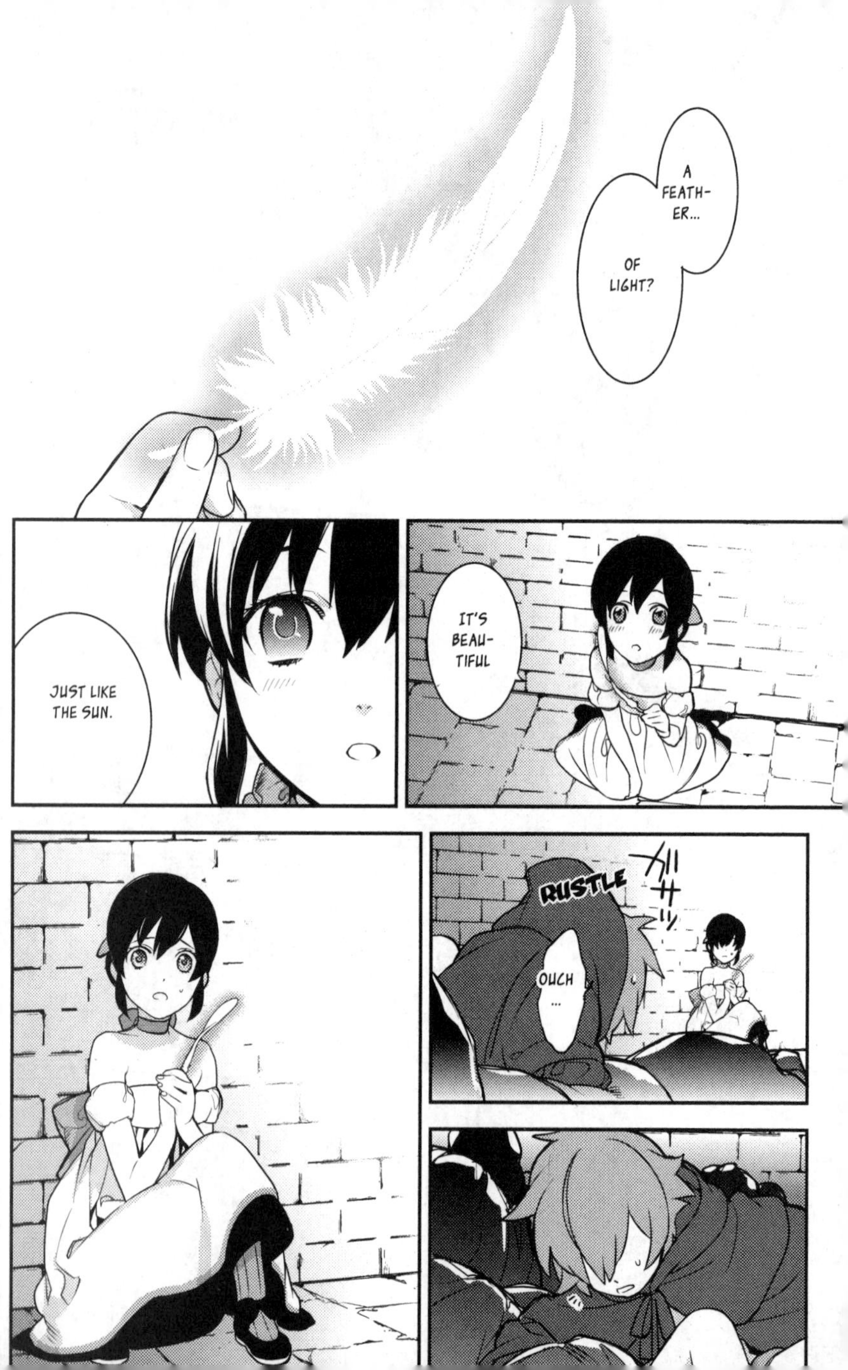
A FEATH-ER...
OF LIGHT?
IT'S BEAU-TIFUL
JUST LIKE THE SUN.
RUSTLE
OUCH ...

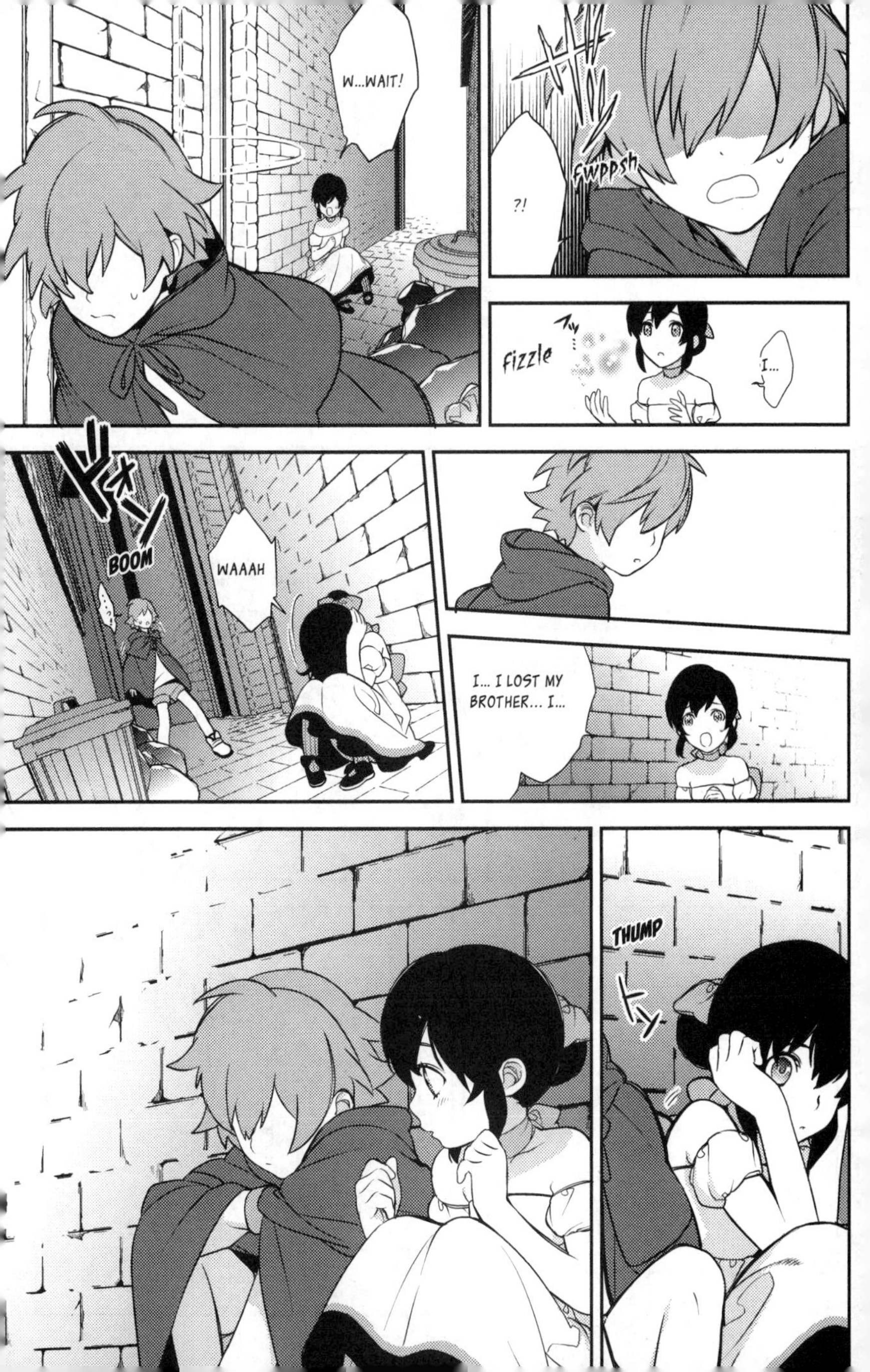

fwppsh
?!
fizzle
I...
W...WAIT!
I... I LOST MY BROTHER... I...
ドォン
BOOM
WAAAH
THUMP
トッ

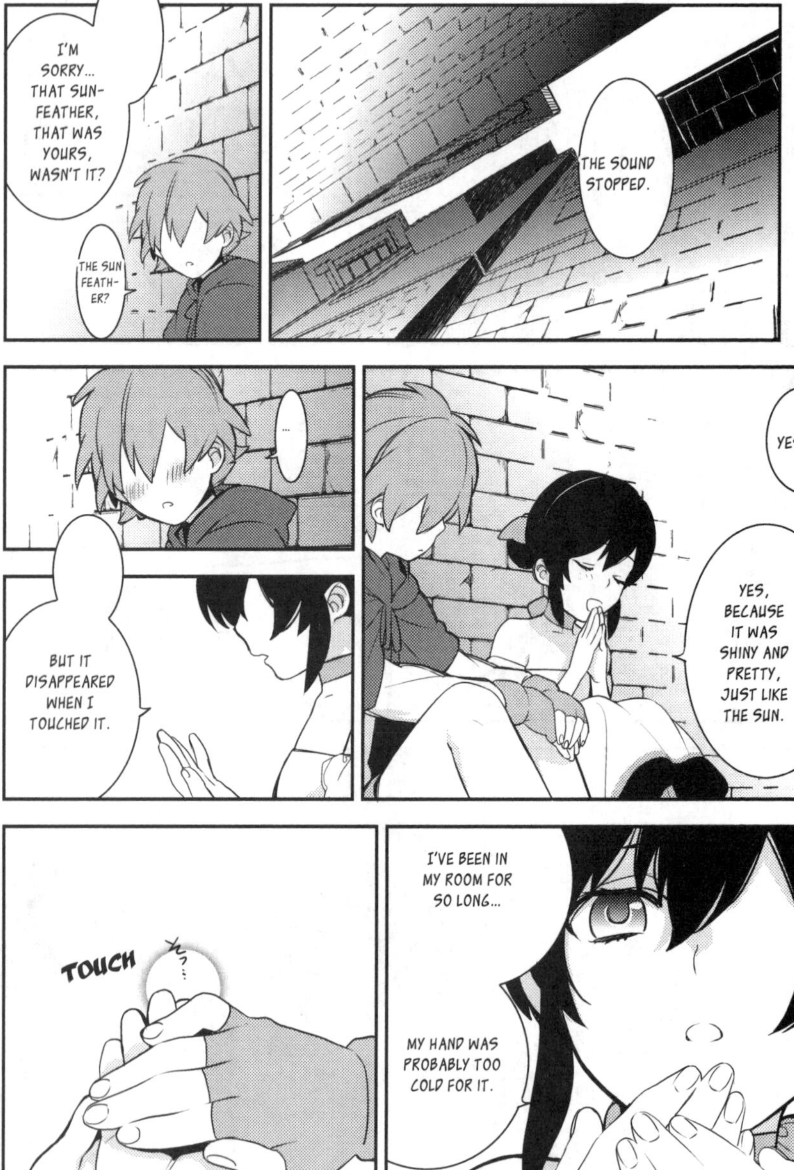
THE SOUND STOPPED.
I'M SORRY... THAT SUN-FEATHER, THAT WAS YOURS, WASN'T IT?
THE SUN FEATHER?
YES.
YES, BECAUSE IT WAS SHINY AND PRETTY, JUST LIKE THE SUN.
...
BUT IT DISAPPEARED WHEN I TOUCHED IT.
I'VE BEEN IN MY ROOM FOR SO LONG...
MY HAND WAS PROBABLY TOO COLD FOR IT.
TOUCH

I THOUGHT THERE WAS NOTHING BUT FEAR OUTSIDE.

BUT...

SO... SO...

YOUR HAND.

IT FEELS WARM TO ME...

YOU CAN ONLY FIND THE SUN IF YOU GO OUTSIDE.

MIKONO! THERE YOU ARE!

DASH

I...

BROTHER!

ARE YOU HURT? THAT WAS SCARY, HUH?

I'M OKAY. I WASN'T ALONE!

YOU IDIOT! I WAS SO WORRIED...

HUG

I'M SORRY!

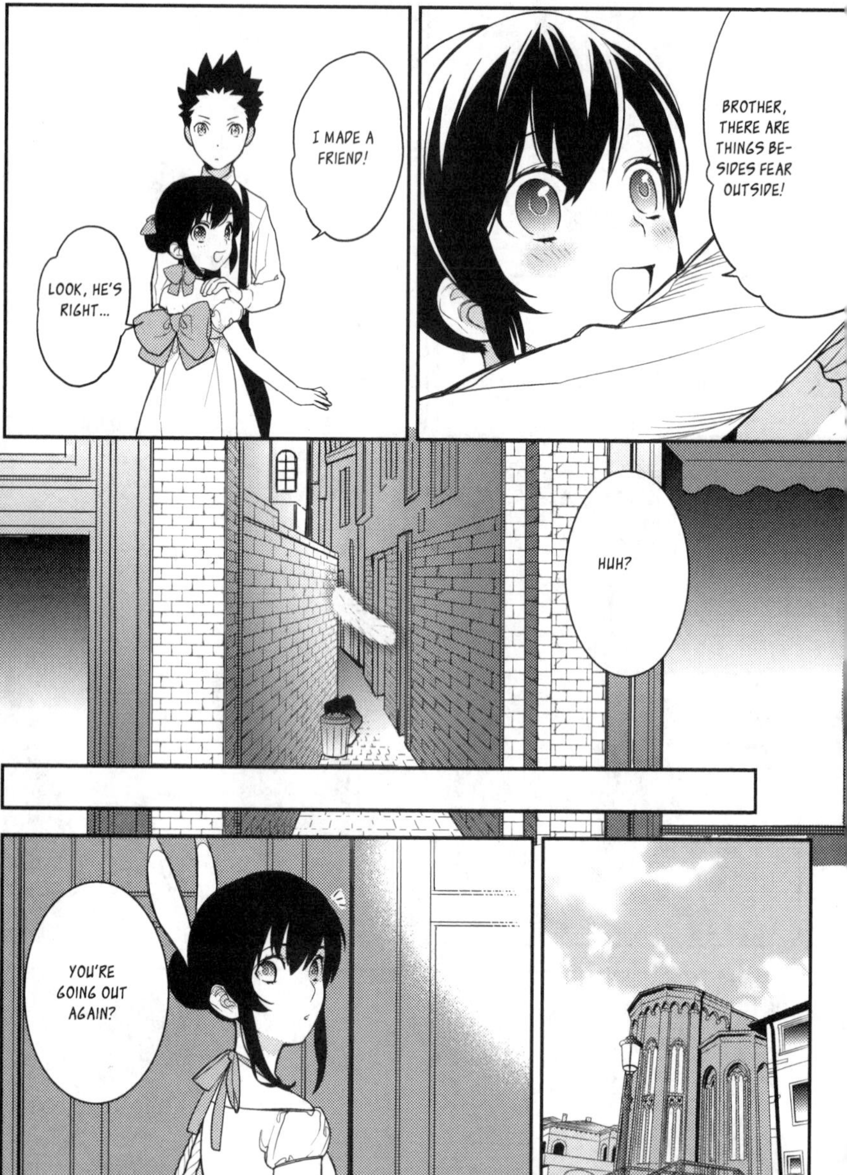
BROTHER, THERE ARE THINGS BE-SIDES FEAR OUTSIDE!
I MADE A FRIEND!
LOOK, HE'S RIGHT...
HUH?
YOU'RE GOING OUT AGAIN?

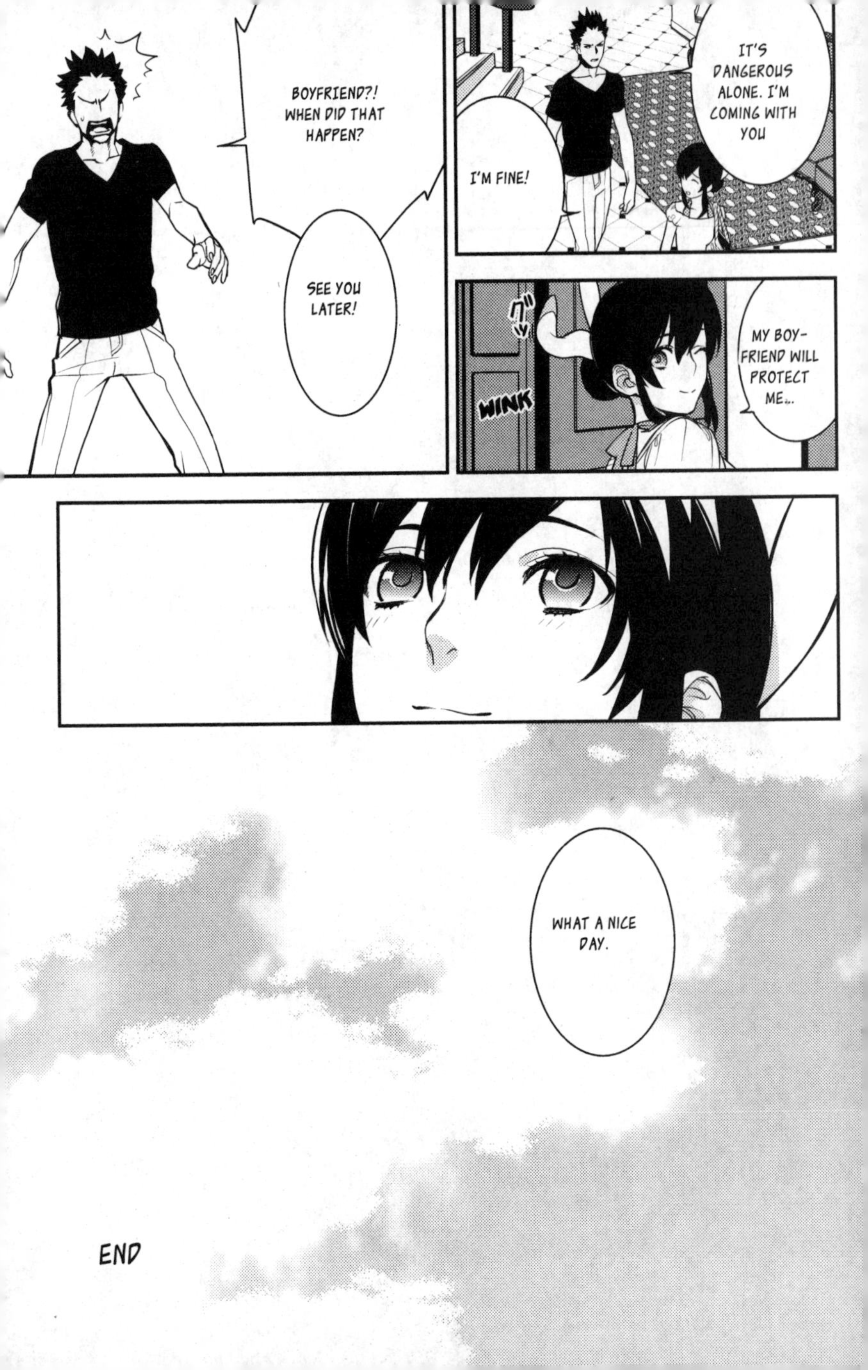
IT'S DANGEROUS ALONE. I'M COMING WITH YOU
I'M FINE!
MY BOY-FRIEND WILL PROTECT ME...
WINK
BOYFRIEND?! WHEN DID THAT HAPPEN?
SEE YOU LATER!
WHAT A NICE DAY.
END